LGBTQ+ Literature in the West

LGBTQ+ Literature in the West

From Ancient Times to the Twenty-First Century

Robert C. Evans

BLOOMSBURY ACADEMIC
LONDON • NEW YORK • OXFORD • NEW DELHI • SYDNEY

BLOOMSBURY ACADEMIC
Bloomsbury Publishing Plc
50 Bedford Square, London, WC1B 3DP, UK
1385 Broadway, New York, NY 10018, USA
29 Earlsfort Terrace, Dublin 2, Ireland

BLOOMSBURY, BLOOMSBURY ACADEMIC and the Diana logo are trademarks of Bloomsbury Publishing Plc

First published in Great Britain 2023
Paperback edition published 2024

Copyright © Robert C. Evans, 2023, 2025

Robert C. Evans has asserted his right under the Copyright, Designs and Patents Act, 1988, to be identified as Author of this work.

Cover image © Wut_Moppie/Shutterstock

All rights reserved. No part of this publication may be reproduced or transmitted in any form or by any means, electronic or mechanical, including photocopying, recording, or any information storage or retrieval system, without prior permission in writing from the publishers.

Bloomsbury Publishing Plc does not have any control over, or responsibility for, any third-party websites referred to or in this book. All internet addresses given in this book were correct at the time of going to press. The author and publisher regret any inconvenience caused if addresses have changed or sites have ceased to exist, but can accept no responsibility for any such changes.

A catalogue record for this book is available from the British Library.

A catalog record for this book is available from the Library of Congress.

ISBN:	HB:	978-1-3503-7182-8
	PB:	978-1-3503-7186-6
	ePDF:	978-1-3503-7183-5
	eBook:	978-1-3503-7184-2

Typeset by Integra Software Services Pvt. Ltd.

To find out more about our authors and books visit www.bloomsbury.com and sign up for our newsletters.

To
Claude Summers and Ted-Larry Pebworth
for many long years of warm encouragement
and to
Nicolas Tredell
for many recent years of warm encouragement

Contents

Introduction		1
1	The Ancient and Classical Periods	7
2	The Middle Ages	27
3	The English Renaissance	35
4	The Seventeenth Century	55
5	The Eighteenth Century	67
6	The Early Nineteenth Century	75
7	The Later Nineteenth Century	87
8	The Early Twentieth Century	109
9	The Later Twentieth Century	155
Conclusion		207
Bibliography		211
Index		219

Introduction

"Homoerotic literature" is, arguably, almost as old as literature itself. Homoerotic themes have been perceived in such ancient works as the Gilgamesh epic, Homer's *Iliad*, Sappho's lyrics, and important parts of the Hebrew Bible. Such themes become even more explicit, in various senses of that word, in the literature of "classical" Greece and "ancient" Rome. They become harder to detect in most literature of the Christian Middle Ages, become more obviously noticeable during the Renaissance, become more and more obvious in the writings of the eighteenth and especially nineteenth centuries, and become increasingly apparent as the twentieth century develops. By the second decade of the twenty-first century, such works reach a height of visibility and even prestige perhaps never seen before. By this latter period, works by and about not just lesbians and gays but also by and about bisexuals, transgender persons, and "queers" (the components of the common acronym LGBTQ) have become openly published, freely discussed, often celebrated, and widely studied. Moreover, the acronym has continued to expand, now often including works by "inter-sexuals," "asexuals," and various other possible sexual orientations (such as "pansexuals"). But the abbreviation seems to have stabilized, at least for the time being, as LGBTQ+.

This book is an attempt to survey, within one volume, the history of critical responses to literature of this kind (or of these kinds) from the beginning down to the present day. For various reasons it focuses on literature of "the West," not only because that is the sort of literature of this type that has been most widely studied but also because it is the sort of literature of this type that is likely to have the most important influence on contemporary writers and be of the greatest interest to current English-speaking readers. This volume could, of course, have been much longer than it is if space were unlimited, but space is rarely unlimited. Instead, this book tries to give readers a clear sense, within a relatively short compass, not only of the development of "queer" literature (perhaps the most encompassing of all the terms) but especially of critical responses to that literature, notably during the past century and particularly the past fifty years.

This book emphasizes, in general, broad studies of the topic, focusing mainly on book-length studies (of which there are many) rather than on essays or articles (of which there are *so* many that trying to deal with them would have been impossible in a volume of this sort). The books emphasized here tend to be books of broad rather than narrow scopes, with special attention paid to reference works such as encyclopedias, dictionaries, scholarly editions, and other kinds of academic surveys. One goal has been to offer a kind of "digest" of previous reference works so that readers will have, in one handy volume, a clear sense of what has been thought and said about "queer" literature by the most trusted experts—the sort of people asked to write about such topics for trusted reference sources. Another goal has been to offer a sense of the arguments made in the most frequently cited studies of the topic. This has meant a preference for scholarly works with a broader focus than is often found in highly specialized monographs. Thus, readers are unlikely to read, here, summaries of probing, in-depth examinations of particular authors or works than summaries of books with more general concerns.

All in all, this book tries to offer a roadmap to much of the excellent scholarship concerning "queer" literature that has arisen in the last half-century—an era of unparalleled interest in the topic and an era that has moved the topic from the distant sidelines of literary study to a place ever closer to the center of things.

* * *

Of course, almost all the terms that make up the acronym LGBTQ+ are inherently anachronistic. No one, for most of the millennia covered in this book, would have used or understood the terms "lesbian," "gay," "bisexual," "transgender," "transvestite," "queer," "intersexual," "asexual," and so on. Historians often make much of the fact that the word "homosexual" was not even coined until the second half of the nineteenth century. But does this mean that homosexuality itself did not exist in prior eras? As will be seen, one of the great debates that ranges (and sometime rages) throughout this book is whether people who *thought* of themselves as homosexuals (and who were thought of by others in that way) existed before the late 1860s. Theorists of literature and history often argue about whether "gay" feelings and thoughts (as opposed to simple "non-straight" sexual behavior) are innate (and thus found in all periods) or whether they are simply "socially constructed." Is there some in-born component to being "queer," or is being "queer" simply a product of nurture, not nature? Or is it some complicated mixture of the two? This key issue arises repeatedly in this book, beginning with coverage of the very oldest literature and extending down to the present day.

Another important topic that is present almost by its absence is the issue of bisexuality. As will be seen, many of the most famous figures and characters in "queer" literary history were bisexual in conduct if not in "inner orientation": they often had sex both with men and with women. Yet bisexuality, as a topic in itself, has been remarkably rarely studied, either by regular historians and theorists or by literary historians, literary theorists, and literary critics. The tendency, instead, has been to want to put people into neat, clear categories of either "heterosexual" or "homosexual" behavior, with very little attention paid, at least until very recently, to people, works, and characters who can't be squeezed comfortably into either box. And, while literature featuring transvestism, as well as discussions of such literature, has been fairly common (especially in studies of English Renaissance drama, when boys played women on that period's stages), discussions of transgenderism have been almost nonexistent until quite recently. Perhaps this is partly because, until recently, the ability to change one's gender surgically and through medication was impossible. Whatever the reasons, however, until recently little has been written about transgender individuals, either by creative writers or by students of literature and literary history. The same is true of people or characters belonging to such other recently named categories as asexuality and intersexuality. For the most part, and for the longest times, attention has tended to focus on writers and characters who would today be called "lesbian" or "gay," with an especially strong interest in the latter.

That strong interest, of course, reflects the fact that until relatively recently, most of the people who either wrote literature themselves or who wrote *about* literature were men, often straight men. That has been less and less the case, especially in the decades since the 1970s, when more and more women began to be hired to research and teach literature in almost all colleges and universities. Moreover, since the 1990s (especially) increasing numbers of academics have "come out" as gay, lesbian, or "queer" and have produced more and more scholarship about literature that was, until then, often ignored, marginalized, or even treated with disdain. "Queer studies" has experienced of boom of interest, both from writers and from readers, during the last thirty years, and society itself has often become more tolerant and even sometimes affirmative in its attitudes toward ideas, works, and people who cannot be classified as heterosexual. In a kind of intriguing feedback loop, growing tolerance for "queers" has helped produce more written works by and about queers, which have in turn helped produce more tolerance and acceptance of people who are not "straight."

Many academic works written about LGBTQ+ literature have been heavily historical, cultural, and sociological in nature. Scholars, in particular, have tended to approach "queer" literature in thematic terms, with a strong interest in the ideas "queer" literary works both explore and express and with an equally strong interest in what the status of queer writers and queer writing at any given time tells us about the societies and cultures in which such writers and writings arose. Relatively little attention has been paid to queer works as *works of art*—that is, as works interesting for their structures, styles, craft, and attention to literary detail. (This is less true, however, of works by such obviously important authors as Sappho and Shakespeare.) But the strong "cultural," historical, sociological and even psychological emphases of much study of "queer" literature are not surprising, especially when one realizes the degree to which *any* discussion of such literature in terms of its queer orientation was once ignored or even suppressed. Many pioneers in the study of such literature have also been pioneers in the advocacy of full civil rights for queer people—advocacy that has resulted, in the west at least, in broad toleration and growing acceptance of people of many different sexual orientations.

※ ※ ※

Inevitably, the present volume pays less attention to the earliest works than to works from the Renaissance and later. Much more evidence, both primary and secondary, exists from the seventeenth century and beyond, with the late nineteenth century providing a cornucopia of works relevant to this book and the twentieth and twenty-first centuries witnessing an explosion of primary and secondary works. It is probably too early, at this point, to say which writers and works from the twenty-first century will seem "canonical" fifty or a hundred years from now. For that reason, most of the "modern" writers covered in this book lived and wrote (or at least began writing) in the twentieth century rather than later. They are also the writers who, almost inevitably, attracted the most public attention in their own days *as* "queer" writers. With the possible exception of Sappho, few writers before the time of Oscar Wilde (and, even in his case, only late in his career) were thought of primarily as "queer." Even Sappho was sometimes seen not as a lesbian writer or even as a writer about lesbians but as, either, a frustrated straight woman or a woman who simply wrote in conventional, non-sexual terms about women playing conventional roles in her society. But in the aftermath of the Wilde trials and the Wilde debacle, more and more writers began to think of themselves, and to be seen and judged by others, as queer. "Gay" writers and "lesbian" authors began to identify increasingly as such and began to write more and more, and more and more openly, about "gay" and "lesbian" topics. For all these reasons, the sections of this book that tend to be most detailed are the later sections—the ones that chart developments from around 1850 to around the year 2000. These are the years and decades in which "the love that dare not speak its name" became more and more audible and then, eventually, even quite outspoken.

But first let us turn to the known earliest works from the earliest known years, the works from the ancient and classical periods, the writing of peoples from such places as Mesopotamia, the various lands of the ancient Hebrews, and the civilizations of ancient Greece and ancient Rome.

1

The Ancient and Classical Periods

The Ancient Period

JONATHAN AND DAVID. "Queer" sexuality has been seen as an important issue in the Old Testament story of Jonathan and David, whose unusually close friendship has long sparked speculation and debate. Some commentators thought it implied either homoerotic feelings, homoerotic sex, or both, while others strongly disagreed. Ward Houser and Warren Johansson (Dynes 1990: 297–8) noted that 2 Samuel 1: 19–27 presents Jonathan as desiring David more than vice versa and quoted later Christians who thought Jonathan's father, Saul, regarded his son as either passively homosexual or at least too submissive.

David Halperin (1990: 88) also emphasized Jonathan's love for David but discounted sexual motives or relations, instead stressing brotherly affection. Martti Nissinen (1998) compared this friendship to those between the *Odyssey*'s Achilles and Patroclus and the *Gilgamesh* epic's Gilgamesh and Enkidu. All three relationships, he thought, stressed "equality, intimate affection, and companionship"—all unusual in ancient times. And although he saw *Gilgamesh* as unusually pessimistic, he noted that all three stories depict one man intensely lamenting another man's death (24). Nissinen emphasized Jonathan and David's unusual closeness, noting how they kiss and weep "when David must depart" (55). But Nissinen downplayed homoerotic interpretations, suggesting instead intimacy between young soldiers. Both men, he noted, were involved with women, and he thought the story was probably not originally intended or interpreted in homoerotic terms (56).

Robert Drake (1998) likewise deemphasized sexual love, instead noting how the relationship's beauty was highlighted by its particularly brutal scriptural context (16). Gregory Woods (1998) mainly noted that Jonathan and David were often *treated* as lovers (or at least as very close friends) by much later writers (3–4). Similarly, Raymond-Jean Frontain (Haggerty 2000: 243–5) traced the legend's influence and noted unsuccessful attempts to contain or suppress its homoerotic overtones. Frontain later (Summers 2002: 89–91) reported some views that even Saul's response to David is implicitly homoerotic and observed that Jonathan and David have long been listed as famously close male friends. David J. Bromell (Aldrich and Wotherspoon 2002: 140) called the story "unusual" because "two individuals from very different family backgrounds 'covenant' together three times ... without stipulated obligations. Their covenant," he continued, "did not concern power and politics, but rather mutual love and personal safety." Moreover, although "Jonathan continued to fight alongside his father, Saul experienced their alliance as profoundly anti-familial, perverted and shameful" and therefore "humiliated Jonathan." The story, Bromell noted, has recently been used both to justify and to forbid gay sex.

Susan Ackerman (2005) compared Jonathan and David both to Achilles and Patroclus and to Gilgamesh and Enkidu but warned against seeing these relationships as "gay." Stressing instead "rites of passage," she thought Jonathan's passivity helped explain and justify David's rise to kingship, since Jonathan often deliberately behaves more as a woman or wife (including, perhaps, sexually) than as an equal male comrade (218–22), thus making himself an unfit king (by ancient Hebrew standards). David, however, presented no such problems.

Anthony Heacock (2007) challenged interpretations of the Jonathan-David relationship as homosexual, stressing instead conventional ideas of male bonding between ancient heroes.

Aaron Hamburger (Canning 2009: 2–7) reported that many liberal scholars consider phrasing in the Jonathan and David tale identical to phrasing used elsewhere in the Bible to describe genuine love. He thought gay readers could relate to this story because gay love need not be exclusively physical (2–3). Only when it is too late, he argued, does David reciprocate Jonathan's love (4–5). Hamburger saw this relationship as "at the very least homosocial" if not actually homosexual, noting its strong influence on many later gay writers and thinkers (7). (Similar arguments have been made, from a lesbian perspective, about the biblical story of Ruth; see Frontain in Summers 2002: 91.)

GILGAMESH AND ENKIDU. The same issues presented by Jonathan and David arise again in *Gilgamesh*, whose title character deeply loves Enkidu. In 1971, Vern Bullough, unsure whether their relationship is homosexual, nonetheless found it intensely homosocial, perhaps because relations with women were not strongly emphasized in a warrior culture (195). In 1982, Jeffrey Tigay, reviewing previous scholarship and considering a homosexual bond a genuine possibility, also cited evidence suggesting merely a strong friendship (184). In 1983, George Held downplayed homoerotic interpretations (136–7), while in 1990 Warren Johansson, considering any homoeroticism "sublimated," nevertheless emphasized the positive powers of the couple's love (Dynes 1990: 479). David Halperin (1990: 87), although noting definite homoerotic imagery, emphasized instead the couple's brotherly feelings (87). In contrast, an anonymous essay (Conner et al. 1997: 159–60) cited scholarship suggesting that both Enkidu and even Gilgamesh may be gender-variant transvestites who, to some extent, dress and behave as females.

Robert Drake (1998: 249–50) thought both men seek something more satisfying than "straight" sex: love with a male equal. Drake, refuting views of them as narcissists, instead considered their love crucial to their maturation (30–4). Hogan and Hudson 1998 (249–50) emphasized their homoerotic friendship and the epic's sexual puns (249). Noting that scholars disagree about how homoerotic the work is, Hogan and Hudson thought it does imply the "positive potential of loving [male] bonds" (250). Martti Nissinen (1998) admitted but minimized homoerotic possibilities, stressing the civilizing impact of homosocial affection, with its unusual equality (20–4). Likewise, Raymond-Jean Frontain (Haggerty 2000: 402–3) stressed the poem's homosocial emphasis and the similarities between these heroic friends and later, similar pairs. Frontain (Summers 2002: 307) also argued that Gilgamesh and Enkidu could love as equals (in a way neither could love a woman), whether or not their love was sexual (see also David McConnel in Canning 2009: 9–15 and Nissinen 2010: 74). In 2010, Nissinen, after reviewing previous scholarship, noted how many characters and themes in the epic blur standard boundaries of all sorts.

ACHILLES AND PATROCLUS. Debates about Achilles and Patroclus in Homer's *Odyssey* strongly resemble disputes about Jonathan and David and about Gilgamesh and Enkidu. Interestingly, many scholars (such as W. M. Clarke in 1978) have conceded that numerous later Greeks considered Achilles and Patroclus lovers, often very explicitly (381; see also Sergent 1986: 251; Dynes 1990: 8, 495–6: Cantarella 1992: 11–12; Percy 1996: 37–40; Woods 1998: 18; Fone 2000: 21; Crompton 2003: 4). Clarke called their emotional bond unusually intense in a poem that largely ignores heartfelt love (389, 392). Patroclus (Clarke argued) uniquely brings out Achilles's potential "tenderness and compassion": they embrace and weep, and Achilles feels deep anguish when Patroclus is killed (392–3). According to Clarke, although Homer nowhere explicitly describes the heroes' physical relationship, he often implies it (393), and Clarke definitely considered these heroes truly in love emotionally (395; see also Clarke in Dynes and Donaldson 1992: 109 and Sergeant 1986: 256; Percy 1996: 39).

Christine Downing (1989: 174-9) noted disagreement among classical authors about whether Achilles and Patroclus had had sex (174) but thought "Homer's account gives us as beautiful depiction as any I know" of intense same-sex affection (175; see also Drake [1998]: 22). Warren Johansson (Dynes 1990: 8) saw them as typifying the strong male bonds ancient Greeks often celebrated.

David Halperin (1990: 83-5) compared this pair's affection to the strong human sociability he had already perceived between Jonathan and David and Gilgamesh and Enkidu: all three couples felt intense, familial, brotherly friendship (however, see Percy 1996: 40). But although later Greeks (and later readers in general) sometimes saw Achilles and Patroclus as physical lovers, Halperin warned against such probable misunderstandings (87; see also Nissinen 1998: 24, 56). Eva Cantarella (1992), however, argued strongly for a physical bond, just as she also contended that homosexuality was "widespread" in Homeric Greece (10; in contrast, see Crompton 2003: 5). But as Clifford Hindley (Aldrich and Wotherspoon 2002: 1-2) noted, Homer never explicitly calls them lovers but does portray "an emotional bond ... far more intense than that between any other pair of heroes. Faced by Homer's opaqueness," Hindley continued, "later writers interpreted the legend in terms of their own times, thus providing icons for themselves and their successors."

Louis Crompton (2003: 5) called the Achilles-Patroclus relationship not typical of the homosexual pairings found later in "classical" Greece (5), while in 2007 James Davidson (2007: 318) considered their intense bond typically youthful: because he has lost a "husband," Achilles's mother (a goddess) encourages him to take a wife.

ANCIENT GREEK LYRIC POETRY. Homoeroticism is implied in various archaic (i.e., pre-classical) Greek lyrics. Archilochus (ca. 650 BCE) has been likened to the later Roman poet Catullus in describing complex sexual feelings, including not only homoerotic passion (Dynes 1990: 496) but also distinct sexual orientations, including lesbianism (Hubbard 2003: 2, 16, 24). Alcman (late 7th cen. BCE?) also described lesbians (Larson 2012: 133, 136-7), while Solon (ca. 638-558 BCE) depicted older males' attraction to younger ones both as completely normal (Dynes 1990: 496) and even as educationally useful (Fone 2000: 19; see also Crompton 2003: 24). Alcaeus (621-560 BCE) also emphasized love between older and younger males (Dynes 1990: 496; Crompton 2003: 20; Hubbard 2003: 338).

SAPPHO (630–580 BCE). Jeannette Foster (1956: 17–22) noted Sappho's fame as both a lesbian and a poet and recommended editions and discussed her life (18). She found Sappho's "variant tastes" not only indisputable (19) but also often evident in her poetry (19–20), and she also surveyed the ways later writers and scholars dealt with Sappho's lesbianism (20–2). Christine Downing (1989: 217–36) called Sappho's poetic voice perhaps the earliest not only of a woman but of someone describing inner feelings, especially about love (217). After recounting not only myths about Sappho but also the few known facts (218–19), Downing discussed modern theories about her life, her social role, and her sexuality (219–20). Downing herself emphasized "the poet's imaginative projections of female emotions and sexuality, not necessarily ... her actual [and much debated] experience" (220–1). Sappho, Downing said, "was a 'true lyric'" poet (222) who emphasized her relationship with the love goddess Aphrodite (222–9). For Sappho, "loving women does not mean *not* loving men," and, like most Greek poets, she emphasized both the appeal and the sad ephemerality of physical beauty (229). Sappho showed "how, in relations among women, the primary infantile bond between mothers and daughters is invoked" (230); emphasized ideal reciprocity between female lovers (231); and stressed themes of "loss and parting" (235).

Eva Cantarella (1992) argued that because affection between women hardly mattered to powerful Greek men, little evidence about it survives (78). Cantarella noted, however, that communities of women (often schools) did exist (Sappho's being the most famous). She also said that passionate love for and among students could be intense (79, 81, 83), although most girls eventually married men (80), and she observed that sex between female students involved equality and could even be considered ennobling (83–4).

Emma Donoghue (1993: 243–53) noted the long tradition of identifying Sappho as lesbian or bisexual (244), disputed critics who downplayed attacks on her lesbianism (244), cited eighteenth-century references to translations of her works (245–7), reported that era's censorship and/or suppression of her texts (247–50), but also cited libertine enthusiasm for her bisexuality and/or lesbianism (250–3). In 1995, Paige DuBois noted that Sappho, while often extolling same-sex desire rather than housewifely duties, also frequently extolled heterosexual weddings (12; see also Hubbard 2003: 22)—facts that have provoked diverse responses (DuBois 13–14).

In 1996, both *Reading Sappho* and *Re-Reading Sappho* (each edited by Ellen Greene) contained numerous important essays. In *Reading Sappho*, Guiliana Lanata stressed Sappho's echoes of previous poetry, both in theme and style;

Charles Segal highlighted her personal and universal concerns and examined her phrasing; and Marilyn B. Skinner, contrasting Sappho with Alcman, emphasized her distinctiveness, especially in her egalitarian emphases and ability to appeal to a wide (even male) readership. Eva Stehle emphasized the fragility of mutual love in a patriarchal culture as a common theme, and Greene reviewed previous scholarship before stressing Sappho's woman-centered, non-patriarchal outlook. Most essays in *Re-Reading Sappho* dealt with the poet's later reputation and influence.

Hogan and Hudson 1998 (493–4) noted that "[a]lmost all of her surviving verse is love poetry addressed to women," reported that the name ascribed to her supposed husband is "almost certainly" a sexual joke (493), and observed that most critics think she was *actively* lesbian: if her feelings were "Platonic" she would not have been criticized. Hogan and Hudson said readers have long admired her poetry despite its lesbianism, and they called her "the only Greek poet ... still widely read" (494).

Martti Nissinen (1998: 74–6) discussed jealousy in Sappho's poems, her own apparent marriage (74–5), resemblances between her works and those of Alcman (75), later Greek mockery of lesbian sex (76), and Sappho's unusual stress on mutual love between equals (76). Jane Snyder (1997) emphasized the female-oriented world of Sappho's lyrics (whatever her own sexual preferences may have been [2]), her frequent allusions to Aphrodite (7) rather than Cupid (15), and her stress on powerful, articulate women (16). Snyder also stressed the poems' sensuality (19); attempts by early and recent scholars to deny Sappho's "lesbian" focus (27–30; 37–8); and the ways she often included men in poems about women (31). Additionally, Snyder discussed Sappho's recurring imagery of fluttering hearts to symbolize sexual passion (32), choices made by various translators (34), her positive presentation of the mythical Helen (often attacked by male writers [63–4]), and much more. Snyder's accessible book highlighted Sappho's literary achievements (see also Zimmerman 2000: 668–9).

Harriette Andreadis (2001: 27–53) noted that Sappho, during the Renaissance, was linked both with female desire in general and with same-sex desire in particular (27). She tended to be depicted as a woman who killed herself when rejected by a man; and/or as the prime example of a somewhat threatening feminine poetic talent; and/or as "an early exemplar of 'unnatural' or monstrous sexuality" (28). Ovid's legend of Sappho and Phaon led many early modern writers to stress her supposed abandonment of women for this attractive younger man (28–9), her punishment for having been a lesbian and a talented artist (30,

35), and her alleged growing discomfort with her lesbianism—a claim especially emphasized as women readers became more common and might be influenced by her (37). For early moderns, Adreadis said, Sappho was "the sole ancient model to which contemporary women writers might compare themselves and to whom they might be compared" (38). But she also became associated with lesbian behavior (39) that John Donne presented in "entirely positive" ways (48) but that other male writers excoriated (51).

Anita George (Summers 2002: 589–94) noted that by classical times the word "lesbians" widely referred to sexually shameful women (not necessarily "lesbian" in the modern sense [590; see also Castle 2003: 13]). She wrote that Sappho was usually regarded as the greatest Greek lyric poet, and although some later scholars tried to deny her lesbianism (see Dynes 1990: 496; 1154), others saw in her work parallels with same-sex love between males (590; see also Dynes 1990: 1153–4; Davidson 2007: 504). George praised Sappho's literary skill (590–1), challenged attempts to deny her lesbianism (591–2), stressed her early emphasis on poetic immortality (592), argued that her own probable marriage implied little about her personal sexuality (593), and discussed marriage's largely social role in ancient Greek culture (593). Suzanne MacAlister (Aldrich and Wotherspoon 2002: 463) noted how Sappho was described by later writers, both in classical times and afterwards:

> We hear of Sappho as mistress of a finishing school, Sappho as married woman, Sappho as whore; Sappho as fat, ugly and rejected by men; Sappho at the centre of either a 'thiasos' (a group of women belonging to a religious cult) or some other Sapphic community of women, and so on.

McAlister said some of these views resulted from "homophobic anxiety, some from the need to 'normalize', some from sheer misogyny, [and] some from visions of a lesbian utopia." For MacAlister and others, however, what mattered most was the poet's obvious talent and her unusual subject matter: Sappho assumes a mutuality not found in the extant writings of ancient Greek men and was "the first extant Greek poet to write expressly about the feelings generated by love" (462–4).

Louis Crompton (2003: 17–19) also stressed Sappho's emphasis on intense feelings (17); noted that she was frequently compared to Homer (18); and described modern disputes about her sexuality (19). Thomas Hubbard (2003: 22–5) suggested that Sappho, while taking marriage for granted, nonetheless celebrated same-sex female love (22). He also noted her stress on natural beauty (22) and valuably summarized earlier scholarship (24–5).

Terry Castle (2003: 13–16) traced later depictions of Sappho, including efforts to deny her lesbianism (15–16), while Maureen Duffy (Canning 2009: 17–24) highlighted her poems' erotic intensity (22). Emma Donoghue (2010: 80–2, 107–8) saw Sappho as partly responsible for the long literary tradition in which "male and female rivals duke it out on the battlefield of love" (82), also noting how Sappho was often depicted, by later straight writers such as Ovid, as a prototypical "monstrous" lesbian (107–8).

Evelyn Newlyn (in Reisman 2012: 177–88) valuably surveyed Sappho's own work and scholarship on it, stressing the poetry's personal nature, its timelessness and vividness, its musicality, and its emotionalism (177–8). Newlyn also noted later attacks on Sappho (179), her nevertheless high reputation generally (180), her use of earlier poetic traditions and methods (181), and, in particular, the skill of various poems (181), including their variety of tones (182), their sensual detail (182), and their careful structure (182; cf. Davidson 2007: 498–512). Newlyn's unusually comprehensive introduction, which discussed Sappho's typical themes (185) and her public and private modes (186), concluded with a helpful annotated bibliography (188). In 2012, Jennifer Larson summarized standard comments on Sappho, emphasizing later attacks (133–4), while Harriette Andreadis in 2014 also stressed later reactions to Sappho (both positive and negative) as well as her literary influence (15–25; see also Larson 2012: 135).

Classical Greece

"Classical" Greek literature is linked with the 500s BCE, the first period in which evidence of homosexuality in Greek culture survives in abundance. Scholars commonly note that adult Greek males from this era were free to have sex both with women and with other (usually younger) males, as long as those adult males were the "active" partners (Crompton 2003: 53; although see Hubbard 2003: 6–8, who finds evidence for blurred sexual roles). Some classical Greeks even idealized male same-sex love while saying little about same-sex relations between women, which many men found hard even to imagine. The affection and desire of older males for younger males were often seen as perfectly natural and were frequently extolled as useful in educating youths, and love between males was often seen as beneficial to society and helpful in politics and war. Many writers assumed that young males would be objects of desire by older males and that young males would in turn feel (and act on) desire for younger males as they themselves aged. Most men who found young males sexually attractive would nonetheless marry and have children, while most young males (it was assumed) lost much of their sexual attractiveness as soon as they began to grow thick beards and generally become hairy. Males who desired other males often sought to function as the active partners in anal sex, although "intercrural" sex—in which the active partner simply penetrated the closed thighs of the passive one—was also common. Classical Greeks generally seem to have had little interest in oral sex and, in fact, typically condemned it. The greatest object of scorn, however, was the adult male who allowed himself (or desired) to be penetrated. Such attitudes influenced classical Rome, although David Robinson (2006) suggested that this standard view of things may be too simplistic, arguing that "even some scholars who espouse the dominant view acknowledge a greater range of ancient thought, feeling, and behavior than the active/passive, penetrator/penetratee schema would suggest" (172). According to Robinson,

> Too often ignored, or briefly acknowledged only to be forgotten, are the signs that in the ancient world, as in the modern and postmodern ones, dominant ideology was *contested*. Not just contradictory, or unstable, or 'precarious', but actually challenged.
>
> (257)

"Subversive views" could be both imagined and practiced, both in private and sometimes in public (257). Robinson and others (see Hubbard 2003: 20) think the standard scholarly emphasis on penetrating and being penetrated is too simplistic.

Most "gay" men in classical Greece and Rome were actually bisexual, and one great debate among scholars involves whether "homosexuality," as presently understood, in fact even existed. Some scholars think sex was then understood in terms of acts rather than basic psychological orientations, although solid evidence exists that some classical Greeks and Romans considered themselves (and were seen by others) as essentially "gay" (see Hubbard 2003: 2-24, *passim*). The poet **ANACREON** (582-485 BCE) has been described as bisexual with a clear preference for young males (Dynes 1990: 497), and his life has even been seen as indicating that strict sexual divisions between penetrator and penetrated often collapsed under the influence of alcohol (Hubbard 2003: 20). Anacreon may also offer the single piece of evidence of a Greek male's sexual desire for a male slave (Hubbard 2003: 24). Sometimes, however, the sexual implications of Anacreon's poems have been called unclear (Larson 2012: 134; cf. Davidson 2007: 515-17).

THEOGNIS (6th cen. BCE) has been seen as "more serious and moralizing than Anacreon" and as stressing the ideal, educational function of an older male's love for a youth (Dynes 1990: 497), even though his complaints about uncooperative youths have bothered some readers (Dynes 1990: 1305). Although married, he wrote nearly fifty poems to one young male, acting as his "counselor and guide" without much emphasis on eroticism but describing both the pleasures and frustrations of such love (Aldrich and Wotherspoon 2002: 520–1). Louis Crompton (2003: 23) stressed Theognis's importance as a writer about same-sex male love, especially its emotional ups and downs: some poems stress contentment, some offer warnings, and others issue complaints, and both the loyalty and the fickleness of youths are stressed. Older males typically had to *compete* for affection and attention from younger males—a fact that contributed to many poems' complicated tones. Thomas Hubbard (2003: 2–24, *passim*), offered Theognis as one among many examples of writers who seemed to imply the existence of distinct same-sex orientations (2–3, 24), and Hubbard also found in Theognis evidence of same-sex desire and activity *among* youths, not just between youths and older males (5). Hubbard thought Theognis stressed lovers' sexual competition and the helplessness lovers often felt (also a theme in Sappho [2–3, 12, 22]), while also noting that "Theognis" may not have been a single individual, even though "his" poems share many themes and attitudes (23). Jennifer Larson (2012: 107–8) also emphasized this poet's interest in educational love, frustrated desire, and the annoying need to compete.

IBYCUS (sixth century BCE) is notable for writing (unusually) about homoerotic desires among the elderly. Cicero "considered him more amorous than Alcaeus or even Anacreon" (Dynes 1992: 573; cf. Crompton 2003: 20; Hubbard 2003: 22), and his poems inspired many others in the *Greek Anthology* of early lyrics (Dynes 1990: 497, 573; cf. Crompton 2003: 20). He was called a "lover of lads" (Crompton 2003: 20) and wrote about male beauty and "gay" lovers from Greek myths (22–3; cf. Davidson 2007: 510–12). **PINDAR** (518–438) extolled handsome, gifted aristocratic youths whose athleticism heightened their appeal to men and women, young and adult (Dynes 1990: 497; Hubbard 2003: 4). He portrayed the Greek male ideal (especially nude athleticism [Hubbard 2003: 23]) while emphasizing the ephemerality of beauty and strength (Dynes 1990: 995–6). Although he sometimes praised an athlete's character as well as his handsomeness, some considered him excessively homoerotic (Crompton 2003: 50). Hubbard (2003) thought Pindar offered further evidence not only that fundamental sexual orientations did exist for the Greeks but also that some homoerotic relationships could involve persons (especially youths) of the same age (Hubbard 2003: 3–4, 5). Pindar was one of many Greeks who described the desire male gods could feel for handsome mortal youths, such as Ganymede (Davidson 2007: 274–7; see also 209–46).

DRAMATISTS. Classical Greece is especially known for important dramatists, such as **ARISTOPHANES** (ca. 450–ca. 385 BCE). Avowedly heterosexual (Hubbard 2003: 3, 86), he attacked effeminacy, passive males, male prostitution, transvestites, and uncontrolled desire (Dynes 1990: 75; Nissinen 1998: 80; Fone 2000: 30–3; Crompton 2003: 2, 54; Hubbard 2003: 6; Larson 2012: 108). He rarely mentioned anything positive about contemporary male-male love but sometimes alluded to male beauty, heroism, and comradeship (especially in prior eras) and admitted the widespread existence of homosexual desire. "The ideal cherished by the conservative Aristophanes is the smooth-skinned, muscular, shy, serious boy of the past, not the avaricious hustler or effeminate youth of the present" (Dynes 1990: 75–6; cf. Aldrich and Wotherspoon 2002: 32–3). He seems to have accepted some potentially positive aspects of male-male erotic relations (although see Hubbard 2003: 87) but satirized corruption of that and other ideals (Dynes 1990: 75–6; Fone 2000: 31–3; Crompton 2003: 26). Aristophanes may even have accepted the idea of distinct sexual orientations (Dynes 1990: 75–6; Fone 2000: 31–3; Crompton 2003: 26; Hubbard 2003: 2–3), and, like most Greeks, he apparently had no problem with male bisexuality (Crompton 2003: 54) or with male sexual relations with male slaves (Hubbard 2003: 10, 87). Mainly he attacked effeminate men and transvestism (Aldrich and Wotherspoon 2002: 32–3; Hubbard 2003: 86–7). Much relevant evidence is cited and quoted by Dover (1978: 135–53).

AESCHYLUS (525/4–456 BCE), in a lost play, explicitly described sex between Achilles and Patroclus, making them lovers despite their similar ages (Dynes 1990: 16; Crompton 2003: 4; Hubbard 2003: 183). **SOPHOCLES** (497/6–406/5 BCE) dealt with male-male love in various works (Percy 1996: 88–9, 185; Crompton 2003: 51), apparently having written four plays (out of 123, most lost) about this topic (Dynes 1990: 16). Considered a handsome youth and lover of other males, he famously tricked one lad by stealing a kiss and was himself tricked by another youth after sex (Crompton 2003: 51–2; cf. Hubbard 2003: 78). **EURIPIDES** (ca. 480–ca. 406) made one character attack effeminate males (Fone 2000: 30), depicted an example of one male kidnapping and raping another (Percy 1996: 57, 186), and even (despite his general enthusiasm for women) himself fell in love in old age with a younger adult male (Dynes 1990: 16; Percy 1996: 186; Crompton 2003: 52). All the works devoted to male-male love and written by all these playwrights no longer survive, perhaps because they were destroyed by later Christians, but the dramatists may simply have been less interested in this topic than various poets were (Dynes 1990: 16; cf. Crompton 2003: 2, 51).

LATER POETS. Among ancient Greek poets who dealt with same-sex desire, **CALLIMACHUS** (310–240) is significant (Crompton 2003: 87; Hubbard 2003: 268–9), but **THEOCRITUS** (ca. 301–260) is especially important, particularly for his influential pastoral poems. Roughly a quarter of his thirty *Idylls* deal entirely with homosexual love, treating it positively and as existing even among the gods. Various poems advise youths and depict love's complexities, and one deals with love between same-aged youths (Dynes 1990: 1304–5). Theocritus thought an older male's love for a youth could inspire virtue (Percy 1996: 189), and he often distinguished between lust and love: the first offered quick physical satisfaction, the second offered both painful and pleasurable emotions, including the realization that love and life are transient (Woods 1998: 25–7; Aldrich and Wotherspoon 2002: 519–20; Summers 2002: 652–3) and sometimes frustrating, especially for older lovers of youths (Hubbard 2003: 269). Much later, **MELEAGER** (ca. 100 BCE) thought sex with women more mutually pleasurable than sex with youths (Halperin 1990: 134), and one early scholar rightly or wrongly saw his many poems about youths as more "a matter of fashion than passion" (in Woods 1998: 34, but see Aldrich and Wotherspoon 2002: 362–3), while Crompton stressed the complexity of this poet's views (2003: 86). Meanwhile, Hubbard (2003: 86) found evidence in Meleager's poems for same-sex attraction between youths of the same age.

THE "GREEK ANTHOLOGY." This massive, influential, and constantly growing collection of poems includes works that span 1000 years (starting in 600 BCE [Crompton 2003: 86]), though actually compiled in the tenth century (C.E.) from earlier collections. Books 11 and 12 are largely devoted to adult males' desires for male youths, expressed in tones that richly vary and are often realistic and revealing (Dynes 1990: 504; Woods 1998: 28; Fone 2000: 428: Hine 2001: ix), particularly when depicting youths who play frustratingly hard to get and who later have to deal with similar youths themselves (Woods 1998: 29–30; Hine 2001: xxiii–xiv). Few poems are explicit (Fone 2000: 428; although see Hine 20001: xvi) but most do provide especially important sources of information about male-male love. Among the authors represented in the "Anthology," **STRATON OF SARDIS** (125–150 CE) exulted in the sexual details of desire for youths in poems that are often both clever and explicit (Aldrich and Wotherspoon 2002: 501–2). According to Gary Simes, traditionally

> Straton's epigrams have received scant and scornful attention from literary critics and historians not only because of their overt and exultant homoeroticism but also because of their sexual explicitness—their 'indecency', their 'pornographic' quality. ... The tone varies from the blunt through the punning to the metaphorical and witty.
>
> (Aldrich and Wotherspoon 2002: 502)

Classical Rome

Many scholars think the classical Romans were less likely than the ancient Greeks to idealize love. Often Romans treated this topic satirically and/or humorously (Richlin 1992). Moreover, although Romans typically took same-sex desire for granted, it was not as central to their culture's highest aspirations as in Greece, but important exceptions existed (Boswell 1981: 74–5; 81–2; 85–6; Fone 2000: 46). As in Greece, lesbianism was rarely discussed by male Roman authors; usually it was presented negatively, although exceptions did occur (Boswell 1980: 82–3). In dealing with male homoeroticism, Romans adopted many Greek attitudes and behaviors but were sometimes cruder or more explicit in the ways they treated (and increasingly satirized) homosexuality, frequently offering less emphasis on love than on lust, domination, and penetration (Richlin 1992, *passim*; Fone 2000: 47; Summers 2002: 555). Adult homosexuality of certain kinds (with youths and with slaves) remained legal throughout Rome's prosperity, although sex between adult males was typically considered degrading to the passive partner, especially if the person penetrated was a citizen rather than a slave or if both partners were young Romans (Boswell 1980: 74–5; Richlin 1992: 220–6; Summers 2002: 557). Even slaves, however, were not entirely powerless, especially if they were handsome (in Summers 2002: 555). Persons who actually preferred passive roles were often ridiculed (Boswell 1980: 74–5) unless (but sometimes even if) they were very powerful (among other complicating factors [Boswell 1980: 75]). Male prostitutes were especially scorned (Boswell 1980: 77). During Rome's heyday, however, adult male desire for youths (especially young slaves) was both legal and widely practiced (Boswell 1980: 62–5). (Youths, in fact, were typically desired, whether male or female [Richlin 1992: 211; Woods 1998: 32].) The idea that Rome "fell" partly because it tolerated homosexuality has been widely disputed, and in fact the "best" homoerotic literature dates from Rome's days of glory (Boswell 1980: 71–4).

As in Greece, bisexuality was the Roman norm (Woods 1998: 32; Summers 2002: 557). The playwright **PLAUTUS** (died ca. 184 BCE) took it for granted and emphasized lust for young male slaves (Dynes 1990: 1002–3, 1112; Richlin 1992: 222; Summers 2002: 556; see esp. Hubbard 2003: 309; Larson 2012: 110; Hubbard 2014: 71), sometimes comparing it with heterosexuality (Hubbard 2003: 310). Significantly, Plautus shows slaves often expecting and receiving rewards for sexual services (Hubbard 2014: 71-2). Among Roman poets, **CATULLUS** (84–54 BCE)—often called "Rome's first major love poet" (87)—was both vivid and influential in dealing with bisexuality, with Sappho as a key source of his style, if not his subject matter (since he strongly emphasized his passion for an aristocratic youth named Juventius [Dynes 1990: 206; Cantarella 1992: 122–3, 125, 128; Nissinen 1998: 70, 73; Drake 1998: 67; also see Hubbard 2014: 73]), whom Catullus may have wanted to embarrass for keeping his distance (Hubbard 2003: 310; cf. Cantarella 1992: 123). Catullus attacked "pathic," penetrable adult males (Richlin 1992: 221; Woods 1998: 33; Fone 2000: 50; Crompton 2003: 88; but see Williams 1999: 155) and effeminate men (Crompton 2003: 53)—perhaps because he was suspected of such "pathic" desires himself (Cantarella 1992: 123-4; Nissinen 1998: 73; Williams 1999: 164–5). He assumed that most men would eventually marry women (Cantarella 1992: 126; Nissinen 1998: 71; Woods 1998: 34; Summers 2002: 138). In Catullus, even freeborn youths might love each other before marriage, but not after (Cantarella 1992: 126; although see Hubbard 2014: 74). His poems have been called earthy, insulting, argumentative, sometimes lyrical, and mainly realistic, featuring strongly vernacular phrasing (Woods 1998: 32–3) and a highly personal tone (Summers 2002: 139) that is often humorous and ironic (Summers 2002: 519). Male-male penetration is a key concern in his works and usually implies domination (Hubbard 2003: 310–11), and Catullus ridiculed men who performed oral sex (Cantarella 1992: 124). His poems to Juventius have sometimes been seen as less convincing than those to a woman he nicknamed "Lesbia" (Aldrich and Wotherspoon 2002: 108–9). In fact, Hubbard (2014) has argued that Catullus was less sympathetic to homoeroticism in general than is often assumed (73–4).

VIRGIL (70 BCE–19 CE), widely considered perhaps the greatest Roman poet, largely avoided male-male love in his important epic *The Aeneid*, aside from that between the heroes Nisus and Euryalus. But Virgil himself never married and was known as a lover of youths (although see Hubbard 2014: 77; cf. Aldrich and Wotherspoon 2002: 549–50). Some of his lyrics, especially his second eclogue, do emphasize homoeroticism and proved enormously influential.

The second eclogue both imitated and helped transmit the trope of youths (even slaves) playing hard to get (Dynes 1990: 1367; Drake 1998: 69; Woods 1998: 39; Summers 2002: 557, 668). In *The Aeneid*, Virgil elevated male-male love to heroic status, echoing the love between Achilles and Patroclus in Homer's *Iliad* but making it more pronounced, with Nisus as the lover and Euryalus as the handsome beloved. *The Aeneid* touches on such love elsewhere, but this theme had little influence on later writers of epics and was often omitted or obscured by translators (Williams 1999: 116–18; Summers 2002: 669; Crompton 2003: 85–6). In fact, it is possible to read the Nisus-Euryalus episode as slightly critical of the lovers (Hubbard 2003: 345; although see Drake 1998: 77–80). Drake calls Aeneas himself a handsome "stud" and finds much of the poem homoerotic (1998: 73, 76; cf. Hubbard 2014: 77–8; although see Williams 1999: 145–6). In any case, it was the second eclogue, influenced by Theocritus, that became "the most celebrated expression of male love" in Latin, partly because of its realism, irony, and humor (Crompton 2003: 92; see also Drake 1998: 70; Hubbard 2003: 345 and Larson 2012: 110). It idealized male-male love in ways uncommon in much other Roman literature (Hubbard 2014: 77).

HORACE (65–8), another important poet, has been called "bisexual, with [a] homosexual preference"; his poems to male youths strike some as more convincing than his poems to women, and his attitudes toward sex in general have been called mostly rational, casual, and sometimes humorous (Dyne 1990: 562–3; cf. Crompton 2003: 557; although see Drake 1998: 88). Cantarella argued that Horace takes for granted the common idea that men will be attracted to non-hairy youths but will also court adult women (1992: 139–40), and Woods (1998: 32) saw Horace as convincingly bisexual (cf. Summers 2002: 346–47; see also Hubbard 2014: 74). His "gay" interests seem to have been in young, handsome male slaves, but he also stressed intense male friendships that have struck later readers as romantic (Summers 2002: 347–8). He may have been indifferent to his slaves' own feelings or desires, and his poetry has been called neither idealistic nor passionate (Crompton 2003: 93).

TIBULLUS (50–17), another important poet, also deals with "gay" themes. He imitates Catullus (Dynes 1990: 1123), praises both youths and women, and attacks corrupt male youths (Dynes 1990: 1307; Hubbard 2014: 75). Cantarella (1992) stressed his real insights into male-male relations, the ways he echoes classical Greek ideals of "gay" love, and the ways these echoes indicate changes in Roman culture (128–35; cf. Hubbard 2014: 75–6). He describes "proper" male love (Nissinen 1998: 73), writes more subtly than Catullus, emphasizes that youths are complex, and also stresses that time brings change (Woods 1998: 34–5; cf. Crompton 2003: 88). He even offers advice on how to court youths, celebrates their modest confidence, and probably describes free youths rather than slaves while taking bisexuality for granted (Summers 2002: 556–7; cf. Crompton 2003: 90; Hubbard 2014: 75–6). Crompton (2003: 90), discussing Tibullus, suggests that "sensitive Romans must have renounced the rights of sexual access the law theoretically gave them and declined to force themselves" on young reluctant slaves, courting them instead. Hubbard (2003: 345) similarly highlights the sometimes complicated romantic elements of Tibullus's elegies.

OVID (43 BCE–17/18 CE), the influential poet, although bisexual, considered heterosexual eroticism superior to male-male sex because it pleased both partners (Halperin 1990: 134; Cantarella 1992: 138–9; Drake 1998: 85; Summers 2002: 557). In fact, Drake considered Ovid less than a kindred "gay" spirit (1998: 85). This poet's famous *Art of Love* says little about male-male sex and condemns such sex between adults; yet his *Metamorphoses* beautifully depict several same-sex relationships (Woods 1998: 40; cf. Fone 2000: 46; although see Hubbard 2014: 78), including one involving Orpheus, a story often later condemned by Christian artists (Summers 2002: 558; cf. Crompton 2003: 206). Ovid is unusual in depicting what seems to be transgender and/or lesbian love, but this sexual "problem" is resolved when a goddess changes one girl into a boy (Summers 2002: 558; cf. Hubbard 2003: 17). Louis Crompton (2003) has called Ovid "a tolerant heterosexual" who, in the *Metamorphoses*," treats the bisexuality of Greek myth without prejudice" (94). Crompton also termed Ovid's positive treatment of lesbian love "all but unique in classical literature" (Crompton 2003: 97; although see Aldrich and Wotherspoon 2002: 395–7 for his negative comments on Sappho and lesbianism). Like most classical writers, he satirized effeminate men (Hubbard 2003: 6), and he may even have been less positive about homosexuality in general than is often assumed (Hubbard 2003: 346, although see Larson 2012: 135–6). But the *Metamorphoses* provided, in later centuries, some of the most widely read accounts of same-sex love (Aldrich and Wotherspoon 2002: 395–7). David Robinson (2006: 163–250) reviewed at length various critics' interpretations of the Iphis and Ianthe tale (165–6) and later argued that Iphis, as well as the story itself, "ultimately treats lesbian sex as unnatural not merely in the sense of going against what Nature intended, but in a far more absolute sense: lesbian sex is an oxymoron, it cannot happen, it is literally, physically impossible." But Robinson also contended that "other characters in the *Metamorphoses* are willing, even able, to brave Nature," so that lesbian and other homoerotic desires and acts are presented more positively by Ovid than might be suggested by the Iphis and Ianthe story alone (171). Emma Donoghue (2010) discussed at length Ovid's treatment of lesbian themes (21–49; 107–8), stressing in particular his account of Iphis and Ianthe and the echoes of that tale in later literature (21), which sometimes varied Ovid's own emphases (24, 27–9). Donoghue credited Ovid with popularizing not only the "female bridegroom" motif but also the "male amazon" theme—two of the many standard literary treatments of "lesbian" ideas Donoghue explored.

PETRONIUS ARBITER (27–66) objectively detailed "gay" sex (among many other kinds) in his fragmentary *Satyricon* (Dynes 1990: 978–9, 1124), also known as *Satyrica*, which combines prose and verse (Aldrich and Wotherspoon 2002: 407–8). Even lesbianism is depicted (Cantarella 1992: 165), and even "pathics" are positively presented (Richlin 1992: 221)—both rare developments in classical literature. John Boswell saw evidence in the book of close, enduring bonds between same-aged, same-sex couples (1994: 66–8). In fact, many if not most of the book's characters are gay (Woods 1998: 38–9), including the central pair (Fone 2000: 47), and this work has been called not only "the first novel" but also "the first gay fiction," with male-male relationships "at the center of its rambling plot" (Fone 2000: 99). Drake called the book chaotic but remarkable in its emphasis on pleasure (1998: 91), while Hubbard argued that this text, like others by Petronius and Martial, shows that "some men were genuinely incapable of sex with women" (2003: 3, 383–4, 386), thus providing evidence of actual sexual orientations. Hubbard, who called the *Satyricon* campy (2014: 81; cf. Aldrich and Wotherspoon 2002: 407–8) also thought it showed that Roman slaves could rise socially and economically through male-male sex (2003: 14).

MARTIAL (40–104), a witty, unrestrained, often satirical writer of epigrams, has been called bisexual with strong homosexual preferences; he admired handsome, non-effeminate youths (although see Crompton 2003: 104), viciously attacking adult "pathics" and lesbians and urging adult males to love their wives (Dynes 1990: 771; 1124; cf. Cantarella 1992: 150; Woods 1998: 35, Summers 2002: 558–9; Crompton 2003: xiii, 53; Hubbard 2014: 79). Like other Romans, he fancied young male slaves (Cantarella 1992: 148; Richlin 1992: 221; Hubbard 2003: 10, 384) and treated sex, in general, with irony, humor, and even ridicule, but he thought celibacy impossible (Woods 1998: 35–8). He mentioned "the special pleasures of anal intercourse" (Williams 1999: 89; cf. Larson 2012: 110), at least for the active partner, since he mocked men who were either effeminate and/or desired to be penetrated. But he also satirized men who wanted to seem more "macho" than they really were (Fone 2000: 48, 52–3; Hubbard 2014: 79) and attacked lesbians who sought to penetrate other women. He felt special contempt for anyone—male or female—who performed oral sex (Crompton 2003: 98, 104; cf. Larson 2012: 135). He admired male slaves who took the initiative erotically, presenting themselves to be penetrated (Hubbard 2003: 13), and he implies that some gay males were forced to behave as heterosexuals (Hubbard 2003: 13, 386). Gary Simes argued that many of Martial's poems

> leave us in little doubt that his primary sexual orientation was homosexual; he responded to male beauty, and desired the affectionate company and attentions of and sex with younger men, though he speaks of occasional encounters with women. It seems highly unlikely that he was married, despite a few references to a wife. In the circles in which he moved, it did not matter, for men, whether one preferred one's own sex or the other or both, and he makes it known that he preferred his own.
>
> (Aldrich and Wotherspoon 2002: 355)

JUVENAL (47 CE–?), a ferocious satirist, attacked such figures as effeminate males, male transvestites, and male hustlers, but he also recommended the sexual pleasures young males could provide (Dynes 1990: 651–2) while mocking some forms of gay marriage (Dynes 1990: 1123; Fone 2000: 44, 48). Once he even suggested that effeminate men were uncontrolled heterosexuals (Richlin 1992: 222), and "pathics" were high on his target list (Cantarella 1992: 153–4; Nissinen 1998: 72–3; Fone 2000: 44, 50), as were male prostitutes, men who proffered oral sex, overly (suspiciously) "macho" men, "lispers," male hustlers who lured other men away from their wives, hypocritical teachers who lusted after their male students, and masculine women (Fone 2000: 48, 50–1, 53; Crompton 2003: 104; Hubbard 2003: 385). His second satire has been called "the longest pronouncement on homosexuality by any Latin writer in any genre," but he was as much a misogynist as a homophobe (Cantarella 1992: 152). He even said that male youths could be less troublesome than wives, and he may have preferred youths himself. One scholar has in fact suggested that his attacks on effeminate men may have been self-protecting (Summers 2002: 559; Crompton 2003: 104–5) while also acknowledging that such attacks were typical of many bisexual Roman poets (Crompton 2003: 53). Men overly concerned about their appearance disgusted him (Crompton 2003: 104). Hubbard cites Juvenal as one of various Roman poets who suggested that some men were exclusively gay, even suggesting that Juvenal provides evidence of a gay subculture in Rome (2003: 3–4, 386; cf. Hubbard 2014: 70) as well as evidence of male prostitutes hired to service both husbands and their wives (2003: 3–4, 385). But some scholars have suggested that the often-vicious speakers of Juvenal's satires are so over-the-top that they themselves are implicitly mocked (see Hubbard 2014: 80).

Later Roman creative writers also dealt with homoerotic themes. **STATIUS** (45–96) famously and affectionately lamented a friend's loss of his fifteen-year-old beloved, a male slave whose beauty and character inspired deep feelings (Summers 2002: 558; Crompton 2003: 103; Hubbard 2003: 13, 384), although one scholar noted that Statius made the youth sound less like a slave than a hero (Larson 2012: 110). **ATHENAEUS** (fl. ca. 200 CE) emphasized male-male relationships (Dynes 1990: 87–8, 501; Crompton 2003: 118), sometimes satirically (Nissinen 1998: 80), but he himself also wrote homoerotic poems (Summers 2002: 560). **LUCIAN** (125–ca. 180), unusually, wrote (in Greek) about lesbianism (Dynes 1992: 751–3; Hubbard 2003: 468–73; Davidson 2007: 506; Larson 2012: 135), while **LONGUS** (second century BCE?), although using Greek to satirize gay lust (Nissinen 1998: 80–1; Hubbard 2003: 445–6), also described a handsome youth. **PHILOSTRATUS** (ca. 170/72–247/50) composed roughly thirty fictional love letters to youths (Summers 2002: 560) and may even (unusually) provide evidence of love between adult males (Hubbard 2003: 5). Numerous other writers might also be mentioned, but describing them would merely reiterate much that has already been said. Hubbard concluded his own survey by asserting that "Roman literature of the classical period (from roughly 200 BCE to 200 CE) reveals such a diversity of perspectives toward same-sex love and lust that it defies generalization" (2014: 82). Suffice it to say, however, that as the classical, "pagan" period waned, the Christian "middle ages" were in the offing and would take a much harsher view of homoeroticism.

2

The Middle Ages

Early Medieval Europe: 350–1200

The earliest surviving homosocial poems from the Middle Ages are anything but explicitly sexual, perhaps because they and many later, similar medieval poems were written by Christian clerics. Thus, **ALCUIN** (735–804), an English monk, wrote a humorous, affectionate poem for a young monk who left his abbey and a poem of loving friendship to an older monk (Wilhelm 1995: 142–5) and otherwise expressed the "passionate friendship" typical among religious people of his era (Aldrich and Wotherspoon 2002: 15–16). John Boswell argued that Alcuin's writings indicate that same-sex affection (at least between males) was taken for granted in his era and that even same-sex behavior involving males could evoke chuckles rather than harsh condemnation (1981: 189–91). (He also quoted, however, a vicious poem from this period attacking lesbians [1980: 185], and Boswell's interpretations, in general, have been challenged by many critics; see Frantzen 1998).

Like Alcuin, **HRABANUS MAURUS** (776–856) composed Christian poems of "eroticized friendship" for a fellow abbot (Fone 1998: 103–4). **GOTTSCHALK** (805–69), an imprisoned monk, wrote a consoling, deeply affectionate poem at the behest of a young friend (Wilhelm 1995: 145–7; see Boswell on the poem's complexly amorous language [1980: 192–3]). And **WALAFRID STRABO** (ca. 848–9) expressed chaste love for his own young friend (Wilhelm 1995: 147; Fone 1998: 104–5). **NOTKER BALBULUS** (ca. 840–912), a Swiss monk, expressed intense regard for a physically and emotionally distant youth, while that youth and another—**SALOMO** (860–920) **AND WALDO**—expressed joint regard for Balbulus (Wilhelm 1995: 148–9). Meanwhile, an anonymous poem titled *O ADMIRABILE VENERIS IDOLUM* (ca. 900), "often considered the first real love poem of the modern world," expressed increasingly intense affection for a youth who had departed from the (presumably male) speaker (Wilhelm

1995: 149: 50). Boswell argued that probably neither the poem's subject nor tone "struck educated contemporaries as indecorous" (1980: 187).

BEOWULF (ca. 8th–11th centuries) has been seen as part of a generally "homosocial" ethos of Old English literature, in which sometimes-intense male friendships outweighed relations between men and women (Lochrie 2014: 91–2; cf. Frantzen 1998: 92–9). Poetic graffiti in a ninth-century manuscript repeatedly attack sodomy, but such jottings also describe a handsome youth (Wilhelm 1995: 172–4). **MARBOD OF RENNES** (1035–123), eventually a bishop, alternately described intense homosocial (perhaps homoerotic) affection; warned of hellish punishment for homosexual acts (Wilhelm 1995: 153–4); and echoed Horace in describing at length a youth's physical beauty (only to stress that it would not last [Fone 1998: 105–6]; cf. Aldrich and Wotherspoon 2002: 350–1). John Boswell suggested that Marbod's prominence "made his attitudes toward gay sexuality extremely influential. Copies or imitations of his gay poems occur in manuscripts all over Europe, from England to Germany" (1980: 248–29). According to Robert Aldrich, however,

> Marbod's verses, like those of Baudri of Bourgueil (one of his students) and Hildebert of Lavardin (to whom Marbod dedicated a work), exemplify a tradition of medieval poetry which celebrated same-sex friendship while generally denouncing the wickedness of sexual relations.
>
> (Aldrich and Wotherspoon 2002: 351; see also Frantz 1998)

GODFREY OF WINCHESTER (d. 1107) wrote ambiguously, but sometimes disapprovingly, about homoeroticism (Wilhelm 1995: 150–1). **BAUDRI OF BOURGEIL** (1046–130), closely connected to the court of William the Conqueror (Goodich 1979: 6), stressed that handsome, beloved youths age; mourned the death of a handsome, talented youth; wrote warmly to a male friend; lamented a friend's departure; bemoaned that friend's absence; and praised another youth's many traits, including his beauty (Wilhelm 1995: 157; cf. Fone 1998: 106). Boswell saw Baudri as epitomizing the transition from "the ascetic passions of the monastic love tradition … to the baldly erotic poetry more characteristic of the eleventh and twelfth centuries" (1980: 244) and also argued that even

> Baudri's disclaimers reveal profoundly altered attitudes toward gay people and feelings. … Baudri may have been troubled about the reactions of the laity to his erotic relationships and poetry, but for his own part he clearly accepted love as good in and of itself and had no difficulty in addressing his love to a person of the same gender.
>
> (1980: 247)

Poems by **HILDEBERT OF LAVARDIN** (ca. 1055–133) vigorously condemned widespread sodomy while also describing Jove's desire for Ganymede and Apollo's love for Hyacinth (Wilhelm 1995: 158–9). In fact, Boswell argued that Hildebert was far less anti-gay than he seemed, suggesting that he attacked infidelity in marriage more than gay sex itself (1980: 236–8). **FOUR ANONYMOUS POEMS FROM AN ELEVENTH-CENTURY GERMAN MANUSCRIPT** attacked a corrupt male, described how a handsome youth made other males burn, mocked gay clergy, and condemned a gay bishop (Wilhelm 1995: 171–2).

PETER ABELARD (1079–142) sensitively rehearsed the love of David and Jonathan (Wilhelm 1995: 159–63; cf. Boswell 1980: 238–9 and Boswell 1994: 282). **HILARY THE ENGLISHMAN** (ca. 1125) wrote "overtly homosexual" poems. In one he intensely praised a handsome youth; in another, he elaborately extolled a blond youth's androgynous beauty, saying it appealed to young people of both sexes; in still another, he declared his desire for another beautiful youth who was handsome enough to satisfy Jove both in bed and out (Wilhelm 1995: 163–6; Fone 1998: 106–7; cf. Goodich 1979: 6). Boswell noted that Hilary's poems to females are usually seen as far less convincing than his poems to males (1980: 249; see also 372–4). In an important passage, Michael Morgan Holmes observed that although

> the tradition of medieval homoerotic verse is much 'narrower' than the heteroerotic stream, the so-called renaissance which affected much of twelfth-century Western Europe created a cultural climate in which a relative flourishing of masculine same-gender literature occurred. As Stehling argues, because these representations of homoerotic longing appear only in Latin and never in the vernacular, male religious communities such as monasteries form the likeliest source for these comparatively erudite writings. Unlike the prose treatises of a roughly contemporary Englishman, **AELRED OF RIEVAULX**, however, Hilary's do not integrate the love of God with desire for other males. Hilary's homoerotic poems instead share with those of his near contemporaries **MARBOD OF RENNES** and Baudri of Bourgueil an exclusive focus on the amorous feelings of a man for a boy; attraction for another grown male never enters their pictures.
> (Aldrich and Wotherspoon 2002: 247–8)

Holmes cautioned against some critics' tendencies to assume that the homoerotic verse of Hilary and others merely imitated classical traditions, and he cited other scholars to support his view (Aldrich and Wotherspoon 2002: 248).

BERNARD OF CLUNY (mid-twelfth century) heatedly denounced filthy sodomy, which he said was widespread and openly practiced

(Wilhelm 1995: 166–7; cf. Boswell 1980: 232–3). **SERLO OF WILTON** (ca. 1110–81) playfully implied sexual desire for another male (Wilhelm 1995: 167–8). **WALTER OF CHÂTILLON** (ca. 1135–after 1184) condemned rampant sodomy (Wilhelm 1995: 168–70), but Boswell observed that

> when he came to comment on the actual moral gravity of such behavior, he pictured God as simply 'laughing at' clerics guilty of it—a rather casual reaction to behavior which would within a hundred years be considered second only to murder.
>
> (1980: 236)

TWO LESBIAN LOVE LETTERS FROM A GERMAN MANUSCRIPT (1100s? 1200s?) are unusual in the Middle Ages simply in expressing women's love for other women, although the language of neither letter is very physical (Wilhelm 1995: 174–6). Boswell called one of these verse letters "perhaps the outstanding example of medieval lesbian literature" and quoted it in full (1980: 220–1).

In a lengthy, popular, poetic late twelfth-century **DEBATE BETWEEN GANYMEDE AND HELEN**, youthful Ganymede defended sex exclusively between males, said it is practiced by powerful persons, claimed youths could enrich themselves by selling their bodies, attacked old men who lusted after youths, and mercilessly mocked women. Abruptly, however, he admitted losing the debate, and the watching gods firmly condemned sodomy (Wilhelm 1995: 176–85; cf. Goodich 1979: 6), as did much of the penitential literature of the Middle Ages (see Frantzen 1998). John Boswell considered this poem so aesthetically important and culturally influential that he not only discussed it at length (1980: 255–60) but also translated it in full (1980: 381–9). He noted, variously, that it was "recited aloud" and "known by heart" (256), that it may indicate a developing gay subculture (256), that it unusually gave a woman a major role (257), that it may therefore imply the growth of women's social prominence (257), that it gave the woman an unconvincing victory (257), and generally that it resembled an Arab poem from the same period (257–8). Boswell also contended that the poem (a) implied widespread homosexuality among prominent people (259), (b) made witty pro-gay arguments that were long remembered (259), and (c) implied a tolerant audience (260). The poem, he concluded,

> was the product of a society in which gay people were an important segment of the population, where defenses of gay love were sufficiently common to have

taken on a defiant rather than apologetic tone and to have inspired poetic genius in representing them. The poem's extreme popularity in many areas of Europe may be due either to the fascination it exercised on less tolerant societies or to the ubiquity of the sort of circumstances that gave rise to it.

(1980: 260)

Boswell also quoted from other poems from this period that both attacked and defended love and sex between males (1980: 261–5). Nevertheless, at around the same time, **ALAN OF LILLE** (ca.1128–ca. 1202) wrote a hymn that "voices homophobic feelings in the most negative way possible" (Wilhelm 1995: 169; cf. Boswell 1980: 310). In a prose work, Alan "argued that sodomy and homicide are the most serious sins, since they call forth the wrath of God" (Aldrich and Wotherspoon 2002: 14–15; cf. Goodich 1979: 33–5). Keiser 1997 (71–92) argued that the poet who created the poem *Cleanness* (probably the same poet who authored *Sir Gawain and the Green Knight*) drew on a literary context that included Alan's *Complaint* for his "polemic against homosexual deviance" (71). According to Keiser, Alan condemned, as unnatural, any kind of non-reproductive sex and thus contributed to a social climate of intolerance within which the *Cleanness*-poet depicted "homosexual desire as a singularly monstrous and unconscionable vice" (72). Although Keiser noted some differences between the treatise and the poem (83–5), she maintained that both works condemned sodomy, sodomites, and the biblical citizens of Sodom (85–6). Commenting on earlier interpretations of Alan's *Complaint*, Keiser disputed, in particular, the views of John Boswell (86–7), concluding that although that work never vindicates eros, it does "contribute to what might be termed the mystique of heterosexism as cosmically ordained" by God (91).

In an anonymous thirteenth-century poetic **DEBATE BETWEEN GANYMEDE AND HEBE**, the frustrated Hebe sarcastically attacked Ganymede, who responded fairly modestly that his beauty appealed both to male and female gods (Wilhelm 1995: 187–90). Boswell discussed this poem at length, noting its erudition, classical allusions, and blatantly pro-gay agenda (1980: 260–1). He called the poem an original, apparently personal statement; noted its misogynistic elements, its use of contemporary gay slang, its implication that gays were gay by nature (and therefore "inculpable"); and, therefore, the possibility that there was a growing acceptance of that view (1980: 261). Perhaps even lesbian desires were felt by some: a song by the female troubadour **BIETRIS DE ROMANS** (early 1200s) fervently celebrated the beauty and virtue of another woman (Wilhelm 1995: 263).

Later Medieval Europe: 1200–1500

DANTE ALIGHIERI (1265–321), perhaps the most renowned and influential of all early Italian poets, described, in his *Divine Comedy*, his own imaginary journey through hell, purgatory, and heaven. His relatively benign depiction of sodomites has long provoked debate, with some commentators suggesting that he could distinguish between a sinner's vices and virtues, others implying that he may have had bisexual tendencies himself, and still others arguing that he treated those with fundamentally gay orientations less harshly than those who deliberately chose gay sex (Dynes 1990: 294–6). John Boswell observed that Dante unusually, for his era, depicted sodomites in purgatory as far less guilty, and far closer to heaven, than other sinners (1994: 262–3), while Wilhelm commented that although Dante was not himself homosexual, "he did create one of the most sensitive portraits of a homosexual in world literature: that of his beloved teacher, Brunetto Latini," who is shown in hell, although other homosexuals are shown in purgatory, implying that for them "the way is ultimately open to Paradise" (1995: 265). Gregory Woods (1998: 47–8) noted that Dante's sodomites always appear in groups, as a kind of gay "subculture," and that those in purgatory seem guilty of excess rather than unnatural behavior, although Woods did concede that no sodomites appear in Dante's final vision of Paradise. Two surveys of recent scholarship on Dante outlined the sheer divergence of opinion about his depiction of sodomites, with some scholars arguing that that depiction has little to do with actual sex and others arguing just the opposite (Haggerty 2000: 242–3; Murphy 2000: 40–3). Another such survey suggested that only immoderate same-sex desire seems condemned and that the poem provides early evidence that some people were gay by orientation rather than choice (Summers 2002: 176). Crompton (2003: 208–12) helpfully laid out many key issues. He outlined interpretive difficulties and disagreements; noted that an "association of homosexuality with intellectuals and teachers was common in Dante's day" (209); and suggested that Dante "takes for granted the traditional theological condemnation of homosexuality but treats the sodomites with more respect than any other inhabitants of hell" (210). Crompton detailed the puzzlement this attitude provoked among commentators and concluded that Dante may have been far less homophobic than most of his contemporaries.

An Old French **STORY OF LANCELOT AND GALEHAUT** (early thirteenth century), depicted Galehaut's intense desire to sleep next to Lancelot, recounted their ensuing deep friendship, and reported how Galehaut dies when he thinks Lancelot is dead (Fone 1998: 111–22). In the **STORY OF AMIS AND AMILE** (thirteenth century), Amile, apparently at God's commandment, slays his own children and uses their blood to cure Amis of leprosy, only to find them resurrected (Fone 1998: 122–4; cf. Boswell 1980: 240).

But it is **GEOFFREY CHAUCER** (1341–1400) whose satirical hints about the homoeroticism of a Pardoner seem more typically medieval. Although many early works on gay literature completely omitted Chaucer (although see Wilhelm 1995: 273–6), that tendency is changing. David Frantzen (1998: 255–66) set Chaucer's *Man of Law's Tale* within earlier and later homoerotic contexts, suggesting that "Chaucer made nothing" of the same-sex affection of Hermengyld and Custance—or at least nothing sexual. "Nor should we. But we should not forget that it *is* same-sex love" (261–2). But Elizabeth Keiser (1997: *passim*) commented that *The General* Prologue to the *Canterbury Tales* "suggests that a man's excessive attention to fashionable apparel could signal dubious sexual preference and practice," especially in the Pardoner's case (149). Gregory Woods (1998: 49–52) compared Chaucer's treatments of homoeroticism to those of **GIOVANNI BOCCACCIO** (1313–75), finding Chaucer less explicit and more conventionally Christian. Woods called the Pardoner "the first gay character in English literature, certainly the first major one" (partly because this character seems *essentially* gay rather than opportunistically bisexual), and he recounted critics' efforts to define the character's sexuality and explain his apparent effeminacy. Byrne Fone, in 2000, pulled no punches, crediting Chaucer with having created

> perhaps the most disturbing picture of a [medieval] sodomite. His Summoner and Pardoner are a repellent ecclesiastical pair whose presence constitutes a specific condemnation of a sexually dissolute and corrupt clergy and of sodomites as diseased and abominable outcasts.
>
> (170)

Fone detailed how and why Chaucer's contemporaries would have equated these characters (especially the Pardoner) with sexual deviance (2000: 170–3; cf. Aldrich and Wotherspoon 2002: 114–15). Glenn Burger (2003) not only surveyed disagreements about the Pardoner (140–42ff.) but tried generally to "queer" readers' interpretations of Chaucer by arguing that his sexual views are in fact hard to pin down. Finally, Nida Surber (2010) argued that Chaucer not only tolerated homosexuality but actually (if surreptitiously) endorsed it.

3

The English Renaissance

EDMUND SPENSER (1552–99), author of *The Faerie Queene* and of such important lyric poems as *The Shepheardes Calender*, received no separate, extended treatment in the encyclopedias edited by Dynes (1990), Haggerty and Zimmerman (2000), or Summers (2002). He *was* discussed, however, in the pioneering early work by Rictor Norton (1974: 149–71), who stressed Hobbinol's homoerotic feelings for Colin in *The Shephearde's Calender*, called the gloss by the unidentified "E. K." on that poem's "January" eclogue the first critique of a homosexual theme in literature, commented extensively on E. K's allusions, and suggested that E. K's gloss is far less equivocal than is often assumed. Rictor also discussed later reactions to E. K's gloss, suggested that Spenser's treatment of homoeroticism in the *Calender* was deliberately ambiguous, related that treatment to classical literary traditions, questioned dismissals of the poem's homoerotic dimensions, and particularly stressed homoerotic motives behind Hobbinol's gifts to Colin. He emphasized Hobbinol's constant, selfless love for Colin, the poem's satire of heterosexual lust, and hints associating Hobbinol with spiritual love and, in contrast, Colin's love for Rosalind with mere physical desire. According to Norton, the *Calender* offers "no explicit condemnation or praise of amorous love between men. Spenser's other poems are similarly ambiguous on this point" (169)—a claim Norton justified by examining *The Faerie Queene*. His early discussion of Spenser (which ended by noting the scant evidence of Spenser's own sexuality) is still unusually long and substantial. Bruce R. Smith's seminal work *Homosexual Desire in Shakespeare's England* (1991) argued that Spenser, both in *The Shepheardes Calender* and in *The Faerie Queene*, valued male friendship, distrusted mere sexual desire of any kind, and ultimately celebrated generative, straight married love (94–9). Dorothy Stephens, discussing the varied roles of women in *The Faerie Queene* (in Goldberg 1994: 190–212), argued that

> It is precisely because of the overwhelmingly negative cultural pressure upon women's friendships—superadded to the pressure of romance narrative

structure, which tends so deflect and defer the desires of both sexes—that the few female alliances in the poem take on such importance. While some of the poem's voices attempt to circumscribe or constrict relationships among women, other narrative voices seem on the point of acknowledging that these socially marginal alliances provide the poem with a kind of energy found nowhere else.

(203–4)

Gregory Woods (1998) quoted Spenser's praise of Sir Philip Sidney's physical and moral beauty, related it to homoeroticism in pastoral elegy, and noted the heavy influence (except sexually) of Theocritus on *The Shepheardes Calender* (cf. Goldberg in McCallum and Tuhkanen 2014: 171–3). Woods argued that E. K.'s commentary on the *Calender* condemned homoeroticism explicitly but not unambiguously (cf. Norton 1974; Goldberg 1991: 203–4; Smith 1991: 95; Hammond 1996: 32–3, Fone 1998: 158–63, Hammond 2002: 17; and Goldberg 2014: 170–1). Woods thought Spenser (in the *Calender* as in *The Faerie Queene*) praised intense but non-sexual male friendship (110–13).

Mario DiGangi (1997: 31–45) thought it "important to recognize that male homoerotic desire in *The Faerie Queene*" can take alternate forms, including "androphilia, or orderly love between men. In book 3, the Legend of Chastity, the Hercules-Hylas myth illustrates disorderly homoeroticism (the antithesis of the book's virtue)," while "in book 4, the Legend of Friendship, it illustrates orderly homoeroticism (the exemplar of the book's virtue)" (42).

In a valuable 2000 survey of "Studies in Homoeroticism," Valerie Traub briefly reviewed several essays on Spenser, most of them short and dealing with varied male bondings. Traub did, however, cite Camille Paglia's comments on various "homoerotic incidents" in Spenser's verse, finding, for instance, a "lesbian suggestiveness" in *The Faerie Queene*'s Malecasta and also noting that "Spenser habitually complicates even innocent exchanges by some erotic adjective" (320). Traub also reported others' comments on such matters as Malecasta, lesbianism, and the sexual implication of images of Elizabeth I (320). In her own groundbreaking book *The Renaissance of Lesbianism in Early Modern England* (2002), Traub discussed *The Faerie Queene*'s symbolic use of breast imagery, its depiction of play between naked women, and the voyeurism of a hidden male spectator (147–50). Louis Crompton (2003: 367) suggested that although the epic's ambiguous erotic details "have puzzled readers," Spenser's "devotion to chastity is quite as strong as his passion for beauty" (367).

SIR PHILIP SIDNEY (1554–86) enormously influenced many other writers, and the homoerotic dimensions of his work have begun to receive more and more attention. Rictor Norton (1974: 306–14) discussed Herbert Languet's frustrated, unrequited longing for his young friend ("Faithful Friend"), while Bruce Smith (1991: 139–45) explored complicated sexual shenanigans in Sidney's huge romance, *The Arcadia*, saying it describes both "gay" and "lesbian" desire and hints of androgyny and elements of transvestism—all in a complex plot that ultimately (or at least overtly) affirms heterosexual values (139–45; cf. Bredbeck 1991: 105–8; Hammond 1996: 45–6). Casey Charles (1992) explored similar issues at length, stressing the work's "representation of man's capacity to love another man regardless and in spite of his sexual orientation" (490). In 1997, Richard A. Levin explored lesbianism in *The Arcadia*, and in 2002 Julie Crawford noted that Sidney had not only translated Sappho's most famous lesbian poem but had also used a kind of poetic form known as the "sapphic" to depict same-sex desire between women. Terry Castle (2003) made similar points (86–7) and also said that Sidney, in the *New Arcadia*, depicted "lesbian panic": "the gripping fear that one's erotic longings are at once utterly reprehensible and the deepest part of one's being" (87). Stephen Guy-Bray (2008) discussed Strephon and Klaius in the *Arcadia*, comparing and contrasting their friendship with that of Pyrocles and Musidorus in the same work, while Emma Donoghue (2010: 49–51) wrote that by "far the most probing treatment of a woman's response to a male amazon" is found in the *Arcadia*, where the "feminine names and pronouns act as a sort of prose costume, letting readers forget that the Amazon is really a man" (49). Donoghue argued that many characters—male and female, old and young—fall for the Amazon's charms (49): when one female realizes that her love for the Amazon "is erotic, the language becomes military: an internal war" (50). Even when she realizes that the Amazon is a disguised male," she is not ready to deny … same-sex desire … but in fact "harps on it" (51), as if "she is almost nostalgic for … the time when she was the active desirer rather than the passive desired, and is not yet ready to let go of the imaginary [Amazon] who won her love" (51).

The treatment of homoerotic desires by **CHRISTOPHER MARLOWE** (1564–93) has long fascinated readers, especially since Marlowe may himself have been defiantly "gay." In his enormously influential early book titled *Homosexuality in Renaissance England* (1982), Alan Bray (44–7) suggested that Marlowe probably believed in God, just not in Christ, which would explain his alleged claim that Jesus himself was homosexual (63–4). Rodney Simard (in Dynes 1990: 768–9) mentioned contemporary claims that Marlowe fancied youths, noted the poet's literary allusions to homoeroticism; called *Edward II* "the first gay play in English", and asserted that Marlowe there "surpasses the achievements of many explicitly gay writers" by sensitively and complexly portraying "a doomed and passionate relationship between two men caught up in a repressive and homophobic society." Bruce Smith (1991: 205–22) emphasized Marlowe's strong interest in stories of "masters and minions" (205; cf. Hammond 1996: 50–1), suggested the teasing ambiguities of the playwright's presentation of Ganymede in his play *Dido* (206–7), argued that the effeminate son of the title character in *Tamburlaine, Part Two* is played for laughs (until his father brutally kills him [208–9]), and saw a similar gap between satire and tragedy in *Edward II*, where Marlowe creates sympathy for kinds of characters other writers often mocked (209–10). According to Smith, Marlowe, even while drawing on a source highly critical of the king, depicted Edward and his beloved "mate," Gaveston, as both sympathetic and unsympathetic and presented their opponents as class-obsessed "snobs" (210–18). Marlowe (Smith claimed) showed the King's situation in all its full complexity (218–21):

> As always in Marlowe, we have in *Edward II* a *double* perspective. Marlowe is both the satirist and the tragedian, both the oppressor and the victim …. Marlowe takes up where the satirists leave off. He accepts the satirists' dismissal of the sexual maverick as a social outcast; at the same time he lets us know what it is like to *be* that outcast.
>
> (221–2)

John Clum (1992: 202–8) commented on modern productions of the play, on Marlowe as a modern gay hero, on *Edward II* not simply as a history play but as a play about gay history, and on Edward as a gay martyr. Gregory Woods (Summers 1992: 69–84) discussed how youths, in Marlowe's works, often use their good looks to enhance their social power, while Jonathan Goldberg (1992: 106–41) challenged critics who underplayed homoeroticism in *Edward II*, explored theatrical cross-dressing during Marlowe's era (when boys played women on stage), noted that Marlowe does *not* present transvestism in his play, and stressed the play's emphasis on violations of class restrictions. Responding to Alan Bray's claims about Edward's friendship for and with Gaveston, Goldberg called these characters "sodomites" in far more than merely sexual terms, since "sodomy" in Marlowe's day could signify any disruption of social expectations. Powerful men in the play tolerate a sexual relationship between Edward and Gaveston as long as the powerful keep their own power. Later, discussing *Dido*, Goldberg reviewed critics' comments on sodomy there and elsewhere in Marlowe's works. In general, he explored relations between diverse definitions of sexuality and the relationship of those definitions both to homophobia and to misogyny as well as to Renaissance ideas of male friendship. Goldberg offered one of the earliest, most comprehensive discussions of Marlowe and homoeroticism.

An insightful 1994 article by Claude Summers, however, challenged Goldberg's (and Bray's) tendency to over-emphasize broad Renaissance definitions of "sodomy"—a tendency that Summers thought oversimplified the true complexity of that period's same-sex eroticism. Summers (in comments repeated in 2002) saw in Marlowe key evidence showing how early modern writers could both challenge and be constricted by prejudices against "sodomy" in both sexual and non-sexual terms. Discussing *Edward II* (in Goldberg 1994: 48–53), Alan Bray suggested that "Marlowe describes in this play what could be a sodomitical relationship, but he places it wholly within the incompatible conventions of Elizabethan friendship, in a tension which he never allows to be resolved. The image we see is simultaneously that of both friendship and its caricature" (49).

Paul Hammond (1996: 33–77) noted the contrast between nude male beauty and artificially clothed female beauty in Marlowe's poem *Hero and Leander*, contending that the poem both encourages and contains homoerotic desire—offering sexual pleasure from reading but distancing the object of that pleasure (Leander) by keeping him safely mythological. Discussing *Edward II*, Hammond highlighted a daring sexual pun (49), noted both the attractions and dangers of Gaveston (49–50), observed that Gaveston is criticized as exotically unEnglish (52), and concluded that the love between Edward and Gaveston seems

> doomed not so much because it is between two men, as because it places private satisfaction before public duty, and employs the state's resources of honour and offices as love-tokens. Gaveston is manipulative, Edward is irresolute. But the barons too are seeking their own advantage ....
>
> (53)

Carl Miller (1996: 171–87) commented on twentieth-century revivals of *Edward II* (171–2), reported comments about it by Ian McKellen, Derek Jarman, and Alan Bray (172–3), cautioned against reading it as simply celebrating sodomy (173), recounted its plot and related it to other works by Marlowe (173–7), stressed Gaveston's flaws (178–9), and explored the play's interests in clothing (180–4). Stephen Orgel (1996: 43–9) noted Marlowe's emphasis on physical homoeroticism in *Hero and Leander*; saw *Edward II* as unusual in so explicitly attacking homoerotic behavior; but also thought that the play satirized, perhaps even more strongly, such other "bad" conduct as the queen's adultery and the nobles' hunger for power. According to Orgel, Gaveston is condemned by others in the play less for being queer than for being insubordinate. Orgel also stressed that the play itself does not show the king being killed by a hot poker, as is so often assumed; instead, he is pressed to death.

Mario DiGangi, in his own discussion of *Edward II* (1997: 108–15), argued that

> by shifting our attention away from the disorderly intimacy between Edward and Gaveston, the ambitious favorite, and towards the disorderly intimacy between Edward and Mortimer, the ambitious peer, Marlowe partially defends Edward's relationship with his favorites. "Sodomy," understood not as a sexual act but as a politically transgressive relation between men, occurs most damagingly not between Edward and Gaveston but between Edward and the peers.
>
> (108)

Robert Drake (1998: 129–37) suggested that the barons object less to Edward's love for another man than to his love for Gaveston in particular (132), whom even Drake calls "insufferable" (133). Gregory Woods (1998: 84–92) variously stressed how some young males in Marlowe (such as Ganymede in *Dido*) often want gifts from male admirers (84–5); how other youths (such as Aeneas in the same play) are both handsome and virile (85); how Leander's beautiful body is treated mythologically; how Leander rejects being effeminized by Neptune; and how he is too innocent to recognize his own beauty (86). In contrast, Gaveston and another youth in *Edward II* know their charms and profit from them (86). Noting some critics' homophobia (86–7), Woods also reported that in one modern production, the king's gruesome murder (a burning-hot iron poker is shoved into his anus) was staged as a parodic love scene (87–8). Woods additionally noted that young males in Marlowe are often presented in "fancy dress or drag," showing that "they are either beloved already, or ready to be loved" (91).

In an important overview of homoeroticism in English Renaissance literature, Valerie Traub (2000: 304–8) surveyed much work on Marlowe. She noted sympathetic treatments of Edward II from as early as 1974 (by Leonora Brodwin), 1977 (by Purvis Boyette), 1983 (by Barbara Baines), 1984 (by Ronald Huebert), and 1988 (by Claude Summers). Traub said some critics emphasized Edward's violations of social, class, and political standards more than his sexual transgressions, citing work by Sharon Tyler and Scott Giantvalley (both from 1985), but she also noted Jonathan Goldberg's claim that Marlowe himself endorsed Edward's sodomitical subversions of cultural norms. Traub cited various critics who discussed the grim symbolism of Edward's murder, such as

Jennifer Brady (1991), Gregory Woods (1992), Stephen Guy-Bray (1991), and Gregory Woods (1992). Other critics she discussed included Dympna Callaghan (1996) on ways homoeroticism buttresses male power in *Edward II*; Viviana Comensoli (1993) on homophobia in that play; and Judith Haber (1994) on sodomy and "pointlessness."

Surveying commentary on other works, Traub reported William Zunder's view (in 1996) that *Hero and Leander* explores a "radical sexuality that acknowledges no restriction," Gregory Bredbeck's (1991) study of blazon imagery in Neptune's seduction of Leander, Judith Haber's interest in the poem's sexual and narrative stabilities (1998), and M. Morgan Holmes's argument (1995) that the poem's homoeroticism undermines stable identities. Other studies cited by Traub—such as ones by Constance Kuriyama (1980), Simon Shepherd (1986), Emily Bartels (1994), Patrick Cheney (1997), and Sara Deats (1997)—explore other aspects of masculinity, homoeroticism, and homophobia in Marlowe and in writings about him. Traub next described essays on various historical contexts of male-male eroticism in Marlowe, including work by Lawrence Normand, David Potter, Michael Hattaway, and Daryll Grantly (all from 1996). Hattaway's essay seems particularly interesting: it argues that there is "enough in Marlowe to question the current orthodox opinion that in the early modern period … there was homosexual activity without the emergence of homosexual identity" (307). Traub also surveyed a 1998 essay collection edited by Paul White titled *Marlowe, History, and Sexuality*, describing essays that discussed both sexual and political definitions of sodomy, commented on Derek Jarman's modern film *Edward II*, discussed effeminacy in Marlowe's banned poetic *Elegies*, and explored gender hierarchies in *Dido* (307). For anyone interested in a pre-twenty-first-century overview of Marlowe and homoeroticism, Traub's text is crucial.

Gregory Bredbeck (Haggerty 2000: 569) noted Elizabethan charges that Marlowe was a sodomite who called Jesus one, too; suggested that all major characters in *Edward II* are presented ambivalently; observed that Edward, nonetheless, wins remarkable sympathy despite his sexual tastes; and summarized homoerotic elements in other Marlovian works. Early in the new century, Claude Summers (2002: 432) observed that "Marlowe represents homoerotic situations and incidents more frequently and more variously than any other major writer of his day" and that "his posture is consistently oppositional vis-à-vis his culture's official condemnation of homosexuality even as that condemnation inevitably and powerfully shapes his varied representations." Summers said Marlowe ambiguously echoed a homoerotic poem by Virgil in his famous "Come live with me" lyric, suggested that Leander's encounter with Neptune comically flouts satire and homophobia, saw the early description of Leander's beauty as "exuberantly defiant", and commented on the limits of Leander's own sexual imagination. Summers additionally explored how Marlowe's classical allusions often justify homoeroticism, emphasized *Edward II*'s moral complexity, and stressed how sexuality is intertwined with issues of power in a play surprisingly sympathetic to the murdered king (432–4).

Alan Bray (Aldrich and Wotherspoon 2002: 353) called *Edward II* "the most revealing view left by the sixteenth century of the place homosexuality occupied in the England of [that] time" and intriguingly asserted that critics discussing "the apparently openly 'homosexual' nature of the play" have not realized how "the intense emotion, the passionate language and the embraces we see" between Edward and Gaveston paralleled "conventions of friendship between men in Marlowe's England, where homoeroticism, jokingly suggested (and as lightly denied), was the stuff of everyday life." According to Bray, Shakespeare's Sonnets are "only the most enduring product of that easy homoeroticism," but *Edward II* "gave such feelings real weight without ever making sodomy a fully explicit topic" (354).

Louis Crompton (2003), called Marlowe "unique in the English Renaissance in tacitly avowing his interest in his own sex" (368), stressed his alleged atheism (368–9), noted that his plays' protagonists are typically outsiders (369), highlighted his emphasis on male beauty (370), and suggested that if Leander were really Greek he would not have been surprised by Neptune's erotic interest in him (371). Crompton saw *Edward II* as relevant to the behavior of James VI of Scotland, heir to the English throne, whose interest in handsome men was already known in 1592 (372). Offering much historical detail about the real Edward II (372–6), Crompton called Marlowe's tragedy "the only Elizabethan drama with a homosexual protagonist and, indeed, the only English play to touch on … same-sex attraction" more than peripherally "before the twentieth century" (378). Crompton called its characterization complex and argued that Marlowe had, necessarily, to underplay Edward's obvious sodomy (378–9).

Michael Cornelius (2016: 37–98) argued that "even Marlowe's shamelessly 'pro-sodomite' work complicates Edward's sexuality rather than simply attempting to enshrine it" (26). Later, though, Cornelius stressed that in the depiction of Edward and Gaveston, "there is absolutely no concealment—nor even attempt at concealment." They are not simply friends; "they are lovers." Edward suggests a defiant Marlowe—"an author recognizing the importance of sexuality and same-sex desire" but "an author who likewise ignores" contemporary conventions (29; see also 114).

WILLIAM SHAKESPEARE (1564–1616) has been much studied by scholars interested in homoeroticism. Seymour Kleinberg, for instance (Kellogg 1983: 113–26), argued that *The Merchant of Venice* explores the "rivalry of romantic male friendship with the claims of conventional marriage" (113), noting how psychoanalytic critics had interpreted Antonio's friendship with Bassanio, how later critics had either underplayed that friendship or interpreted Antonio's feelings as perverse (114), how some insisted that the friendship was merely platonic (116), how the play's "happy ending" shows "the triumph of heterosexual marriage over the romantic but sterile infatuation of homoeroticism," and how the "play is filled with ambiguities of sexuality and money, love and hatred" (124).

Joseph Pequigney, in an important book-length study, argued

> (1) that the friendship treated in Sonnets 1–126 is decidedly amorous—passionate to a degree and in ways not dreamed of in the published [commentary and criticism], the interaction between the friends being sexual in both orientation and practice; (2) that verbal data are clear and copious in detailing physical intimacies between them; (3) that the psychological dynamics of the poet's relations with the friend comply in large measure with those expounded in Freud's authoritative discussions of homosexuality; and (4) that Shakespeare produced not only extraordinary amatory verse but the grand masterpiece of homoerotic poetry.
>
> (1985: 1)

Pequigney then developed these ideas for well over 200 pages.

Eve Kosofsky Sedgwick (1985: 28–50) noted that homosexuals have often been attracted by the sonnets, that scholars have been forced, by some of these poems, to discuss homosexuality, that the poems have often been read unhistorically, and that many mysteries surround them. She emphasized the importance of the triangular relationship between the male speaker, the male youth, and the so-called "dark lady," paying particular attention to the "Two loves I have" sonnet, and later suggested that the sonnets "record and thematize misogyny and gynephobia" in ways affected by a larger stress on male bonds (33). However, in an argument central to her book as a whole, Sedgwick also argued that the sonnets *before* the arrival of the dark lady

> present a male-male love that, like the love of the Greeks, is set firmly within a structure of institutionalized social relations that are carried out via women: marriage, name, family, loyalty to progenitors and to posterity, all depend on the youth's making a particular use of women that is not, in the abstract, seen as opposing, denying, or detracting from his bond to the speaker.
>
> (35)

The dark lady, however, threatens to destabilize this equilibrium because "*any erotic involvement with an actual woman threatens to be unmanning*" (36) for at least one man involved in the complex triangle.

Rodney Simard's brief article (Dynes 1990) touched on debates about the poet's own sexuality, found little evidence of gay characters or pro-gay sentiments in the plays, but mentioned that women's roles were played by Elizabethan boys, often giving various scenes and characters a homoerotic edge (1190–1). Simard found many of the first 126 of Shakespeare's sonnets "clearly homoerotic" in ways critics had often downplayed. Simard rejected such efforts, emphasizing the sonnets' psychological and physical implications and suggesting, at the very least, their bisexual sensibility, even if the male speaker is not Shakespeare himself (1191). Simard concluded that

> Shakespeare's sexual identity will probably always be speculative, but this in no way diminishes the achievement of a playwright who could sensitively chart the full range of human involvement in a compassionate portrait of human diversity. But without question, Shakespeare is the author of some of the finest lyric poems to describe gay love and passion.
>
> (1191)

Jonathan Dollimore (1991) discussed Shakespeare's treatment of "perversion," especially in *The Tempest* (107–12), as well as "natural and unnatural forces" in *Othello* (148–65).

Also in 1991, Bruce R. Smith produced an important book on Shakespeare and homoeroticism, arguing that only the *literature* of the Renaissance offers insights into homoerotic feelings or *desire*, whereas other documents mainly record homosexual *acts* (17). Smith emphasized six different "myths," or common cultural understandings, of homoeroticism in Shakespeare's period (21). He labeled these standard stories "Combatants and Comrades," "The Passionate Shepherd," "The Shipwrecked Youth," "Knights in Shifts," "Master and Minion," and "The Secret Sharer" (see contents page and also 22–3). Smith devoted special attention to various plays, including *As You Like It* (144–55), *Coriolanus* (33–5), *Cymbeline* (152–4), *The Merchant of Venice* (67–9; 151–2), *Othello* (61–4), *Romeo and Juliet* (63–4), *Troilus and Cressida* (285–6), *Twelfth Night* (243–4), and *The Two Noble Kinsmen* (69–72). He also discussed *Venus and Adonis* (134–6) and the sonnets (228–70), exploring many poems in detail and concluding that in the first 126 sonnets

> Shakespeare seeks to speak about homosexual desire with the same authority that Petrarch assumes in speaking about heterosexual desire. In pursuit of that

end Shakespeare invokes three different modes of discourse: Horace's language of erotic experience, the traditional language of courtly love, and the language of Christian marriage.

(264)

Gregory Bredbeck (Summers 1992: 41–68), in densely theoretical language, discussed Shakespeare's treatment of sodomy. Ellis Hanson, also in Summers 1992 (135–51), suggested that in *Antony and Cleopatra*, Cleopatra (played by a boy) is presented as a kind of sodomite who disrupts the "natural" order of things much as the young men favored by King James disrupted, in the eyes of many, proper order at the Jacobean court.

Marjorie Garber (1992) noted the importance of cross-dressing of all sorts in the characters, themes, and acting of Shakespeare's plays (32–9; see also 122–5), especially in *As You Like It* (74–6), *The Merchant of Venice* (85–8), *A Midsummer Night's Dream* (84–5 and 89–90), *Twelfth Night* (36–8), and also in connection with Falstaff (124–5). Jonathan Goldberg (1992: 141–75) thought Shakespeare's presentations of various friendships are potentially homoerotic or at least homosocial, especially in *The Merchant of Venice, Twelfth Night, As You Like It, The Merry Wives of Windsor,* and *Troilus and Cressida*. Goldberg paid particular attention to Prince Hal in the *Henriad*, reviewing previous critics' responses to him, discussing the relevance of Falstaff and Hotspur, and suggesting a possible sexual connection between Hal and the fat knight. In a 1994 essay collection edited by Goldberg, his own essay on *Romeo and Juliet* (217–32) sought to complicate understandings of sexuality not only in *Romeo and Juliet* but also in other dramas by Shakespeare. Goldberg argued that "[r]eadings of the plays, written from whatever position, that seek to enforce a compulsory heterosexuality must be complicit with the domestication of women and with the scapegoating of men (often by palming off the ills of heterosexuality on homosexuality)" (227).

Paul Hammond's 1996 book, amid many scattered comments about Shakespeare, also gave him an entire chapter (58–87), arguing that Shakespeare was startlingly able to present male-male relations from numerous perspectives and with practically no negative judgments (except from the sarcastic Thersites in *Troilus and Cressida*), but without revealing much about his own inclinations (58). Hammond thought Shakespeare often presents groups of men distant from women, including in *The Two Gentlemen of Verona, The Tempest, Love's Labours Lost,* and *As You Like It*, although such "imagined worlds are never permanent" nor free of tensions (59). He noted homoerotic playfulness in *Romeo and Juliet* (59), homoerotic overtones in *Troilus and Cressida* (59–61), love between men and emphasis on the emperor's body in *Julius Caesar* (61–2), and an even more erotic stress on male bodies in *Coriolanus* (62–4). Hammond claimed that in *The Winter's Tale*, the arrival of women fractures a male pastoral innocence (64–5), that postponements of marriage occur in *Love's Labours Lost, The Merchant of Venice, Twelfth Night*, and *Much Ado about Nothing*, and that bonds between males help dictate much of the tragedy in *Othello* (65–7).

Hammond also discussed Shakespeare's interest in variously "gendered roles" (67), the playful homoeroticism in *As You Like It*, and especially the issues of homosexual attraction in *Twelfth Night* and *The Merchant of Venice*, particularly the ways homosexual feelings may cause social disruption (68–75). Neither play, Hammond concluded, "quite manages to imagine a permanent place for an older man in love with a youth" (75; see also 107–11). Turning to the sonnets, Hammond stressed such topics as "homosexual infatuation" (76), the ways editors and scholars, from early on, have tried to downplay the poems' possible homoeroticism (76–7), recent criticism emphasizing that very possibility (77), and the ways the early sonnets stress less the pleasures of married love than the need for the handsome youth to leave copies of himself behind by having children (77–8). In later poems, according to Hammond, "the idea of creating another self in the form of a son will be displaced by the idea that the poet himself, as lover, is the youth's other self, and will ensure the youth's immortality through his poetry" (78). Hammond contended that the sonnets, far from presenting the poet and youth as equal friends, instead emphasize the speaker's obsession with the youth and particularly with the youth's androgynous beauty (78–9), however unstable their relationship might prove (80–2). Ultimately, Hammond argued, the sonnet sequence ended in frustration and literal incompletion, with two lines missing from the final poem (87).

Carl Miller (1996: 90–108, 127–47, 192–7, 211–14) discussed the complex plays on gender and sexual language in *As You Like It* (90–100), claimed that the "beauty of love between women gets eloquent expression in *The Two Noble Kinsmen*" (101), stressed the ways women are matched in *A Midsummer Night's Dream* (102–4), and explored the roles of women in other Shakespeare plays (104–8). Later, Miller emphasized that modern terms for sexual identities were unknown in Shakespeare's time (127–8), discussed how variously Shakespeare's treatments of sexuality have been interpreted and performed (128–31), noted that Shakespeare thrice used paired characters named Sebastian and Antonio (131–2), observed the use of male disguises by female characters (played by boys) in *The Merchant of Venice* (132–3), and commented on how that work presents affection between men (133–5). Miller also explored issues of gender and sexuality in *The Two Noble Kinsmen* (136–41), *Much Ado about Nothing* (141–3), *A Midsummer Night's Dream* (143–5), *As You Like It* (145–7), the *Henry IV* plays (192–5), *The Merry Wives of Windsor* (195–7), and *Othello* (211–14). Miller's commentary, however, tended to be cursory.

Stephen Orgel (1996: 57–71) dealt with homoeroticism in *As You Like It*, *Twelfth Night*, and Sonnet 20, finding its treatment in all three works less hostile and more complex than one might have assumed. He also argued that sodomy in Shakespeare's era was usually imagined as the anal rape of a young male and was, for that reason, rarely provable and rarely dealt with in courts of law. Indeed, he asserted that the

> love of men for boys is all but axiomatic in the period; and despite fulminations in legal and theological contexts against the abominable crime of sodomy, most of what men and boys could do with each other did not constitute sodomy, and it was, as we have seen, a crime that was hardly ever prosecuted.
>
> (71)

Mario DiGangi (1997: 38–42) suggested that "within the context of *Twelfth Night*, … a man's desire for a woman may be the least 'natural' or most problematic course of all. The objects of erotic desire in the play are men: Viola desires Orsino; Sebastian and Antonio desire each other" (41). Discussing *As You Like It* (50–62), DiGangi argued as follows:

> Recognizing that male homoerotic desire was acknowledged in early modern England as a potentially dissonant force within marriage, we can understand the ideological motives of texts that attempt to displace, contain, or marginalize this threat to marital (hetero)sexuality. One such text is *As You Like It*. … The crucial mythological subtext of [this play] is the familiar story in which Jupiter replaces Hebe with Ganymede, thereby angering Juno and alienating her from the marriage bed. An analysis of this mythological subtext in the play brings into sharp relief the discordant aspects of Rosalind's enactment of Ganymede, by means of which female homoerotic desire (Celia's for Rosalind) and male homoerotic desire (Orlando's for Ganymede) are both finally rejected. The play's concluding marriages succeed to the extent that premarital female homoerotic desire and postmarital male homoerotic desire have been successfully banished.
>
> (50–1)

Hogan and Hudson 1998 (505) noted that "Shakespeare has been 'accused' of harboring 'unnatural' desires since at least the eighteenth century, and was 'claimed' to be gay as early as the 1830s," despite little knowledge about his personal life. They reported that some critics consider his sonnets "literary exercises, reflecting his era's respect for Greek and Roman homoerotic poets," that some see Sonnet 144 as "a confession of bisexuality," that he alludes to the fickleness of a "boy's love" in *King Lear*, and that "sonnets [commonly] judged homoerotic are numbers 20, 29, 35, 36, 53, 55, 60, 67, 87, 94, 104, 110, 116, and 144."

Gregory Woods (1998) emphasized homoerotic aspects of the relationship between Mercutio and Romeo in *Romeo and Juliet* (93), same-sex relationships in the *Henriad* (93–4), and especially the "gay" nature of Antonio in *The Merchant of Venice* (94). Woods also commented on evasive editorial commentary on the coupling of Achilles and Patroclus in *Troilus and Cressida* and on other characters' criticism of that coupling itself (95–7), on the complexity of Iago's "homosexual" speeches in *Othello* (97–8), on the potential homoerotic aspects of *Timon of Athens* (98), and on similar aspects of *Coriolanus* (98–9). Woods surveyed efforts by previous critics (especially Eric Partridge and Alfred Harbage) to dismiss homoerotic interpretations of the Sonnets (99–103), discussed the subsidiary roles of women in those poems (103), and then focused on interpretations of Sonnet 20 (104–7). Woods concluded that

> [r]eading the sonnets will always flush out the reader's attitudes to homosexuality. To that extent if no further, this sequence of poems is *the* key gay text in English literature. (And Sonnet 20 is *the* key individual poem.) For centuries the sequence has been testing the extent to which canonical English literature will ever be allowed to be 'gay literature' at all.
>
> (107)

Valerie Traub (2000) reviewed numerous essays and books on the Bard, including commentary on such matters as "lonely," "tragic" gays in the drama, "queering" the Shakespearean family (310), the relevance of deconstruction and new historicism, the placement of "bodies in space and time," the complex interactions of history and critical theories in interpretation, the insights recent stagings can provide into Shakespeare's depictions of sexualities, and critical responses to Shakespeare himself as potentially "gay" (311). Traub also reviewed work on crossdressing in the comedies, on responses to Stephen Greenblatt's influential work on this topic, on the (ir)relevance of medical texts to critical readings, and on economic status as a factor influencing sexual availability in Renaissance households (311–12). She surveyed commentary by Camille Paglia, Jonathan Crewe, and Laurie Osborne on androgyny, on transvestism, and on performance studies as evidence of how directors have historically suppressed homoerotic implications in Shakespeare's plays (312–13).

Characterizations of Antonio—an arguably "queer" character in *The Merchant of Venice*—received much of Traub's attention, as did that play in general (313). Traub reviewed work on lesbian desire in Shakespeare by critics such as herself and Theodora Jankowski, on the Duke as gay in *Measure for Measure*; on issues of "coming out" in *Two Gentlemen of Verona*; on debates about homoeroticism and Falstaff; and about varied depictions of sexuality in *The Merry Wives of Windsor* (314). She dealt with essays by Nora Johnson on homoeroticism in *The Tempest* and *The Winter's Tale*, by Gregory Bredbeck, Gary Spears, Linda Charnes, and Eric Mallin on similar issues in *Troilus and Cressida* (314-15), and by Jonathan Dollimore, Arthur Little, Jr., Jonathan Goldberg, Richard Corum, and Paula Bennet on such plays as *Othello* and the *Henriad* (315). Traub discussed relevant essays by Mark Reschke on *Hamlet*, by Jody Greene on *Timon of Athens*, and by Joseph Porter and Jonathan Goldberg on *Romeo and Juliet* (as well as by Goldberg himself on *Coriolanus* and *The Tempest*). Traub mentioned an essay by Paul Hammond on revisions of *King Lear* (315) and various other essays dealing with textual or editorial issues or matters of sexual word-play (315-16). Finally, Traub also surveyed essays by Elaine Hobby and Nicholas Radel on the relevance of homoeroticism when teaching *As You Like It* and also *Romeo and Juliet*.

Reviewing work on homoeroticism and the poems, Traub discussed Joseph Pequigney's pathbreaking 1985 book on the sonnets as well as a more recent essay by Pequigney published in a collection edited by James Schiffer that included much commentary on homoeroticism (317). Traub mentioned Schiffer's valuable introduction, an essay by Heather Dubrow expressing skepticism about finding a homoerotic narrative in the sonnets, an essay by Margreta de Grazia on the scandal of interracial romance in those poems, and an essay by Peter Stallybrass on Victorian responses to the possibility of Shakespeare as a "sodomite" (317-18). Also included in Schiffer's collection were an essay by Bruce Smith on the sexual implications of the poems' use of pronouns, one by Traub herself on sodomy and misogyny, one by Peter Herman on usury and "unauthorized sexualities," and one by Rebecca Laroche on "the legacy of the sonnets to the fate of Oscar Wilde" (318).

Other essays on the sonnets surveyed by Traub included a piece by Robert Crosman arguing "that Shakespeare pretended to fall in love with his patron in order to flatter him, then discovered that he was no longer pretending," one by Judith Kegan Gardiner on male "marriage" in the poems, and one by David Buchbinder similar to Joel Fineman's important book *Shakespeare's Perjured Eye* (328). Traub also commented on relevant work by Eve Kosofsky Sedgwick (on "homosociality"), by Marjorie Garber (on bisexuality), and by Raymond

Waddington, Daniel Wright, and Lisa Jardine on Sonnet 20. Finally, dealing with *Venus and Adonis*, she mentioned writings by Jonathan Bate, James Schiffer, and Goran Stanivukovic (319). All in all, Traub offered an exceptionally valuable overview of Shakespeare and homoeroticism.

Alan Bray, in Aldrich and Wotherspoon 2002 (404–6), asserted that although several Shakespearean characters "have been interpreted as homosexual, ... the most telling moments ... explore the ambiguity of the transvestite conventions" of early modern English theatre, "where the female roles were played by boy actors" (404). Bray, noting that some "commentators have interpreted the first group of sonnets as homosexual," contended that, when extended to other poems, "the argument begins to collapse" (404). "The homoerotic gesture," he continued, was "a commonplace in the friendship between the educated men of Shakespeare's time; and Shakespeare's Sonnets are only one—albeit breathtaking—moment in the convention that could first playfully propose, and then archly deny, a sexual interpretation to the intimacy of a patron and his humanist-educated 'secretary'" (405). Bray questioned gay readings of sonnet 20, calling it instead a humorous depiction of patronage relationships.

Stephen Guy-Bray (2002) focused mainly on *The Winter's Tale* (198–215), arguing that it depicts a competition between a "traditional masculine pastoral, exemplified in the play by the boyhood of Leontes and Polixenes, and the heterosexualized pastoral ultimately exemplified by Perdita and Florizel" (198). Meanwhile, Colm Tóibín 2002 (19–11) did read Sonnet 20 as homoerotic (particularly in terms of an implied desire to penetrate the young man) but also noted how often Shakespeare scholars have resisted or rejected any "gay" readings.

Commenting on several sonnets in particular (especially 5, 6, and 20), and on the "child-bearing" and "dark lady" sonnets in general, Richard Halpern (2002: 11–31) concluded that by displacing "the tropes of sodomy from the young man onto the Lady, Shakespeare thereby invests her with a proto-Sadean sublimity, a sublimity that is sodomitical through and through," thus laying "the basis for an aesthetic that will continue through Sade, to Wilde, and beyond" (31). Paul Hammond (2002: 62–116) explored Shakespeare's presentation of "strong male bonds," the ways "he adapts his sources" to suggest male-male "affective and sexual possibilities where none had existed," and "the rhetorical figures through which male relations are delineated" (62). Hammond said the sonnets "keep playing over the nature of the bond between the speaker and the youth, redefining it repeatedly and obsessively" (68) in ways that suggest desire, possession, and dispossession (68–9) and in language full of "sexual connotations which are not consolidated into puns or metaphors" but are more subtly suggested (70). Hammond maintained that the sonnets were almost certainly influenced by Shakespeare's reading of Richard Barnfield (72–5), not only in sonnets 20 and 33 but especially in 46 (75–84). According to Hammond, the sonnets attracted remarkably little attention, perhaps because their publication might have been seen as reflecting uncomfortably on King James's homoeroticism (87–8).

Turning to the plays, Hammond suggested that Shakespeare often altered his sources to highlight homoerotic possibilities, especially in *The Merchant of Venice* and *Twelfth Night* (87–100). After Shakespeare's death, Hammond maintained, editors and later adaptors often eliminated the homoerotic phrasing and possibilities of his works (101), especially in John Benson's edition of the sonnets, George Granville's re-writing of *The Merchant of Venice*, Nahum Tate's version of *Coriolanus*, and John Dryden's adaptation of *Troilus and Cressida* (100–16). "Restoration adaptations," Hammond concluded,

> were motivated partly by a concern to protect male friendship from the suspicion of homosexual desire and, by removing the productive ambiguities of Shakespeare's language, to preserve the clarity and stability of the definition of masculinity in the face of a new world of homosexual self-definition.
>
> (116)

Terry Castle (2003: 99–101) suggested that "*As You Like It* and *Twelfth Night* might be considered 'honorary' sapphic comedies since both 'feature charismatic cross-dressing heroines who inspire ardor in unwitting females'" (100). She noted that "given 'the extraordinarily attractive *illusion* of female same-sex love in each play', it is not surprising that [these plays] have played a talismanic role in lesbian literary tradition," with many later works alluding to their plots and/or their characters (100). Louis Crompton (2003: 378–81) noted that the alleged homoeroticism of Shakespeare's sonnets has long been debated (378–9), reported that some early evidence had emphasized the possibility by changing some masculine pronouns to feminine (179), reviewed the evidence himself (380–1), and concluded that the poems are at least Platonically homoerotic. Crompton called the sonnets "undoubtedly the most distinguished love poetry written by one man to another" (381).

Denise Walen (2005: *passim*) noted Shakespeare's emphasis on "mistaken sexual identity" in several plays (59–61), arguing that in *Twelfth Night* "Olivia's repeated flirtations create a homoerotic tension," even implying the possibility of "physical intimacy" (59). Walen was even more intrigued by the final scene, which "presents homosexual pairings within heterosexual unions." For example, "Olivia is aware in the concluding scene that Viola is a woman and still endeavors to establish a lasting relationship," although ultimately "female homoeroticism" is kept "ambivalent" (60). In *As You Like It*, a "dual erotic allows an audience conscious of female homosexual practices to perceive the homoerotic potential in Phebe's pursuit of Rosalind" (60). Walen argued that although neither *Twelfth Night* nor *As You Like It* "presumes to break heterosexual authority by presenting mutual female attraction, both … fashion a homoerotic tension between the actual and the perceived" (61). Walen also commented, in passing, on various other plays by Shakespeare throughout her book.

Emma Donoghue (2010: *passim*) noted that Shakespeare sometimes drew on "the most common female bridegroom" storyline of his time—the one involving a "cross-dressed woman who accidentally attracts other women," a plot especially apparent in *As You Like It* and *Twelfth Night* (29–30). In the latter play, Donoghue wrote, "Viola is no cynical role-player: she is expressing the kind of hypothetical desire, an if-only-I-could yearning that is common among female bridegrooms." She thought that in this play "Shakespeare keeps the emphasis, according to stage custom, on the fruitlessness of attraction between women" (30), but she argued that "many of Shakespeare's predecessors, peers, and successors were less cautious on the topic than he was" (31). Donoghue contended that the endings of such plays by Shakespeare often seem mechanical because they suddenly throw the brakes on same-sex desire the plays themselves have dealt with subtly and provocatively (35–37). But she also stressed how Shakespeare's women-pretending-to-be-men, "without having intended to make women fall in love with them," nonetheless "often seem flattered, titillated, and downright triumphant" when precisely that happens (36). *As You Like It*, she contended, "is still the most famous portrayal of female friendship in the literary canon" and features a "prototypical inseparability plot" in which the close relationship between two women makes them seem, and feel, inseparable (64). Donoghue called Rosalind and Celia in this play "an unforgettable duo, with an immense influence on later plays and fiction about love between women," even if their own relationship ends somewhat anticlimactically (65).

In discussing *A Midsummer Night's Dream*, Donoghue noted in passing that at one point, Helena accuses Hermia not of taking her man "but of letting men into the secret garden of girls' love." Donoghue thought it significant that ultimately Shakespeare "does not show Hermia and Helena speaking another line to each other" (74). But the organization of Donoghue's book meant that her comments on Shakespeare and most other authors were scattered rather than concentrated.

4

The Seventeenth Century

JOHN DONNE (1572–1631). Janel Mueller, in Summers 1992 (103–34), argued that Donne's poem "Sappho to Philaenis" stands "alone not only in [Donne's] work but in the entire" Renaissance "for its celebration and defense of a passionate lesbian relation" (103). According to Mueller, Donne's poem showed how friendship between equals—a common Renaissance ideal—could during this era only be achieved by women. She also claimed that Donne's poem "undertakes to imagine the pleasures, sustenance, and ideological implications by which lesbianism, as a mode of loving and being, resists patriarchal disposition and diminution of women" (104) and implies "a fully utopian moment for human possibility" (125).

Donne, famously "witty" as the author of so-called "metaphysical poetry," is usually considered almost exclusively a poet of heterosexual love and/or sex. Many standard volumes dealing with "gay" literature simply ignore him, but he *is* mentioned briefly by Crompton (2003: 397–9), who discusses his single "lesbian" poem but who also suggests that "Donne's attitude toward male homosexuality seems to have been conventionally negative" (398). That "lesbian" poem—"Sappho to Philaenis"—has attracted much attention, but possible homoerotic readings of other poems by Donne *were* explored in detail in an entire book (from 1994) by George Klawitter. Klawitter stressed that he was not arguing that Donne himself was "gay" (x) but noted his close friendships with men (3). He paid particular attention to certain early verse letters to Thomas Woodward, to whom Donne wrote some lines with arguably homoerotic implications (4–18). Klawitter saw similar possibilities in a verse letter to Edward Guilpin, noting homoerotic phrasing in some of Guilpin's own poems (18–26). Klawitter examined "Sappho to Philaenis" at length (47–61), even suggesting that it might involve two men rather than two women (56–61). In addition to discussing Donne, however, Klawitter also surveyed homoerotic possibilities in other poetry of the period, especially that of Richard Barnfield

(63–74), explored homoerotic phrasing common during the time (especially involving fellatio [75–9]), emphasized the importance of manuscript (rather than printed) evidence (95–112), and, in general, suggested that openness to potential homoerotic readings of various poems enriched interpretive possibilities (113–93). Richard Rambuss (1998: 49–60; 114–17), in scattered comments on Donne, discussed homoerotic language in various poems and sermons, asking, for instance, "Are the Holy Sonnets redeeming sodomy, or are they sodomizing redemption?" (60). Elizabeth Wahl (1999: 18, 49–71) argued that Donne's poem about Sappho "conveys a strange mixture of fascination and erotic titillation" and "anxious desire to redefine female homoeroticism as ultimately autoerotic and barren" if it rejects heterosexual reproduction. She thus considered the poem typical of early modern attitudes toward lesbianism, arguing that Donne could write with relative tolerance about a kind of same-sex desire that seemed safely in the distant past (18). According to Wahl, Donne's poem was written before satire of female homosexuality became common, "conveys a deeply rooted ambivalence" toward lesbianism (53), implies *some* degree of dissatisfaction with phallocentrism, and is less rigidly patriarchal than some critics have assumed (54).

In 2000, Valerie Traub valuably surveyed nearly fifteen essays on Donne and homoeroticism, mentioning discussions of his allusions to previous poets (particularly Sappho and Ovid), his treatments of transvestism, and especially his presentation of lesbian themes (299–300). Additionally, George Klawitter's suggestions about the Woodword poems, as well as others critics' readings of "Sappho to Philaenis," were treated briefly in Summers 2002 (185–6). Terry Castle (2003: 125–6) argued that although Donne "borrows the name Philaenis, meaning 'female friend', from one of the most scabrous anti-lesbian satires of antiquity—epigram 67 of book 7 of Martial's *Epigrams*—his handling of the amorous situation is curiously sympathetic." Not only, she continued, "does he try to imagine Sappho's passion from the inside," but "he pointedly modifies Ovid's heterosexualized version of her myth" (125), implying that her love for Philaenis is more enduring than her momentary passion for a male named Phaon (126). "Critics remain divided over how deep this revisionary 'sapphophilia' goes," Castle wrote, "but in rewriting Sappho's tragic fate he nonetheless intervened powerfully and distinctively in the evolving literary history of the lesbian topos" (126). Denise Walen (2005: 31–2) argued that "few early modern texts present as vigorously approving an image of female homoeroticism" as Donne's poem, especially since it "argues not simply that female sexual unions are acceptable, but that they are superior to heterosexual matches" (31). Walen stressed the poem's unusual emphasis on physical sex (31) and said the work "represents an exception to early modern male-authored texts that ignore female homoerotic desire, ridicule it, or construct it as transgressive" (32).

RICHARD BARNFIELD (1574–1620?). Although Alan Bray (1982: 61–2) drew attention to an unpublished commonplace book by Barnfield containing explicit heterosexual pornography and cautioned against reading his homoerotic poems as based in personal experience, Barnfield is widely regarded as one of the most intriguing homoerotic poets of the entire English Renaissance, partly because the "gay" aspects of his work seem so undisguised (Dynes 1990: 109; Hammond 1996: 38; Haggerty 2000: 97–8). His anonymously published first volume of poems, *The Affectionate Shepherd* (1594), echoed Virgil's influential second eclogue by depicting an older shepherd's courtship of a younger male named Ganymede. George Klawitter's 1990 edition of Barnfield's poems broke new ground, especially thanks to its excellent introduction (11–64) and "Explanatory Notes" (195–249), although the biographical information provided on pages 11–19 has, in part, been superseded by the later research of Andrew Worall. Klawitter identified Ganymede with Charles Blount (22), noted one early commendation of Barnfield's work (22), and commented on his reception from 1675 forward into the twentieth century (22–5), reporting that during this whole period he has "most often been treated, when read at all, as secondary or perverse" (25). Klawitter then offered textual introductions to each of Barnfield's works (25–51), deemphasizing similarities between Barnfield's *Affectionate Shepherd* and Virgil's second eclogue (30) and stressing instead potentially dangerous allusions to particular contemporary aristocrats (30–2). Klawitter also discussed later parts of *The Affectionate Shepherd* volume (32–4), explored potential sources for its sequel, *Cynthia* (34–5), discussed the likelihood that the male wooer and wooed in that later poem were of the same age (36), noted some heterosexual emphases in Barnfield's writings (36–7), and generally suggested a movement in Barnfield's feelings from early homoeroticism to later heterosexual desires (37).

Bruce Smith, in 1991, noted Barnfield's poems' explicitness (99), their elements of sexual fantasy (100), the way the speaker imagines himself in an almost "female role" during love-making fantasies (100–1), and their playfully erotic symbolism (101). Smith noted that in Barnfield's second collection (*Cynthia* [1595]), the poet felt obliged to deny homoerotic interpretations of *The Affectionate Shepherd* by claiming he had merely been imitating Virgil (102), although most of his intended readers were in fact young males in their late teens or early twenties who were studying law at the Inns of Court (102) and who were noted for their classical learning and interest in the poetry of Ovid and Petrarch (103). Smith thought Barnfield was taking the homoeroticism of Virgilian pastoral poetry seriously while also having fun with the genre (104), giving it an anti-feminine spin (104), perhaps alluding to real persons (105), and emphasizing the virtuous intent of the gay (as opposed to the female) lover (106) the poems describe. As the affectionate shepherd ages he becomes (in Smith's view) progressively more serious and moral (107), even urging Ganymede to marry (107–8) while finally emphasizing his own religious maturity (108). In *Cynthia*, according to Smith, Barnfield wrote homoerotic Petrarchan sonnets (109–10) but eventually confessed poetic defeat (110–11), partly because his poems could not transcend their "campy," "self-absorbed," and even "pornographic" limitations (112).

Gregory Bredbeck (1991: 151–60), seeing the homoerotic desire described in *The Affectionate Shepherd* as at least more sensible than their "slapstick" heteroeroticism (151), reviewed such matters as the work's complex reception, Barnfield's efforts to distance himself from personal criticism, the complicated relations between the first volume and its sequel, *Cynthia*, and the connections of all these matters to concepts of sodomy and sodomites. Bredbeck, in Summers 1992 (49–61), discussed (among other things) the ways Barnfield both created and disavowed homoerotic meanings (47). Jonathan Goldberg (1992) disputed Alan Bray's argument that Barnfield could not have been "gay" because a commonplace book associated with him supposedly contains heterosexual pornography. Goldberg called Bray's definitions of sexual orientation anachronistic (68–70). Paul Hammond (1996) noted that Barnfield almost invited readers to associate him with the speaker of *The Affectionate Shepherd*, found the work's overall structure somewhat confusing, emphasized its explicit homoeroticism (38), and suggested that the problems with structure and tone may have resulted from the problems of trying to write such an openly gay, openly erotic work during this period (38–9). Exploring the implications of Barnfield's sometimes ambivalent imagery, Hammond found space for actual physical, sexual consummation only in the reader's imagination, not in the poems themselves, which sometimes struck him as full of contradictions (40–1). Gregory Woods (1998), seeing Barnfield's poems as somewhat unsophisticated and even boyish, contrasted him variously with Shakespeare (70–2) while also suggesting that some of Barnfield's poems seem emotionally authentic (72), especially in the sexual yearnings they describe (72–3). Claude Summers, in Haggerty (2000), reported important new biographical facts discovered by Andrew Worral, including a new date for Barnfield's death, evidence of tension with his father (who disinherited him), and evidence that he died a bachelor rather than (as had previously been assumed) a married "gentleman farmer." Summers also discussed the poems' explicit homoeroticism, the ways classical precedents allowed this subject to be dealt with, and the possible influence of Barnfield's sonnets on Shakespeare's (97–8). Valerie Traub (2000) briefly surveyed previous scholarship on Barnfield.

Especially significant to Barnfield studies was the publication, in 2001, of a large essay collection edited by George Klawitter and Kenneth Borris. It contained an important biographical article by Andrew Worral (25–38), whose main conclusions have already been mentioned above, and an equally important overview of criticism prepared by Kenneth Borris (13–24). Borris surveyed reactions to Barnfield from the 1600s to the twenty-first century, including essays in the Klawitter-Borris volume itself. He quoted critics who had praised and/or condemned Barnfield, both as a poet and person, showing how some critics had minimized or explained away his poems' homoeroticism while others had condemned it both morally and aesthetically (13–15). He also discussed the growing interest in Barnfield evident in the late twentieth century (17), the history of nineteenth-century editions and scholarship (17–19), the ways Barnfield was often discussed alongside Shakespeare (to whom some of his poems were wrongly attributed) (19–20), and the implications of Barnfield's work for the whole issue of a distinct "gay" identity during the English Renaissance (20–1). Surveying the contents of the Klawitter-Borris volume itself, Borris noted biographical discussions of Barnfield's works, the nature of Spenser's influence on Barnfield, and Barnfield's possible contributions to another collection of Elizabethan poems (21). Other topics discussed included Barnfield's use of the Bible, the nature and implications of his poems' homoeroticism, and numerous other aspects of his writings and reputation, including his possible authorship of a little-studied work titled *Orpheus His Journey to Hell* (22–3).

Klawitter, in Summers 2002 (74–5), noted that Barnfield may have died either in 1620 or in 1626, expressed doubts about biographical readings of the homoerotic poems, noted the presence of frustrated homoerotic feelings even within the *Cynthia* volume, and reviewed the critical reception of Barnfield's works (75). Also in 2002, Stephen Guy-Bray discussed Barnfield at length, finding his poems sometimes triumphant, sometimes mournful (152). Guy-Bray emphasized Barnfield's debts to English writers (especially Marlowe and Spenser) (152–3), noted the explicitness of some of his phrasing (153–4), and commented on the poet's attitudes toward sexual "sin" (154). Guy-Bray also discussed the ways Barnfield satirized some aspects of heterosexuality (155), the ways his language was sometimes explicitly homosexual (155–6), and the ways his tones altered as the volume developed (157–8), particularly in a growing stress on both heterosexuality and misogyny (158–9). Finally, Guy-Bray ended by commenting on the sexual and other complexities presented in *Cynthia* (160–3). Michael Morgan Holmes, in Aldrich and Wotherspoon 2002 (40–1), suggested that Ganymede, in *The Affectionate Shepherd*, was likely "the handsome courtier Charles Blount," endorsed Klawitter's claim that that volume was probably not censured for its homoeroticism but for reflecting badly on an aristocratic lady (40), and suggested that when Barnfield's poems are read with an "open mind" they "can challenge readers to reevaluate prejudicial understandings of 'natural' desire and sexuality, and thereby broaden their understanding of the varieties of human experience, past and present" (41).

ANDREW MARVELL (1621–78), a famously "ambiguous" poet, has not attracted much critical attention as a possibly homoerotic writer until recently. Valerie Traub, in 2000, did summarize five different articles, most dealing with lesbianism, allegedly lesbian nuns, and satirical treatments of Marvell's own sexuality (308). In 2002, Paul Hammond noted that Marvell was often accused by political opponents of being either effeminate, impotent, masturbatory, interested in men, or some combination of these (186–204). Such accusations led Hammond to explore possible "queer" dimensions in Marvell's verse, especially his focus on male beauty, his occasional use of female speakers (204–25), and his repeated emphasis on "unrequited homoerotic desire and the self-sufficient, even self-loving, observer" (224). Terry Castle (2003: 138–9) noted that Marvell's poem "Upon Appleton House" includes "an important sapphic episode" in which nuns are implicitly depicted as lesbian predators whose intended victim is liberated by a heterosexual young man (138). The whole poem, Castle suggested, "deserves to be considered part of that influential corpus of 'homoeroticized' anti-clerical writing extending from Chaucer (with his sodomitical Pardoner) to Diderot and the Marquise de Sade" (139). George Klawitter, in 2017, published an entire book on Marvell and sexual orientations in the seventeenth century. Klawitter argued that few of Marvell's "straight" poems seem especially convincing, that some poems can be read as addressed either to women or to men, that a poem titled "The Unfortunate Lover" seems especially homoerotic, that autoeroticism may be suggested by other Marvellian lyrics, and that celibacy is yet another possibility that perhaps underlies various poems by this author (25–6). All in all, Klawitter argued for a more fluid, less prescriptive view of the sexual dimensions of Marvell's work than has hitherto been common.

KATHERINE PHILIPS (1632-64). Lillian Faderman (1981: 68-71) saw Philips's poetry as a proto-lesbian expression of "romantic friendship" between women, emphasized both its conventional and personal traits, and cited evidence of Philips's passionate feelings for other women. She noted that Philips did not describe such passion in physical terms, explaining how this poet used erotic language to describe spiritual relationships. "It is impossible," Faderman wrote,

> to be certain what Katherine Philips's passions meant to her, but we can be fairly sure that they were regarded by those who believed her to be a model of the perfect romantic friend as an expression of platonism which delighted not in physicality but in the union of souls and in philosophizing and poetizing. Men viewed these relationships as enobling.
>
> (71)

Arlene Steibel, in Summers (1992: 153-71), argued that standard readings of Philips's poetry "have ignored or denied the lesbian aspects of [her] verse by dismissing them as asexual representations of well-known literary conventions." Instead, Steibel maintained that such conventions "present a complex and sophisticated lesbian sexuality" and also deal with other sexual taboos (153). Faderman 1994 (17-19) said that all of Philips's "most important emotional relationships seem to have been with women" (17), traced the poet's various romantic friendships with females (18), and noted that many of her love poems to women were seen by her "contemporaries as pure expressions of idealized, platonic love," even though they are often "imbued with ambivalence, anger, jealousy, and sensuality such as is generally more consonant with eros than friendship," at least as friendship is seen in modern terms (18).

Elizabeth Wahl (1999: 130-70) argued that Philips portrayed ideal friendship between women as egalitarian in ways marriage could never be (130). She surveyed the ways these friendships were sometimes negatively portrayed by later scholars (133-9), sought to set Philips's ideas about close relations between women in an appropriate historical context (139-47), and noted the complex relations her poems often depict (147). Wahl suggested that the friendships Philips idealized inevitably competed with marriage (153), considered her poetry more subversive than its supposed Platonism would allow (154-8), and doubted the wisdom of calling Philips a "lesbian" in the modern sense (161). Wahl nevertheless saw erotic implications in some of her poems to and about women (162-3) but commented on the pressure Philips felt to emphasize "spiritual" love (168-9).

Harriette Andreadis (2001: 55-83) suggested that modern lesbians had sometimes treated Philips as one of their own without trying to situate her in her precise historical contexts (57). Andreadis saw her as "a woman whose emotional focus was primarily on other women and whose passionate involvement with them guided much of her life and inspired her most esteemed poems" (57). Philips, according to Andreadis, expressed "a desexualized—though passionate and eroticized—version of platonic love in the love of same-sex friendship" in a way reminiscent of male writers' (especially Donne's) love poems about women (58, 62). Philips's best poems, Andreadis said, were inspired by her love of particular women, and when those women were no longer parts of her life, "the well of her unique creativity dried up" (75). Her use of the conventions of male poetry helped her reputation and acceptance (81), but as her same-sex attractions came to seem more sexual, her reputation declined (83).

Kate Lilley, in Aldrich and Wotherspoon 2002 (347–8), commented that "Philips's reception amongst contemporary [i.e., recent] feminist and queer readers stresses the primacy of relations between women in her poetry, focusing especially on the embodied erotics and fraught dynamics of her 'friendship' poems addressed to women, compared with the less sublime and more formal character of those addressed to her husband and other men" (348). Arlene Steibel, in Summers 2002 (511–12), wrote that roughly "two thirds of Philips's printed poems are about erotic relationships among women. Although the female lovers she addresses were married, as was Philips, their marriages were the conventional domestic arrangements of the period, implying neither love nor sexual attraction" (511). Steibel called Anne Owen Philips' "lover," suggested that sex without penile penetration was not considered sex in Philips's day (512), and asserted that Philips "demonstrates clearly the sensibility that prioritizes erotic attraction between women, acts on it, and celebrates it, not merely as an idea but in fact" (512).

Terry Castle (2003: 158–60) argued that Philips's poems to other women

> register the growing importance of female romantic friendship in post-Restoration English society. Intense emotional bonds—feverish, fantastical, oddly eroticized, yet also usually deeply sublimated—became increasingly common between educated middle-class women in the seventeenth and eighteenth centur[ies], even, paradoxically, as the cultural taboos against homosexuality intensified.
>
> (158–9)

Ironically (in Castle's view), because "the literature of romantic friendship helped to habituate Western civilization to the notion of passion between women, it was not entirely distinct in its cultural effects from contemporary pornography" (159).

Louis Crompton (2003: 398–9) wrote that whether Philips' poems "belong to the new tradition of romantic friendship between women or whether they reveal a lesbian element in her psyche remains an open question" (399).

APHRA BEHN (1640–89). Arlene Steibel, in Summers 1992 (153–71), argued that although much of Behn's verse was once read as merely conventional, it actually "epitomizes the disguise that reveals [lesbian] meaning" (162). Lillian Faderman 1994 (24–5) asserted that most of Behn's "love poems to other women ... appeared especially in her volume *Lycidus* (1688)," although they "may not have been viewed as presenting particularly significant challenges to the prejudices of her day" (24). But Behn, Faderman suggested, sometimes "seems to play with ... conventions of romantic friendship ... by hinting at the possibility of going beyond them" (24).

Hogan and Hudson 1998 suggested that Behn is now best-remembered for her "playfully erotic—often homoerotic—poems," that her heterosexual affairs were topics of gossip in her time, that she "also had same-sex romances" (77), but that she kept "generations of readers guessing whether her lesbian relations were sexual" (77–8).

Elizabeth Wahl (1999: 55–60) found Behn's poem "To the Fair Clarinda" rare for its day since a "woman writer depicts female-female desire" (55). In this poem, said Wahl, Behn "wittily subverts stereotypes of male and female sexual behavior" (56), implies that lesbian desire can "lead to pain and betrayal" (57), concludes with a play on words on the bisexual figure of the hermaphrodite (59), and shows modern readers' need to be sensitive to early modern "euphemisms and indirect allusions" (60). Harriette Andreadis (2001: 88) saw both Behn and Margaret Cavendish as writers who tried to create "a discourse of female same-sex erotics that was not in the least evasive but that also avoided identification with the vulgar and unnatural sexuality identified as tribadism" (88, 90). Kate Lilley, in Aldrich and Wotherspoon 2002, highlighted Behn's friendship with a noted bisexual male and argued that throughout

> her career as a writer Behn stages a canny and necessarily complicit enquiry into the cultural hegemony of heterosexual relations, but also acknowledges the heterogeneity, perversity and instability of desire. At her most utopian she gestures towards the reciprocity and fluidity of desire between and across the divisions of sex, gender, rank and 'race' in such a way as to call into question both the priority of heterosexuality and the truth of gender, always returning to a shrewd analysis of the multifarious operations and seductions of power.
>
> (47)

Arlene Steible, in Summers 2002 (81–3), surveyed Behn's life and career, cited contemporary comments suggesting Behn's homoeroticism, and noted phrasing by Behn herself presenting "the classical concept of the androgyne or hermaphrodite as the basis for same-sex eroticism" (82). Steible suggested that Behn wrote about same-sex relations both between men and women, reported that her closest male friend in later life was a gay man, and thought that Behn was attracted by the idea of androgyny in both men and women (82). Steible emphasized Behn's "explicitly lesbian love poem" *To the fair Clarinda, who made Love to me, imagin'd more than Woman*" and stressed the poem's focus on erotic mutuality (83).

Terry Castle (2003: 170–2) argued that Behn "took a lively interest in female charms" and showed, in various poems, "neither embarrassment nor coyness" but instead displayed "a kind of worldliness and esprit that would become all too rare" in women writing in the coming century. In Behn's bohemian milieu, "love between women was simply one of a number of sophisticated erotic options" (172). Louis Crompton (2003: 401–2) wrote that most of Behn's "erotic verse is directed to men, but some shows a fascination with women which suggests that she was bisexual" (401). He cited one poem by Behn which he thought might be "the first in English in which one woman unambiguously declares her infatuation with another" (402).

JOHN WILMOT, EARL OF ROCHESTER (1647–80). Dynes (1990) stressed Rochester's bisexuality and cast doubt on his authorship of *Sodom*, a play sometimes printed under his name (1: 1111). Paul Hammond (1996: 92–3) argued that in some poems by Rochester, homosexuality "is generally imagined only as a hypothetical possibility, rather than as part of a narrative of desire, and the young male body is only sketchily represented. ... In Rochester's writing it is women who generate the writer's emotions—tenderness, lust, contempt, disgust—while the homosexual pleasures remain motifs which help to establish the speaker's libertine credentials and to remind women that they are not indispensable" (93). Cameron McFarlane (1997: 46) stressed Rochester's emphasis on penetration as the defining male sexual act. Gregory Woods (1998: 125–7) discussed Rochester as an archetypal libertine, at least in his writings if not in his actual behavior (125) and emphasized that the sexual partners of libertines, whether male or female, were usually needy persons who were bought and paid for (126). But even Rochester, Woods argued, had to compromise with his era's official values (127). In 2002 (226–54), Paul Hammond placed Rochester in the context of Restoration ideas about relations between males as well as in the context of Rochester's own life. Hammond discussed different manuscripts and editions of the poems, varied contemporary reactions to them, various kinds of censorship (226–51), and the ways Rochester tends to exclude homoeroticism from ideas about mutual love (251), as well as the ways he tends to treat homosexuality as merely a supplement to heterosexuality (not a true alternative [252]). Amy Farmer, in Summers 2002 (553–4), emphasized Rochester's satires on heterosexuality (553), discussed several such poems, and suggested that his poems "participate in the libertine ethic of bisexuality so prevalent during the Restoration" (554).

Louis Crompton (2003: 396–7) humorously said that whether or not Rochester wrote *Sodom*, its characters "are not people but vocal private parts" (397). Raymond-Jean Frontain, in Frontain 2003 (89–114), argued, concerning *Sodom*, a work attributed to Rochester, that "rather than signaling Rochester's agreement with the presumptive biblical imprecation against sodomy and consequent divine vengeance, the conclusion of the play" indicates just the opposite (90). Reading the play "in terms of Mikhail Bakhtin's theory of the carnivalesque grotesque" (91), Frontain contended that the play "subverts the biblically authorized theology of marriage and sexual intercourse" (106).

5

The Eighteenth Century

JOHN CLELAND (1709–89). Kevin Kopelson, in Summers 1992 (173–83), emphasized how variously the sodomitical episode in *Fanny Hill* is unusual, even unique (175). It is, for instance, "the only instance known to Fanny of successful anal penetration" and also "represents the only sexual act" Fanny considers "morally outrageous" (175–6). Also in Summers 1992 (185–98), Donald Mengay contended that the entire book suggests strong appreciation of the almost classically beautiful male body and that even Fanny herself is more masculine than the heroines of many other eighteenth-century texts (190). "In the final analysis," Mengay concluded,

> *Fanny Hill* is not the straightforward celebration ... of bourgeois heterosexuality ... most critics claim it to be. Cleland subtly undercuts this notion at too many junctions ... [so that] if he doesn't *replace* it with a trenchant paradigm of homosexuality, or, more aptly, bisexuality, he certainly *juxtaposes* it next to the socially accepted one, offering it as a possibility.
>
> (196)

Fanny, in this reading, is a kind of male in drag in a text often as stimulating to gays as it is to straights.

Paul Hammond (1996: 113–16) argued that Cleland's *Memoirs of a Woman of Pleasure* creates "an opportunity for homoerotic pleasure even as the act is being condemned" (113). According to Hammond, this book, unlike Smollett's *Roderick Random*, "does not assume that the narrator's ignorance and revulsion" at homosexuality "will be shared by the reader," and Hammond even suggested that the novel's gay pornographic aspects might have been instructive to young men rather than discouraging, especially since the two youths described engaging in gay sex experience "mutual affection and give mutual pleasure" (115). McFarlane (1997: 163–73) noted that Cleland often provides readers with "a detailed, lingering, and fascinating description of the male body that focuses on the genitalia" and observed that Cleland describes the genitalia of males far more frequently than those of females (164). Lisa Moore (1997: 53–75) argued that the novel's representations "of female homosexual desire and agency," as in an early episode, "challenge the novel's explicit plot of heterosexual social ascension" (59), and she also contended that the book's very emphasis on female sexual desire undermines any simple ideas of the "naturalness of heterosexuality" (64). Elizabeth Wahl (1999: 238–43) argued that Cleland's novel not only deemphasized the clitoris but also implied the rise of lesbian "tribadism" and suggested male fears of that development (243). Terrence Johnson, in Summers 2002 (156), called *Fanny Hill* "the first (and probably the funniest and most humane) pornographic novel in English," avoiding "all unattractive elements of sexuality and prostitution" and "claiming pleasure as the ultimate goal." Johnson noted that the book describes lesbians, that in creating a female narrator, "Cleland himself is doing a female impersonation," and that in several ways an "apparently heterosexual text thus becomes a masterpiece of homoeroticism." According to Johnson, Fanny implies that "women who seduce other women ... can be as responsible for the downfall of women as men," and that Fanny felt contempt for men who have sex with men. But Johnson observed that Fanny "describes having more sexual pleasure with women than she admits to" and that she "thinks all sodomites are effeminate, but none of the men she describes fit that description."

Terry Castle (2003: 286–7) argued that Cleland's *Memoirs* contains "one of the most influential scenes of lesbian seductions in eighteenth-century fiction." She asserted that while "Cleland obviously relishes the opportunity to deliquesce on female-female love-making—the scene is salacious in the extreme—it turns out to be a prelude" to later episodes of straight sex (286). Cleland thus "establishes one of the cherished conventions of pornographic lesbian representation: that female sexuality is at best a sort of warm-up to heterosexual sex" (287).

David Robinson (2006: 37–84) observed that few "critics have ventured to suggest, and only in passing, that Cleland purposely wrote a homoerotic text. Yet the case for reading *Memoirs* as, at least in part, closeted homosexual writing is remarkably strong" (37). Later he argued that scholars "seem not quite to have realized, or at least not to have articulated, how extraordinary Cleland's treatment of male-male sex actually is." In Robinson's view, the "*Memoirs* contains, in the once-expurgated, now-famous sodomitical scene, one of the most positive treatments of male homosexuality in seventeenth- and eighteenth-century British and French literature" (45). Elaborating on this point, Robinson contended that

> whereas recent gay history leads us to expect, in accounts of eighteenth-century male-male sex, *either* masculine libertines *or* effeminate mollies, Cleland presents a youth *both* masculine *and* effeminate, on the basis of his anatomical and erotic capacity both to penetrate and to be penetrated. Such a depiction is unheard of in the eighteenth century.
>
> (47)

Robinson thought it not surprising that "the two paragraphs in which the simultaneously feminine and masculine, penetrated yet erect youth appears are absent from most editions of *Memoirs*, even pirated ones, and explained away in others as an 'interpolation' by someone else" since Cleland "violates too thoroughly the period's conventions for representing male homosexuality" (49).

THOMAS GRAY (1716-71). George Haggerty, in Summers 1992 (199-214), argued that "Gray's 'Elegy Written in a Country Churchyard' commemorates a problematic sexuality that traditional readings of the poem's 'melancholy' usually ignore," so that the poem "shows how the poet's awareness of his own homosexuality shaped the familiar features of the most popular poem of the eighteenth century" (199). Haggerty later, in Summers 2002 (317-18), suggested that Gray long "suppressed his deeply emotional attachment to members of his own sex, and only later in life did he actually express the love he felt for another man," whose name was "Charles-Victor de Bonstettin." Poems on Richard West and on Eton College, along with the famous "Elegy," are other works Haggerty mentions as relevant to Gray's homoeroticism (318). Louis Crompton (2003: 456-9) called Gray "the most distinguished poet of his generation"—a "shy, affectionate man" whose "emotional life centered on intense male attachments" (456).

HORACE WALPOLE (1717-97). Peter McNeil, in Aldrich and Wotherspoon 2002 (472-3), commenting on Walpole's architectural innovations, noted that "Timothy Mowl has interpreted [his building projects] as a war of style, in which the homosexual outsider Walpole attacked the values and norms of his father's generation, creating 'an introspective and fantastical retreat' when he designed his own home." Despite plenty of evidence to the contrary, McNeil observed, "Walpole's homosexuality was ignored and even rebutted until the 1960s" (472). Haggerty, in Summers 2002 (673-4), mainly surveyed Walpole's life.

Max Fincher (2007) read *The Castle of Otranto* as "a cautious warning against suspicious narratives and paranoid interpretation which characterizes homophobia in the eighteenth century, looking particularly at extortion and the drive to see queer desires in effeminate bodies" (45). Fincher commented on Walpole's familiarity with other texts dealing with extortion (49), saw Walpole's book as "queer" because it "represents gender as a performative act" (53), and perceived the novel as "demonstrating (implicitly) how eighteenth-century homophobia is concerned with the elimination of effeminacy in male subjectivity" (52; see also 55). Fincher saw connections, in this novel, between extortion, surveillance, penetration, masquerading, and same-sex desire (58–9). He concluded that the "novel's dynamics show how speculative gossip can function as a powerful instrument to incite paranoia" and how it reflects the "paranoid dynamics of homophobia in the inability to control narratives about the self and to identify the queer body and its desires" (64).

Duncan Fallowell (Canning 2009: 32–40) called Walpole an "unwavering bachelor" (32) who travelled widely (33–4), eventually became an earl (34), was considered "effeminate, not merely foppish," and "was at the center of a practicing homosexual network," although his letters don't mention "personal sexual events" and he was not a member of a club of the time devoted to "group masturbation" (35). Instead, he presented himself as an "English adult male virgin," subject to occasional "emotional infatuations" with other men (35). The Yale edition of his over 3,000 letters "extends to over fifty volumes"; his writings annoyed Victorian critics who objected to his "inconsistent whims and affectations" (37) and sense of humor and failed to recognize the literary merits of his letters, in which he expressed strong opinions against slavery and both for and against important figures of the time (38). Fallowell praised Walpole's style (38–9), called him a dandy, and compared him to Wilde, Proust, and various later English writers, including various gay authors (38–9).

TOBIAS SMOLLETT (1721–71). Paul Hammond (1996: 111–13) suggested that the increasing visibility of so-called "effeminates and sodomites" in the late seventeenth and early eighteenth centuries produced an anxiety observable in Smollett's *Roderick Random*, especially in chapter 34 (111). Hammond thought some of Strutwell's language echoed contemporary defenses of homosexuality: that it "was permitted by the Greeks, praised by the poets, and is widely practiced abroad," so that "its condemnation by British laws is due more to prejudice than reason" (113). Cameron McFarlane (1997: 108–44) argued that Smollett depicted sodomites as unmanly men who corrupted ideal relations between males, especially where they should be strongest, as in military or patronage relationships (111). He also noted that Smollett excoriated sodomy repeatedly, not just in *Roderick Random* (144). Gregory Woods (1998) thought the book provided "early evidence of the practice of blackmailing same-sex lovers in English society" (136). Byrne Fone (2000: 243-9) argued that "Captain Whiffle and Lord Strutwell respectively represent the effeminate and the monstrous aspects of sodomy" (243), with Whiffle shown as a weak seeker after similar men and Strutwell as a perverse but potentially persuasive defender of a kind of immorality that many considered increasingly threatening in eighteenth-century England.

David Robinson (2006: 61–77) suggested that Roderick's relations with his male sailor friends are depicted as so close that Smollett had to try to prevent readers from interpreting those relations as homoerotic:

> To protect his characters from anti-sodomitical suspicion—and to protect himself, given the semi-autobiographical source of the *Thunder* material—Smollett presents identifiably homosexual characters as foils, as if to say, '*Those* are sodomites. Roderick and his friends are nothing like *them*'. And thus, although Smollett might know sodomy to be common among sailors, he can on no account acknowledge the fact; such masculine sodomites would bear too close a resemblance to the protagonist and his friends, arousing rather than allaying suspicion. Instead, he employs two scapegoating stereotypes—the corrupt, debauched nobleman and the effeminate molly—fleshed out for maximum contrast with Roderick and friends.
>
> (73-4)

According to Robinson, Smollett repeatedly "distinguishes what Roderick and his friends feel and do" from sodomites' feelings and behavior. He "condemns *sex* between men, in order to present what matters most to him: *love* between men" (77).

WILLIAM BECKFORD (1760–1844). Louis Crompton (1985) discussed Lord Byron's fascination with Beckford, a gay exile from England. Crompton also commented on homoeroticism in Beckford's novel titled *Vathek* (1787) (118–23). He described English ostracism of Beckford and reported that the philosopher Jeremy Bentham hoped to collaborate with Beckford on a work attacking homophobia (270–3). Wayne Dynes (1990: 123) saw evidence of Beckford's early homoerotic sensibility reflected in *Vathek* (originally published only in French), noted that Beckford chose exile rather than suffer from English prejudices, and reported that when Beckford eventually returned to England, he expressed his homoeroticism mainly in private letters (Dynes 1990: 123). Paul Hammond (1996: 120–3) discussed the symbolism in *Vathek* suggesting homosexual taboos (121) and also reported on gay episodes not published in the main text (121–2). Robert Drake (1998: 143–5) read *Vathek* as a plea that gays might have chances to lead happy lives. Gregory Woods (1998: 131–3) interpreted *Vathek* in terms of "camp" (131) and considered the book only artificially profound (132).

George Haggerty, in Summers 2002 (80–1), mainly surveyed Beckford's life, noting in particular that his "extreme" letters to William Courtenay were also "indiscreet" (81). Rictor Norton, in Aldrich and Wotherspoon 2002 (45–6), reported that *Vathek*'s "deliberately decadent style ... directly influenced" novels by Ronald Firbank, Joris-Karl Huysmans, and poetry by Mallarme and Swinburne and that several "additional *Episodes* contain explicitly homosexual tales" (45). Norton said Beckford had "become a potent symbol for the homosexual outcast who defends himself with arrogant disdain for propriety" (46). Max Fincher (2007) discussed how *Vathek* represents "queer bodies and sexualities" and also how "queerness is celebrated" but also complexly associated with evil (65). Fincher explored the book's publication history (65–6), its English and French editions, the possible role of its translator as a part-author, and the ways the book potentially resists definitive interpretation (66), thereby "mirror[ing] the feat of those queer bodies whose gender and sexuality cannot be easily read and remain suspicious" (67). Fincher also examined perceived connections between queerness and monstrosity (68–71), the "problematic" pleasures of destroying "boundaries between reality and fantasy" by displaying "excess" (71), and *Vathek*'s emphases on transvestism (76–7), effeminacy (78–9), luxury (80–3), masturbation (85), and sexual excess (85–6). Fincher thought the book's "overarching narrative ... is that an unregulated, private desire that questions the boundaries of a hierarchical order or consumes itself at the expense of the individual or public welfare is destructive," so that queerness in the eighteenth century was increasingly "described in terms of monstrosity" (86). The novel thus "suggests an unholy alliance with a homophobic ideology, one which scrutinizes and destroys the queer body that will not permit its desires to be defined and regulated by the authoritarian discourses of law, religion and a heteronormative culture" (86).

MATTHEW G. ("MONK") LEWIS (1775–1818). George Haggerty, in Summers 2002 (415), mainly surveyed Lewis's life, arguing that "whether or not anything about Lewis's own sexual behavior can be proved," his novel *The Monk* is a great work in the gay and lesbian literary tradition (415). Max Fincher (2007) thought the novel "contains just about every conceivable possibility of anti-heteronormative sexual interests: incest, sado-masochism, auto-eroticism, necrophilia, voyeurism and same-sex desire" (87). Fincher suggested that Rosario, in *The Monk*, could be seen as queer, effeminate, and subservient (88). He maintained that "[f]emininties are the source of [the book's] physical horror and supernatural terror" (90), asserting that "Matolda's queerness precipitates Ambrosio's final violation of Antonia and her mother" (94). Fincher also explored the book's treatment of "problematic gender" identities (95), Ambrosio's "sexual attractiveness" (97), the novel's "anti-clericalism" (100), the significance (for queer readings) of "certain kinds of looks or gazing" (102), and debatable readings of the novel as "camp" writing (105–9). According to Fincher, the "queer-camp aesthetic ... underlines the persistent ambiguity of whether *The Monk* is politically conservative or reactionary" in treating "gender and heterodox desires" (109).

6

The Early Nineteenth Century

GEORGE GORDON, LORD BYRON (1788–1824). Louis Crompton's lengthy 1985 book titled *Byron and Greek Love* discussed, in rich detail, homophobia in Byron's culture, the poet's own bisexuality and homoeroticism, his involvement with various youths and men, and numerous other relevant matters. The book discusses Byron's confessions of homosexuality, his efforts to suppress and disguise it, his fear of it, his ostracism and exile, the centrality of homosexuality to his life, its connections with his heterosexuality, the development of his awareness of his homoerotic desires, the ways scholars suppressed evidence of those desires and related activities, and much else. Crompton additionally examined influences of the poet's complex sexual attitudes on his life and literature.

Crompton also, in Dynes 1990 (179–80), noted that Byron abandoned England for Italy in 1816 after his wife left him, emphasized his "many affairs with women," noted his early love for the Cambridge choir boy John Eddleston, and reported that many of Byron's poems about Eddleston had to be published as if they were about a woman (see also Aldrich and Wotherspoon 2002: 77). Crompton reported that Byron, while in Europe, was involved with several Greek youths, that he named one his heir, that he often referred to them in coded letters, and that his final poems were written about a Greek youth who did not reciprocate the poet's affection (see also Aldrich and Wotherspoon 2002: 77). Byron's bisexuality, wrote Crompton, was not widely known until 1935, although an anonymous poem titled *Don Leon*, an open defense of homosexuality written shortly after his death, was attributed to him. Marjorie Garber (1992: 316–20) discussed Byron's interest in cross-dressing males and females, both as a source of erotic attraction and also as a theme in *Don Juan*. Robert Drake 1998 (146–8) mentioned that Byron translated a homoerotic passage from Virgil's *Aeneid* (see also Aldrich and Wotherspoon 2002: 77), found subtle homoeroticism in Byron's own *Childe Harold's Pilgrimage*, and noted the homoeroticism of some of Byron's final poems.

Mark Lilly (1993: 15–27) noted Byron's affairs with women as well as men (15–16), stressed his interest in "human freedom as forbidden" (16), suggested that Byron's emphasis on romantic heroes resonated in later gay literature (16), and announced a particular focus on the significance of Byron's work titled *Lara* (17). Lilly saw in Byron's life a tension between desiring conformity and yearning for freedom (19), noted the poet's interest in the theme of concealment (19), contended that Byron's description of a pirate named Conrad was relevant to the poet's own sexual life (20), and contended that in *Lara* an emphasis on "emotional and physical extremes" is used to "blot out the experience of perceiving the world as meaningless"—a perception rooted in Byron's troubled youth (21). According to Lilly, Byron thought Islamic societies lacked the West's "sexual hysteria" (22), sometimes used the Orient to symbolize "the possibility of gay love" (25), sometimes used cross-dressing as a way to treat gay themes (25), and, in his translation of part of the *Aeneid*, stressed homoeroticism (26).

Paul Hammond (1996: 119–20) described how Byron, in *Lara*, cleverly "implicates the reader in imagining a dangerous homosexual relationship before moving us back into a less threatening version of exotic passion" (119). Carl Miller (1996: 253–4) suggested that Byron's *Manfred* might deal, covertly, with homoeroticism, while Garry Wotherspoon, in Aldrich and Wotherspoon 2002 (77), reported that among Byron's works is "*Hours of Idleness* (which includes his translations of homoerotic classical poems)" and observed that as "Louis Crompton has noted, critics, scholars and [the] public managed, despite overwhelming evidence, to ignore Byron's blatant bisexuality until recent years." Crompton, in Summers 2002 (119–22), emphasized Byron's bisexuality (119–20), his youthful poems to other boys, his numerous homosexual experiences in Greece, and the coded letters he received "giving many details about homosexual scandals in England" and the harsh penalties gays faced there (120). Crompton suggested that Byron lived abroad partly to avoid such punishments, that he worried about being blackmailed, that a woman he knew spread damaging rumors about him, and that he consequently left England (120–1). Among works with homoerotic aspects (including cross-dressing), Crompton discusses *Lara* (influenced by Beckford's *Vathek*), *Don Juan*, and a little-known text titled "Detached Thoughts." Crompton suggested that Byron's bisexuality may have been "one source of the anguished guilt felt by the Byronic hero," also opining that "under the homophobic conditions of the day, Byron could refer to male love affairs in a published work only if he appeared to condemn them." Crompton reported that Byron "fell desperately in love" with a Greek youth who exploited Byron's interest (121), that a friend burned Byron's unpublished memoirs after the poet died, but that soon, however, someone published "a pseudo-autobiography"—*Don Leon*—that was surprisingly accurate on Byron's homosexual affairs. Crompton discussed the poem's provenance, suggesting it was *not* by Byron (since it mentioned historical events from after the poet's death) but calling it "one of the most remarkable documents in gay literary history" (122).

Max Fincher (2007) examined how "Byron and writers like [John William] Polidori tap into a public climate of suspicion about [Byron's] sexual desires for men, and how we can describe Byron as queer" (131). According to Fincher, "self-empowerment via a climate of repression is the defining quality of Byron's queerness" (131). Fincher discussed the disguised homoeroticism of Byron's elegy "To Thyrza" (132), his interest in gender reversals (132–3), his need to be secretive (133), worries that he might be assassinated (134), and his queer "defiance, particularly in his attempt to defy the communal power of gossip by manipulating the suspicions of the reading public" (135; see also 156).

AUTHOR OF *DON LEON* Crompton (1985: 343–61) described the anonymous *Don Leon* as a "polemical narrative" claiming "to be [Lord] Byron's own account of his homosexual experiences" and called it "one of the major puzzles of English literary history" (343). He noted that the poem is nearly fifty pages long, is followed by fifty pages of notes, is remarkably accurate about Byron, but was long ignored by Byron's biographers. After reporting speculation about its authorship, he praised its wit and style, emphasized its anti-homophobia, noted its arguments against the death penalty for gay sex, and described its extended defense of homosexuality and its suggestion that homoeroticism was widespread in English culture. Crompton observed that the poem sometimes paradoxically uses homophobic language, is playfully erotic near the end, reflects positive changes in British culture since the time of Byron's birth, and may have been completed as early as 1833. Fone (1995: 25–39) argued that *Don Leon* presents fear of homosexuals as the cause of their persecution, suggested that it was groundbreaking in seeing gays as a distinct population far earlier than Foucault claimed, saw the work as an important document in the growth of a self-confident gay consciousness, speculated about its authorship, stressed its emphasis on homoerotic ideal friendship, and justified its closing sexual explicitness. Paul Hammond (1996: 135–7) called *Don Leon* "uneven" but said that its defense of homosexuality echoed both Enlightenment and Romantic themes even while the accompanying notes documented "the plight faced by homosexual men in the nineteenth-century police court" (137). Byrne Fone (2000: 258–65) called

Don Leon "a well-reasoned plea for sanity, the first and most direct challenge yet sounded in English literature to the persecution" of gays resulting from homophobia. According to Fone, the anonymous author not only regarded gays as "an identifiable minority" following their own natural impulses but also drew on otherwise unknown personal information about Byron. The poem defended gays from "crimes" that harmed no one, regarded homoerotic desires as innate, and presented both itself and its author as challenges to "homophobic prejudice."

ALFRED, LORD TENNYSON (1809–92). Crompton (1985: 187–91) noted contemporary attacks on *In Memoriam*, Tennyson's elegy for his beloved friend Henry Hallam, for being too unrestrained. Richard Dellamora (1990: 16–41) suggested that Tennyson "carefully fences intense male bonding from sexual activity" (16), had to have known the homoerotic tradition of the pastoral poetry that helped inspire *In Memoriam*, and was part of an intimate male group while studying at Cambridge (19). Dellamora challenged later editors who claimed Tennyson had been ignorant of homosexuality (28), disputed the critical tendency to deemphasize the poem's homoeroticism (30), and compared Hallam in *In Memoriam* to Dante's Beatrice (31–3). Showing that Tennyson's revisions toned down the poem's homoeroticism in response to criticism (33–4), Dellamora examined its homoerotic but often aesthetically asexual phrasing (38–9).

Dynes (1990) emphasized that the poem, although eventually very popular, sounds homoerotic to modern ears and sounded so even to some of Tennyson's contemporaries (86–7; see also Drake 1998: 192–4). Christopher Craft (1994: 44–70) noted early and later reviewers' discomfort with its homoerotic tones, suggested that Tennyson could express intense love for Hallam only because Hallam was dead, and explored the poem's links between love and death (47–52). He stressed how Tennyson dealt with a difficult topic by using Christian ideas, making Christ a substitute for Hallam (53–8), and noted Tennyson's symbolism of touching hands to imply true love (56–8). Hallam, he concluded, remained central to *In Memoriam* (70).

Paul Hammond (1996: 145–58), discussing Tennyson's affection for Hallam, noted that the poet repeatedly associated their relationship with an 1830 visit to a valley in the Pyrenees mountains, where, perhaps, Tennyson declared his affection for his friend. Hammond also noted how frequently Tennyson wrote about women longing for men, suggesting Tennyson may have felt similar desires (145–8). Discussing *In Memoriam*, Hammond noted criticisms that it was too homoerotic and also explored how it deals with the theme (and phrasing) of "love" (151–3), including by using both the language of marriage to depict the

Tennyson-Hallam relationship as well as its often "extraordinary physicality" (153–4). Hammond thought Tennyson's revisions often suggest "a nervousness and uncertainty" precisely "when he is trying to find words for his intense love" and "is trespassing on the dangerous grounds of erotic consummation" (155). Gregory Woods (1998: 118–20) commended Tennyson for unusually resisting "the pressure to stay silent" about his feelings, crediting this conflict for creating "a very productive inner tension" that benefits the poem (119).

Seymour Kleinberg, in Aldrich and Wotherspoon (2002: 437–8), described how Tennyson's father psychologically abused his twelve children. Kleinberg also said Tennyson and Hallam "formed a friendship of such intensity that the word 'love' barely describes it. After Hallam died suddenly in 1833, Tennyson suffered from "mourning and melancholia" for twenty years (437). His "love for Hallam," Kleinberg observed,

> has remained until recent decades critically sacrosanct, the ideal friendship, a relationship of platonic perfection. This was partly the result of the prudery of academic critics and scholars, but also because all the letters between Hallam and Tennyson were burned by Hallam's father immediately after his son's death and because Tennyson's eldest son, his literary executor and first biographer, Hallam Tennyson, destroyed many more letters after his father's death. *In Memoriam* was viewed as a metaphysical poem laden with symbolic and allegorical meaning, and interpretations that might be regarded as psychological or personal were dismissed as irrelevant. Only since the reprinting of his early poems, hitherto either unpublished or never reprinted after their first appearance, have critics begun to reexamine the nature of Tennyson's love for Hallam. Now it seems clear that their relationship was both passionate and romantic, though it is doubtful that it was ever consummated.
>
> Tennyson's love for Hallam, undeniably homoerotic, was also unselfconscious, that is, free from remorse or guilt or a sense of the illicit. The idea of homosexuality denoting a psychological identity did not yet exist, and since the men were chaste, they had nothing to reproach themselves for, regarding the sin of sodomy.
>
> (437)

Donald Hall, in Summers 2002 (650–2), emphasized both Tennyson's heterosexuality and his interest in androgynous males and in homoerotic and homosocial relationships. Hall thought Tennyson defies easy categorization, observing that some of his early Arthurian poetry celebrates androgynous males and chaste affection between men. Such poems include "Morte d Arthur," "Sir Galahad," "The Princess," and "The Holy Grail." Tennyson condemned "debauchery," sometimes associating it with homoeroticism, but celebrated his own "profound emotional attachment" to Hallam (651). Hall discussed *In Memoriam* in detail, particularly noting how Tennyson edited it to make it seem less homoerotic. According to Hall, Tennyson condemned effeminacy, was defended by his son against any hints of homoeroticism, wrote very little (and that disapprovingly) about lesbianism, and saw male bonding as socially beneficial but female bonding as a threat to social cohesion.

HERMAN MELVILLE (1819–91). Georges-Michel Sarotte (1978: 72–5, 78–85) noted that Melville once wrote of the homosexuality common on ships (72), frequently described the ship-board contempt for effeminate men (73), and sometimes linked naval homosexuality with sadism (73). Sarotte said Melville described brotherly feelings among seamen (74) and showed a consistent appreciation (often shared with other sailors) of masculine beauty (74–5), especially in *Billy Budd* (75). According to Sarotte, Melville describes Billy as "adored, innocent and pure, passive yet dominating and subjugating his fellows." He is also "the perfect androgyne, cast into a world of men without women" and treated as a "demigod of the Beautiful, the Good—what each man wants to be or dreams of being" (75). Sarotte said this kind of character,

> the Handsome Sailor, is a type that appears to have obsessed Melville from *Typee* to *Billy Budd*, as his *homosexual temptation*. [Melville] is forced to disguise and sublimate this temptation in aesthetic admiration (mythological references, the relationship between a gentlemanly soul and an attractive appearance, the Platonic theory of the handsome body reflecting a noble inner man, a celestial gaze denoting innocence and purity, etc.). Billy is the essence of masculine beauty (strength) animated by feminine tenderness.
>
> (79)

Sarotte thought Melville associates Billy with instinct, the id, and pleasure and therefore gives him no real past, but he also denies a past to Claggart, Billy's agonized, sadistic antagonist, whom Melville associates with repression, oppression, and the Freudian superego. Only Vere, first symbolizing the Freudian ego but eventually resembling Claggart in his repressiveness, is given a clear past. Later Melville lets Vere show his love for Billy but refuses to describe it directly (79–81). Sarotte said Melville here "relied upon tradition, custom, and martial law to control his deepest sexual tendencies, which so many critics ... have discerned" (82). He often used "complex symbolism that enabled him to write about his insoluble dilemma: how to love a young man purely and innocently" in nineteenth-century America. He imagined an "unfettered" utopia of symbolic male love objects. Despite rebelling against social repressions, "Melville had too much respect for his own culture to make Billy Budd, the embodiment of his obsessive homosexual temptations, into a man of flesh and blood" (82).

David Bergman (1991: 143–9) discussed "Cannibals and Queers" in Melville's early novel *Typee*, concluding that the book "presents two sorts of homosexual relations: those egalitarian in nature, and those mediated by the feminine. The latter are free from anxiety because they reproduce the familiar privileged relations of male power." Surprisingly, Bergman thought "the prospect of an egalitarian homosexual relationship" terrifies Melville—"a terror he converts to the more understandable and acceptable fear of being eaten"—because "equality represents for him a new, untried loss of power and privilege" (149). Byrne Fone also (1995: 49–52) emphasized homoeroticism in *Typee*, especially Tom's relationships with handsome youths who represent different homoerotic ideals. Warren Johansson, in Dynes (1990), argued that homoeroticism in "Melville's writing is subtle, pervasive, and rich in symbolic overtones." Johansson credited Leslie Fiedler for first noticing this (although in fact it had been perceived much earlier). He elaborated on Fiedler's views, stressed Melville's intense interest in strong male friendships, and saw this interest as subtly subversive of his era's official culture (799). Robert Drake (1998: 163–4), noting Melville's attractions to other men (including Nathaniel Hawthorne), called *Moby-Dick* "the wondrous queer heart of American literature." Gregory Woods (1998: 163–6) called Melville "an informed connoisseur of working men" who dramatizes individual relationships (163). Woods thought Melville, emphasizing masturbation rather than penetration, seemed unable to imagine any lasting love between men (164). Woods also thought Billy Budd's "perfection is flawed because it inspires the imperfections of others" (165).

Robert Martin, in Summers (2002: 439–43), surveyed Melville's life and career, emphasized his homoerotic descriptions of life in the South Seas and his particular interest in marriage customs there (involving two men and one woman), attributed some of Melville's psychological difficulties to a "too-loving mother," and stressed *Redburn*'s importance to Melville's views of America and of relations between men (440–1). Martin said Melville "seeks a balance between the sexes, neither too masculine nor two feminine," as well as balance between imperial and colonized cultures. He increasingly tried to depict "male friends in a real social space," as in *Redburn*, where one episode covertly celebrates masturbation, while in *Moby-Dick* Melville contrasts Queequeg's positive masculinity with Ahab's negative version (441). Martin thought the relationship between Ishmael and Queequeg showed how homophobia could be linked to racism, said Melville implies an etymological link between whales and phalluses, and wrote that the novel "calls repeatedly for a reclamation of pleasure," particularly in the "sperm" episode, which celebrates homoerotic, homosocial play (442). Martin also emphasized sly homoeroticism in *Pierre*, Melville's treatment of Claggart in *Billy Budd* as a "repressed homosexual," and his presentation of Billy as a powerless androgynous victim (443).

David Garnes, in Aldrich and Wotherspoon (2002), wrote that although

> there has been much conjecture regarding the precise nature of [Melville's] relationship with the novelist Nathaniel Hawthorne (their close friendship suffered an abrupt, unexplained rupture in 1852), Melville's writings provide the best case for including him in the gay literary canon.
>
> Homoerotic overtones in the early seafaring novels are unmistakable, from extended descriptions of the male beauty of the South Sea islanders to romanticised depictions of sailor friends and comrades on board ship. In *Moby Dick*, male bonding is notable in the 'marriage bed' episode involving Ishmael and Queequeg, as well as in the intensely erotic and metaphoric 'squeeze of the Hand' chapter describing the camaraderie of sailors extracting spermaceti from a dead whale.
>
> *Billy Budd*, written at the very end of Melville's life, is both the most explicit and sombre of his writings in terms of gay content.
>
> (307–8)

Vestal McIntyre (Canning 2009: 41–7) commented briefly on gay motifs in *Moby-Dick* and *Billy Budd* (43–4), compared gays of his own generation to Ahab in their attraction to what others considered the "dark, dangerous, and wrong" (44), jokingly compared Ahab's quest to gay "cruising" (44–5), and recounted his own attraction to Melville's masterpiece (45–7).

WALT WHITMAN (1819–92). Robert K. Martin (1979: 3–89) noted frequent critical efforts to downplay or deny Whitman's homosexuality, discussed at length his poems "The Sleepers" and "Song of Myself," and suggested that in these works "the experience of orgasm … gives rise to Whitman's 'cosmic consciousness'" (28). Martin thought Whitman could not make his gay orientation as explicit as he wanted to, said he appropriated the term "adhesiveness" to imply his homoerotic ideas, and thought Whitman continuously developed this concept throughout his works. Martin especially emphasized homoeroticism in the "Calamus" poems, reported both negative and positive responses to this collection, traced its various themes and sources (such as Platonism and Quakerism), and discussed the collection's overall structure.

Eve Kosofsky Sedgwick (1985: 201–18) discussed Whitman's influence on and relations with such English intellectuals as J. A. Symonds and Edward Carpenter, recounted his strong denial, to Symonds, that his homoerotic poems implied physical relations, noted his popularity nonetheless among gays on both sides of the Atlantic, and discussed the often negative ways in which Whitman's ideas affected others' views of women. Richard Dellamora (1990: 86–93) discussed Whitman's influence on Hopkins, Swinburne, and Symonds, arguing that his "practice clarifies by contrast the hesitations, compromises, [and] at times the panic" of English "gay" writers, including Hopkins and the especially ambivalent Swinburne, who sometimes valued Whitman and sometimes turned against him (87–93).

Edward F. Grier, in Dynes (1990: 1387–9), noted how Whitman listed men's names in notebooks, emphasized his early mysticism, and reported his eventual relationship with "a young streetcar conductor, Peter Doyle." Grier noted a later relationship with eighteen-year-old Harry Stafford, asserted the impossibility of determining "the nature of Whitman's homosexuality," and criticized naivety on both sides of the debate. Grier suggested Whitman may have had sexual experiences with both men and women, noting that Whitman's heterosexual passages truly shocked some of his contemporaries (1388). According to Grier, the "second and third sections of 'Song of Myself' use homosexual imagery," with a "tremendous sweep of eroticism from section 24 to the climax of fulfillment in male intercourse in section 29" (1389). Grier explored Whitman's idea of "adhesiveness," stressing especially the homoerotic "Calamus" poems (1388–9). David Bergman (1991: 48–52) also stressed these poems, situating them biographically, reporting previous critical reactions, and finally concluding that

> Whitman's genius is not that he was able to establish a gay identity—would we expect such a thing of him?—but that he points out the difficulties so clearly. *Calamus* is ultimately a moving portrait of psychological isolation against which his grandiosity is clearly a strategy to prevent the most profound depression. Even so, Whitman does not evade the hardest truths: his love for men and the impossibility of sustaining such a love within the context of the 1860s. Of these desires and frustrations, he writes with a frankness, a tenderness, and an unaffected passion never expressed before.
>
> (52)

Fone (1995: 57–73) examined Whitman's intriguing early homoerotic story titled "The Child's Champion," relating it to some later poetry, especially *Leaves of Grass*, "Song of Myself," and the *Calamus* poems. Neil Miller (1995: 3–13) mainly surveyed Whitman's life, his ambiguous relationships with other men, the ways he was admired by various British writers, and the ways he denied, in his later years, that he advocated actual gay sexual behavior.

Paul Hammond (1996: 158–66) discussed Whitman's impact on such English writers as Hopkins, Symonds, Carpenter, Lawrence, and Ivor Gurney (158). He explored the ambiguous erotic language of one poem (160–1) and said "Whitman's poetry often shapes the landscape as a site of erotic longing and satisfaction" (163). His work, Hammond continued,

> characteristically celebrates achieved love between adults, rather than a longing for the transient beauty of unattainable boys. The muscular strength of the working body attracts him, rather than the lustrous surface of the boyish form. His poetry is more tactile than visual, his lovers are not translated into works of art, and no invisible boundary separates a gazer from the erotic object: Whitman does not frame the body so as to preserve it for the eye and keep it from the touch.
>
> (163–4)

Robert Drake (1998: 180–91) discussed homoeroticism in "The Child's Champion," noted that Whitman sometimes protectively changed the genders of people mentioned in his early poems, and quoted from much of Whitman's later poetry. Hogan and Hudson (1998: 572–3) emphasized the "Calamus" poems (572), which some early readers interpreted as non-erotic celebrations of male comradeship, finding his heteroerotic poems more disturbing. Hogan and Hudson, noting that many critics long denied Whitman's homoeroticism, reported recent discoveries suggesting that he was intimate with male students during his early years as a teacher. They concluded by emphasizing his wide literary influence (573).

Gregory Woods (1998: 154–9, 176–80) argued that Whitman's poems "have turned out to be the most influential of American homo-erotic texts, and indeed influential *as* homo-erotic texts" (154–5). Woods emphasized how New York City and other sites inspired Whitman's gay sensibility (155): he sought "to demonstrate that the urban industrial revolution cannot obliterate the virility of the pioneering spirit" (156). Woods disputed claims that Whitman avoids depicting intimacy (156–7), suggesting that the Civil War poems demonstrate how "it often takes a war to persuade men to love each other at all demonstratively" (158). Calling Whitman the "most influential modern homosexual writer in late nineteenth-century Britain" (176), Woods claimed that Whitman "sent shockwaves through the furtive gentility" of Britain's gay literati, transforming "their nostalgia for pastoral Greece into a yearning for a utopian New World of open frontiers and open-necked shirts" (177).

Charley Shively, in Aldrich and Wotherspoon (2002: 483–5), noted Whitman's intense affection for his mother, emphasized how his poems celebrate sexual love, claimed that *Leaves* "pivots upon [a] dalliance with a young man," and reported that in "1889, the poet told an interviewer, 'Sex, sex, sex: sex is the root of it all'" (484). Shively emphasized Whitman's working-class origins and interests, the notes he kept detailing his frequent sexual relations, and the inspiration Fred Vaughan provided for the intensely homoerotic *Calamus* poems. He described Whitman's chance erotic encounter and then long-term relationship with Peter Doyle, the mixed reception of *Leaves of Grass* (which Abraham Lincoln admired), and the ways his later poems became "less homoerotic" and "more abstract" (484). Shively detailed Whitman's reputation and tastes, commented on his various lovers, emphasized his love of opera, and described the enthusiasm of some recent admirers (485).

Robert Martin, in Summers (2002: 685–91), emphasized "The Child's Champion," noting this story's stress on an older male as a protector of a younger male, whom he actually comforts in bed in the first version of the story (a detail Whitman later removed) and whom Whitman depicts as a champion against vice. Martin discussed Whitman's significant visit to New Orleans, the possibility that he may have had a homoerotic relationship there, and the likelihood that the homoerotic "Calamus" poems may have been inspired by a failed relationship with Fred Vaughan (685). According to Martin, Whitman rejected the "foofoo, or dandy … in favor of the freckled outdoorsman, whose beard associates" gay men with masculinity. The poet's own marginal position allowed him to sympathize with women and slaves, and in his famous poem about twenty-eight young males swimming naked while being observed by a yearning woman, the "repressed desires of the woman and the young men come together, in a scene that derives its power from its violation of convention. The sexuality here is hetero, homo, auto, perhaps truly queer, that is, lacking fixed definition." But Whitman's main interest was in "the male working-class body," frequently visible while cruising in the city, "a world of constantly repeated flirtations and erotic possibilities." Martin said Whitman wanted to reunite body and soul (686), reject Emerson's emphasis mostly on the latter, and also make poetry more deliberately social and political. However, Whitman was not an easy optimist; he knew the reality of pain but believed "in the power of male love to work against patriarchal authority," often speaking "through the voices of others who have suffered" and thus becoming "a general voice of the outcast and forbidden." Martin found evidence of Whitman's homoeroticism even in poems before the "Calamus" lyrics (687), such as an explicit passage (later cut) from section 21 of *Song of Myself*, but he suggested that *Song*'s first edition is "highly erotic" but mostly lacks a "sense of identity or community." But *Song*'s second edition, in its "Song of the Open Road," allowed Whitman "to deal at once with his mission as a national poet and as a lover of men." Martin thought Whitman differed from Emerson in his thoughts about the functions of eyes and, in the "Calamus" poems, wrote in the tradition of Virgil's "Bucolics" (688). Whitman's "Calamus" lyrics emphasize the power of love but "lack much of the frank sexuality of 'Song of Myself'. They insist, not on homosexual *acts*, but on homosexual being in the world," evoking darkness "primarily in personal terms," as resulting from "isolation" and failed personal love. "Whitman wonders whether his love for other men is actually shared by others; he seeks community" (689), but even private masturbation was condemned in his era. In Martin's view, the "dream of a united America, and the search for a personal friend, give way in the later poems to a desire for fulfillment in death"—a desire independent from "personal sexual identity." Martin concluded that Whitman's writings quickly won him many gay admirers, both at home and abroad (690).

Colm Tóibín (2002: 10–13) noted that the great critic F. O. Matthiesen, himself a closeted gay, said almost nothing about Whitman's sexuality in a chapter of over a hundred pages on the poet, although Matthiesen did report Whitman's important influence on such other gay writers as James and Hopkins. But when Matthiesen did mention Whitman's sexuality, he did so disparagingly and insultingly. Philip Clark (Canning 2009: 48–55) thought academics had damaged Whitman's image but recounted positive responses to Whitman by such figures as Emerson and Edward Carpenter and a devoted woman reader named Anne Gilchrist, who hoped to marry him. Clark suggested that "sexual expressions in Whitman's poetry were particularly powerful for female readers ... trapped by the Victorian purity cult" (54).

7

The Later Nineteenth Century

EMILY DICKINSON (1830–86). Jeannette Foster (1956: 145–8) briefly surveyed Dickinson's attachments to both men and women, relying heavily on a 1951 biography by Rebecca Patterson for evidence of the poet's possibly lesbian feelings. Lillian Faderman (1981: 174–7) noted that nineteenth-century women often addressed one another in terms that seem almost erotic today, reporting that by the twentieth-century such expressions had come to seem suspect and that an early editor omitted many such passages from Dickinson's letters. In Dynes (1990: 315–17), Faderman stressed Dickinson's "strong emotional attachments" to certain other women, noting that she did not always write passionately to or about *all* women, and suggesting that about forty to fifty of her poems could be called lesbian (even though Dickinson was also attracted to various men). Faderman quoted from Dickinson's various letters to other women, noted that language used there often also appears in the poems, and surveyed previous scholarship on Dickinson's lesbianism. She said "Dickinson's homoerotic poetry seems to span" her whole career and observed that roughly ninety percent of the poet's letters no longer exist (315–17). According to Faderman, the "speaker in Dickinson's homoerotic poems is usually the lover and pursuer"; the poems often admit the impermanence of such love; Dickinson seemed pained by romantic inconstancy; and the poems are "never joyous," mainly because Dickinson understood the pressure women felt to marry men (317).

Faderman (1994: 43–6) reported little evidence of Dickinson's romantic feelings for men (43), observed that she felt strongly attracted to various women (43–4), emphasized especially her feelings for Sue Gilbert (44), and suggested that Dickinson eventually felt that if "she could not share her life with Sue, she would share her art" (44). Faderman thought many Dickinson poems resemble lesbian "love lyrics" and often echo "the sentiments of Dickinson's letters" (44). Faderman said critics had long tried to "explain away" lesbian aspects of Dickinson's poetry but thought this approach had begun to diminish, with one critic even focusing on some poems' supposed "clitoral" imagery (45). But even skeptics, Faderman claimed, would find it hard to deny that Dickinson sometimes "passionately loved women" (45). Hogan and Hudson (1998: 184–5) noted that one of Dickinson's early advisers attacked Walt Whitman and Oscar Wilde, that early biographers simply assumed Dickinson was straight, but that she is now commonly seen as homoerotic or bisexual (184).

David Garnes, in Aldrich and Wotherspoon (2002: 127–8), noted that in recent years the woman-loving aspects of Dickinson's poetry have been frequently stressed. Garnes wrote that Dickinson was especially affected by her relationship with her brother's eventual wife, Susan Gilbert Dickinson:

> Often communicating to relatives and friends through short poems and letters, Dickinson lavished on 'Sue/Susie' literally hundreds of dense and often passionate communiques. Even allowing for the liberal affectional conventions of nineteenth-century female friendship, Dickinson's expressed feelings for her school friend and later sister-in-law and lifelong neighbour argue for a lesbian interpretation. Whatever the exact nature of the relationship, however, what is indisputable is that Susan Dickinson provided the poet with the inspiration for some of her most deeply-felt writing.
>
> (128)

Nancy Hurrelbrinck, in Summers (2002: 181–4), noted that Dickinson sent more of her poems to women than to men; reported that early editors downplayed her relationship with "Sue" Gilbert; observed that, when young, Dickinson often wrote humorous texts; and named several of her friends and mentors. Hurrelbrinck thought Dickinson "avoided those she loved because they affected her too powerfully" (181), adding that her feelings about Gilbert and about Samuel Bowles were particularly intense and noting that she sent three times more poems to Gilbert than to anyone else. But Gilbert, after initially reciprocating Dickinson's affection, "apparently began to feel suffocated by the poet's demands for attention" after Gilbert married Emily's brother. Dickinson, said Hurrelbrinck, wrote to Gilbert for various reasons and "was clearly in love with her," as her impassioned writings showed. "The prevalence of both hetero- and homoerotic imagery," Hurrelbrinck observed, "suggests that Dickinson was bisexual, but did she regard herself as such? … she may not have acknowledged [to herself] the homoerotic strain in her letters and poems." Hurrelbrinck considered some evidence ambiguous, suggested that Dickinson sometimes toned down her poems to Gilbert (182), and argued that Dickinson, when writing to Gilbert and others, "wanted to conceal the details of her passions but had a consuming need to disclose their intensity"—tactics evident in the writings to Gilbert. Hurrelbrinck contended that Gilbert's

> role in the development of Dickinson's writing cannot be overemphasized: As the source of love and frustration, of literary camaraderie and competition, she provided the poet with both a source of material and an ideal reader. Sue's early friendship inspired [Dickinson] to express her love candidly in poems and letters, but her perceived defection [after she married the poet's brother] forced Dickinson to resort to poetic language to communicate with her.
> (183)

Terry Castle (2003: 482–4) noted that so "fiercely erotic are some of [Dickinson's] female directed poems" that several "early editors felt obliged to alter the pronouns in order to disguise their unusual nature" (482). Castle assumed that Sue Gilbert was Dickinson's most probable addressee but observed that "what could not be said in person was channeled into verse: into some of the most amorous, mysterious, and magnificent writing one woman has ever addressed to another" (483).

CHRISTINA ROSSETTI (1830–94). Lillian Faderman (1994: 60–2) compared Rossetti to Emily Dickinson in her living arrangements, freedom from normal work and family obligations, and enigmatic emotional life. Rossetti, Faderman said, had no enduring heterosexual relationships, despite her brother's emphasis on them, adding that images in *Goblin Market* "impute evil to male sensuality and value the sensuality ... possible between two women" and that although "Rossetti seems to have been depicting salvation through romantic friendship in this poem," many illustrations of the poem, "even in the late nineteenth century, hinted at lesbian sexuality" (62). James Najarian, in Summers (2002: 567–8), reported a change in Rossetti's personality from happy to serious, her two broken engagements, her "lifelong interest in 'fallen women,'" and her emphasis on female sexuality in "Goblin Market" (567). Terry Castle (2003: 443–4) said Rossetti's poetry could be both pious and "wildly erotic," adding that she shares with Emily Dickinson both a "sublimated yet potent sensualism" and a profound susceptibility to "the power of the feminine" (443). Castle called *Goblin Market* both childlike and "shockingly homoerotic," making it "one of the strangest of Victorian love poems" (444).

ALGERNON CHARLES SWINBURNE (1837–1909). According to Richard Dellamora (1990: 69–85), Swinburne thought great poets were bisexual either literally or metaphorically (69). Citing numerous examples of Swinburne's interest in non-standard sexual behavior, Dellamora focused particularly on his treatment of lesbianism, even while also noting that although nothing directly indicates Swinburne's homosexuality, he was "imaginatively receptive to male-male desire" (70). Dellamora emphasized that legal restrictions prevented Swinburne from writing freely, indicated his interest in androgyny, saw him as an English conduit for unconventional French literature, and stressed how he echoed Sappho and showed a strong interest in lesbianism (70–5). Discussing in detail Swinburne's Sapphic poetry, Dellamora ended by focusing on Swinburne's interest in flagellation (75–85).

Donald Gray, in Malinowski (1994: 363–7), thought Swinburne's early works (provocative, sexually charged, and sometimes even pornographic) differ from his later, more conventional writings. Gray noted the controversy caused by the early works, their flirtations with sadism, their author's interest in hermaphrodites, lesbians, and bisexuals (Sappho in particular), and Swinburne's treatment, in *Lesbia Brandon*, of all kinds of "controversial sexual situations, including adultery, potential incest, homoeroticism expressed or displaced in sadism and masochism; the confusion of genders in androgyny, cross-dressing; and the narcissism of loving oneself in a brother or sister" (366). James Najarian, in Summers (2002: 645), noted Swinburne's interest in flagellation and his poems on masochism (such as "Delores"), bisexuality (such as "Hermaphroditus"), and lesbianism (such as "Anactoria"). Najarian said Swinburne "was fascinated by lesbianism and bisexuality not only for their erotics but because he interpreted them as gestures of social and cultural rebellion."

Terry Castle (2003: 459–61) wrote that Swinburne, like "Baudelaire, who influenced him greatly," was "deeply attracted by the lesbian theme," especially when using it to express "sadomasochistic sexual fantasies." She referred to one poem's "morbid and fetishistic" traits and its "peculiar fusion of high-art ambition and dizzying tastelessness" (460).

WALTER PATER (1839–94). Richard Dellamora (1990) at first set Pater's homoerotic thinking within its immediate social and historical contexts at Oxford University (58–68), later detailing his responses to Leonardo da Vinci, whom Pater saw as sexually unconventional (130–46). An ensuing chapter (147–66) challenged "the common view that Pater criticized Victorian religious beliefs and social mores in his first book, *Studies in the History of the Renaissance* (1873), then spent the rest of his life backing down" (147). Instead, Dellamora emphasized Pater's bravery in anticipating later unconventional thinking, especially about homosexuality in the earlier Christian eras (166). Finally, in one more chapter on Pater (167–92), Dellamora claimed that Pater read certain classical myths as "coded protests" by "marginalized groups" (173), partly because of his "particular interest in relations between men within a patriarchal order" (176), especially "uncontrolled homophobia" (192)—a topic Dellamora also discussed later (167–217).

Warren Johansson, in Dynes (1990: 953–4), mentioned an early indication of Pater's sympathy for Greek homoeroticism, noted his interest in the companionship of young, handsome men, reported his "rejection of Christianity and affinity for paganism," and observed Pater's unsuccessful efforts to hide his erotic interests. According to Johansson, Pater idealized aesthetic ecstasy and intense male friendship, found evidence of both in the Middle Ages and the Renaissance, and wrote fiction dealing with tensions between paganism and Christianity. Johansson stressed the beauty of Pater's prose and noted his eventual emphasis on a sort of disciplined Platonism. Pater's "refined and academic hedonism," Johansson concluded, "mark him as a ... homosexual with profound aesthetic sensibilities" (954). Gregory Woods (1998: 167–9) briefly discussed Pater's homoerotic writings. Scott McLemee, in Summers (2002: 505–7), discussed Pater as a stylist, an advocate of art for art's sake, a historian, theorist, and possible practitioner of homoerotic desire, and both a controversial and influential author because he was seen by some as immoral and by others as amoral, despite his own rejection of such claims. Jason Boyd, in Aldrich and Wotherspoon (2002: 339–40), discussed Pater's influence on such concepts as aestheticism, decadence, and Hellenism, as well as his "perceived relativism, agnosticism, amorality, and paganism." Boyd noted his strong influence on Oscar Wilde and mentioned two of Pater's works of fiction in which male pagan gods come back to life during the Middle Ages.

JOHN ADDINGTON SYMONDS (1840–93). Geoff Puterbaugh, in Dynes (1990: 1271–2), noted Symonds's childhood dreams about nude men, saying Symonds felt his homoeroticism was innate but was nonetheless "disgusted" by the gay sex he saw at school and even reported the school's headmaster (who was then dismissed) for loving a particular youth (1271). Puterbaugh said Symonds married on his father's advice, sired four daughters, had a distant relationship with his wife, "and continued to pursue young men as soul mates," eventually having franker homosexual relations and relationships. According to Puterbaugh, Symonds gradually became increasingly committed to defending homoeroticism, publishing two important but limited-edition books on the subject, working with sexologist Havelock Ellis on another book, and leaving behind revelatory letters not published until 1984 (1272). Byrne Fone (1995: 129–45) reported Symonds's interest in the beauty of young men, noted that his poetry reflects his homoeroticism, discussed in detail his two important prose works on ancient and modern homosexuality, and commented that the "central emotional crisis of Symonds's life, and in the lives of so many homosexual writers of the nineteenth century, was the contradiction they perceived between the spirituality of homosexual desire and the sensuality of homosexual sex" (133). Fone found various limitations of class, race, and gender in Symonds's thought, including occasional misogyny, but credited him for writing "the first published defense [in England] of homosexual desire" (137). Symonds, rejecting views of homosexuality as a sickness, advocated for decriminalization. Fone quoted Symonds as writing that once he had accepted and acted on his homosexual impulses, rather than fighting them, he attained true creativity as well as real "'mastery and self-control'" (144).

Eve Kosofsky Sedgwick (1985: 203–17) discussed Symonds's intense regard for Walt Whitman, his persistent but unsuccessful attempts to get Whitman to concede that Whitman's poetry implied or sanctioned physical love between men, and his friendship with Edward Carpenter (whom Sedgwick considered far more cheerful than Symonds). She also explored Symonds's conservative attitudes toward both homoeroticism and women, as well as Carpenter's doubts about Symonds's real commitment to gay liberation. Dowling (1994: 127–32), noting Symonds's disgust with anti-gay laws, said he developed growing distrust for merely "Platonic" gay relationships and rejected his professor Benjamin Jowett's emphasis on precisely such relationships, feeling he had been miseducated by Jowett and seeing in ancient Greek homoeroticism a counterweight to modern theories of homosexuality as unnatural or sick.

Joseph Bristow (1995: 127–46) began by discussing Symonds's long-suppressed autobiographical memoirs which, by detailing his homosexuality and defending homosexuality in general, "comprise one of the first modern male homosexual autobiographies in England" (132), although the memoirs never used the word "homosexual." Bristow noted the memoirs' connections to contemporary German sexology, reported Symonds's sexual self-classification, related his thinking to the later ideas of Michel Foucault, and emphasized the *Memoirs'* stress on Symonds's awakening physical lust. Bristow discussed Symonds's regard for Whitman, his relations with Havelock Ellis, his need to see his erotic impulses as ethical, and his rejection of any notion that he was passive and effeminate.

Paul Hammond (1996: 166–74) noted Symonds's importance in a developing gay canon, emphasized the impact of Plato and other classical Greeks on his thinking, recounted his various love interests, and emphasized how difficult Symonds found it to translate Greek ideals into everyday Victorian existence. He suggested that Symonds tended to view homoerotic "sexual pleasure as aesthetic pleasure" limited by death, asserting that Symonds often "licenses his erotic gaze ... by killing the object which it contemplates" (173). By emphasizing Death so strongly, Symonds removed beautiful youths "from the grasp of Time or other lovers, arresting their growth (or decay) into adulthood," although Hammond also saw a "sadistic streak" in this tendency (173).

Alan Stewart (1997: 3–8) commented briefly on the ways Symonds associated homosexuality and the Renaissance. Hogan and Hudson 1998 (532–3) noted that Symonds, as a boy, claimed to be repulsed by "crude" gay sex, that he reported his headmaster for an affair with a boy, that the headmaster was forced to resign, and that Symonds, ostracized by former friends, "was never able to resolve his 'ambivalent remorse'" (532). After reading Plato, Symonds himself fell in love with various youths but nevertheless married and sired children while writing homoerotic poetry and then, later, began having sex with men in London parks, with Swiss peasants, and with Venetian gondoliers, including one with a girlfriend and children. Hogan and Hudson commented that Symonds was especially interested in working-class men, an interest he perceived also in the works of Walt Whitman, who (perhaps under pressure) nonetheless rejected Symonds's homoerotic interpretations of Whitman's poems. Hogan and Hudson called Symonds's *A Problem in Greek Ethics* "[p]robably the first scholarly work on homosexuality published in the United Kingdom" (533).

David West, in Aldrich and Wotherspoon (2002: 429–30), called Symonds an "unsuccessful poet and discreet advocate for homosexuality," noting that after "early explorations with obliging male cousins, the sexual and emotional repression of his early years ... was interrupted only by brief but intense friendships with young men" (429). West reported that one relationship with a man lasted for over ten years (until his death), reported that Symons was an early user of the new term "homosexual," which was imported from Germany (429), described the influence of various sexologists on Symonds' own thinking; and said that Symonds, arguing "cautiously only for decriminalisation of this 'sport of nature,'" took "pains to emphasise the 'anti-sexual' bias of the Urning [i.e., homosexual], who is more interested in intense friendships than in sodomy, who is not necessarily effeminate, and who has no inclination to corrupt minors." West attributed Symonds's impact on gay liberation at least as much to his extensive friendships and "carefully worded" correspondence as to his limited-circulation pro-gay pamphlets (430). Joseph Cady, in Summers (2002: 646–8), wrote that various poems by Symonds from the 1860s and 1870s—"such as *Lyra Viginti Chordarum, The Lotos Garland of Antinous and Diego, Pantarkes, Rhaetica, Tales of Ancient Greece, Crocuses and Soldanellas, Old and New, Fragilia Labilia*—are some of the frankest Victorian homosexual writing, if not always distinguished as literature." Cady called Symonds's long-unpublished *Memoirs* "the first self-conscious homosexual autobiography known to us" and said his letters are "the first surviving examples in history of extensive and candid homosexual correspondence." Cady then mentioned many different texts by Symonds containing open or coded homoerotic material (such as *Many Moods, New and Old, Animi Figura*, and *Vagabundili Libellus*). He noted the importance of Symonds's translation of Michelangelo's sonnets, commented on his publications in Victorian "gay" journals, and cited three homoerotic essays published in his book *In the Key of Blue* (646). Cady emphasized Whitman's importance to Symonds, reported some harsh responses to his works, noted the problems that resulted from attempted publication of some of his non-fiction, and observed that Symonds was the subject of "the first [biography] to discuss any Victorian homosexual frankly." Finally, Cady suggested that Symonds's life challenges the "social construction" view of homosexuality, which assumes that homosexuals in the modern sense did not exist before the late 1800s (647).

Matt Cook (2003: 129–33) thought an ambivalence toward London in "escapist fantasies" appears in Symonds's *Memoirs*, that he found aspects of city life both enticing and distressing, that he enjoyed at least one exciting sexual encounter with a lower-class soldier in a male brothel there, and that various sights and experiences in London erotically aroused his imagination. Morris Kaplan (2005: 10–18, 213–16) recounted some of Symonds's sexual history, outlined some of the intellectual influences on his attitudes, described his sexual ambivalence and his complex but often lofty and egalitarian views of same-sex desire, and reported the ways Symonds thought such desire could bridge artificial divisions of "age, social class, and nationality" (18). Later, Kaplan offered further details about Symonds's sexual history, tastes, and habits (213–16).

HENRY JAMES (1843–1916). Georges-Michel Sarotte (1978: 197–211) compared James to Tennessee Williams, noting that as boys both were "sissies" who sought refuge in literature. Both feared women, were fundamentally androgynous, gave evidence of "spiritual transvestism," and were "obsessed" by an "unattainable virile ideal" (197). After discussing James's "domineering and suffocating mother" and his "weak father indulgent toward his children" (198), Sarotte explored James's young manhood (including an *obvious desire to pass for a eunuch*' [italics in original]), the ways mothers in his novels are "either terrifying and domineering or passive and withdrawn" (199), his history of somewhat distant friendships with women (200), and his attraction toward young men. According to Sarotte, "James's attitude toward overt homosexuality" was "ambiguous": although his fiction is "highly homoerotic," his *"public* attitude" toward "professed homosexuality was fairly distant" (202). Some people who knew him considered him somewhat effeminate, resembling, in various respects, his hero Lambert Strether in *The Ambassadors*. Sarotte explored this novel in detail, calling it "above all an allegory of James's emotional life" (210).

Richard Hall, in Kellogg (1983: 83-97), reported that Leon Edel, James's biographer, agreed with Hall's suggestion that "James's apparent asexuality derived not from a repressed homosexuality, injury, or hormonal dysfunction but from a profound and lifelong fixation on his [older] brother William"—a fixation that "preempted Henry's homosexual feelings and constituted the core of his affective life" (84). Hall noted, however, that although Edel accepted Hall's "theory of homosexual incest" (84), he had only hinted at it in his published volumes, partly because stating the theory too openly would have prevented sources from cooperating with his research. Later, Hall discussed James's friendship with the closeted gay English intellectual, Edmund Gosse, the details of Henry's relationships with William and others, and the significance of various kinds of imagery in James's works.

Elaine Showalter (1990: 27-31) reported on James's disappointment with the reception of *The Bostonians* and described the varied ways the characters and plot can be interpreted. Warren Dynes, in Dynes (1990: 631-2), noted that *The Bostonians* portrays "a close emotional relationship" between two women, while James dealt with male homoeroticism in "The Pupil" and "The Turn of the Screw." Dynes, suggesting that James may have suppressed homoerotic themes in many works, then surveyed various interpretations of his own mysterious sexuality, maintaining that James exhibited personality traits common among upper-class gays of his day, especially "fastidiousness," "sensitivity to art," and "extraordinary attention to social nuances" (632). Terry Castle (1993: 150-9) noted that some critics have attempted to deny a lesbian theme in *The Bostonians* even while conceding that the book's central female character is a repressed homosexual. Castle emphasized the book's "European" rather than "American" themes, arguing that lesbianism was one of the former.

Marjorie Garber (1995: 457–70) discussed efforts to deny lesbianism in *The Bostonians*, considered its bisexual aspects, noted the importance of "class, age, and gender role" in the relationship between Verena and Olive, and reported common criticisms (in the 1990s and earlier) of bisexuals as fickle. She concluded that bisexuality in *The Bostonians* "is really an effect—an effect of the difficulty of satisfying women's desire with regard to power and pleasure" (466). David Van Leer (1995: 106–13) discussed James's story "The Beast in the Jungle" (106–7) and particularly assessed the strengths and weaknesses of Eve Kosofsky Sedgwick's reading of the tale (107–13), finding her unsympathetic to the idea of "gay self-knowledge" (113). Robert Drake (1998: 170–9) discussed James's own sexual reticence and reserve, emphasized gay aspects of *Roderick Hudson*, and suggested that that novel provided a model of the kind of close friendship that has often existed between homosexuals. Gregory Woods (1998: 326–9) commented on homoerotic overtones in *The Turn of the Screw*.

Seymour Kleinberg, in Aldrich and Wotherspoon (2002: 268–9), commented on the probability that James never had sex, reported his late interest in various young men (such as Hendrik Andersen), observed that his male characters are rarely passionate (unlike his women), and commented that Leon Edel, when revising his huge biography, dealt more forthrightly with James's sexuality. Priscilla Walton, in Summers (2002: 370–3), mentioned James's "lack of sexual interest in women" (370) but close friendships with many, the fact that his interest in men was not widely studied until the 1980s and 1990s debates about whether James was ever sexually active, and the intensity of his attraction, late in life, to certain young men, especially Hendrik Andersen. According to Walton, James "was ambivalent about his own sexuality"; never advocated for gay rights, was "horrified by [Oscar] Wilde's flamboyant sexuality"; and refused to publicly support Wilde's release from prison. Walton observed that James portrayed women insightfully but focused especially on relations between men (371). He cited some examples of James's fiction dealing with same-sex relations (both male and female), suggested how he perceptively commented, as an outsider, on straight relationships, and cited various works with gay themes, such as "The Pupil," "The Author of Beltraffio," "The Middle Years," *The Beast in the Jungle*, and "The Jolly Corner." Walton praised James's treatment both of women and of male friendships, suggesting that he was able to "channel his own marginality into literary texts that document" his era's "anxieties" (372).

Colm Tóibín 2002 (28–34) noted James's growing interest, as he aged, in attractive young men, speculated that he may have had a youthful dalliance with Oliver Wendell Holmes (28), reported James's intense interest in John Addington

Symonds's sexuality (28–9), found it "astonishing" that James managed so much to suppress his own sexuality in his work (29), and faulted both James and his artistic achievement in some works (such as "The Pupil" and "The Beast in the Jungle") precisely because James's reticence damaged his writings (31–4). Terry Castle (2003: 555–7) thought *The Bostonians* might be "the first 'lesbian novel' written in English—that is, the first nonpornographic work ... to engage fully and self-consciously with the love-between-women theme" (556). Although Castle found the book's "attitude toward female homosexuality" hard to pin down, she saw some evidence for James's sympathy toward the lesbian protagonist (556–7).

Richard Dellamora (2004) argued that although there are "many significations of queer desire" in James's novel *The Tragic Muse*, "James always retains the option of deniability" (154). Regina Marler (Canning 2009: 64–70) recounted her initial dislike but growing admiration for *The Bostonians*, summarized its plot and initial reception, and commented on the mixed reactions to its lesbian dimensions, although Marler regretted some negative aspects of the book, including its "mean-spirited" characterizations, negative depictions of lesbian desire, and denigration of flat-chested women (70).

Emma Donoghue (2010: 93–7), noting both resemblances and differences between James's *The Bostonians* and a novel by Eliza Lynn Linton, praised James's "perceptive characterization, intense drama, and wry narrative style" while also commenting on the book's effective imagery. She thought that by describing the rivalry of a woman and man for a second woman's affection, James depicts "a fairly level playing field" and "never makes it clear who will win, which gives suspense another turn of the screw" (95), even though he ultimately characterized the women's relationship as "morbid"—"one of those words (like *sentimental, intense, languid,* and *dangerous*) often used as code for *lesbian* in the late nineteenth century" (96). Donoghue saw Oliver Chancellor as "the archetypal lesbian loser. Her gloomy shadow not only falls on later characters whose debt to her is obvious ... but on every woman who gives up her beloved to a man rather than fighting no-holds-barred" (97).

"MICHAEL FIELD" ([Katherine Bradley (1846–1914) and Edith Cooper (1862–1913)]). Lillian Faderman 1994 (88–90) said Bradley and Cooper "formulated ideas together, did research for their historical plays together, and wrote pages, speeches, and even single lines together," often "champion[ing] same-sex love in the guise of romantic friendship" (88–9). Sometimes, Faderman wrote, their work "seems to display an erotic awareness" foreshadowing modern lesbian writing: "sexual imagery abounds" but "alternates with images that are much less erotically charged." Faderman concluded that whether they saw themselves as lovers, friends, or both, "their total commitment to each other" is clear (90).

GERARD MANLEY HOPKINS (1844–89). Richard Dellamora (1990: 42–57), examining an unfinished poem describing young male swimmers, compared its reticence with a similar, more outspoken poem by Walt Whitman, and reported a parodic poem about homoeroticism Hopkins composed at Oxford. Dellamora noted that although as adolescents Hopkins and two close friends were "all romantically involved with other males" (47), Hopkins was troubled by his sexual impulses and chose Catholicism partly because it emphasized "the worthiness of the redeemed human body" (50). He often wrote to "rejoice in the naturalness of the body" (52) while also sometimes implying a phobia "against both intercourse and male masturbation" (53). Exploring imagery of male virginity and male social relations in several poems, Dellamora stressed how Hopkins often "denied the worth of sexual desire between men" (56).

Robert Drake's discussion of Hopkins (1998: 232–3) was brief and biographical. Gregory Woods (1998: 171–3) suggested that Hopkins sometimes disguised and censored his homoerotic thoughts (171) but added that "beautiful men remind [Hopkins] of Christ: 'seeing such men', he desires them; his desire makes him feel guilt; and his guilt draws his attention to the moral system, to which he himself so strongly subscribes, which denounces male-male desire in the name of Christ" (172). Woods thought the "more one reads Hopkins, the more one becomes convinced that his particular torture was to have realized the intensely carnal nature of his own spirituality" (172)—a realization that even contributed to his poetry's intensely physical rhythms.

George Piggford, in Aldrich and Wotherspoon (2002: 213–14), noted Hopkins's early familiarity with homoerotic literature, his apparently agonizing struggle with the impulse to masturbate, and his seemingly chaste affection for various young men. He destroyed all his early poems, celebrated, like Whitman, both body and soul, and wrote poems implying homoeroticism, such as "The Bugler's First Communion," "Brothers," and his dark, so-called "terrible sonnets," including "I Wake and Feel the Fell of Dark, Not Day," which emphasizes sexual despair and suggests "a struggle with masturbation." Piggford maintained, however, that

> Hopkins's most clearly homoerotic poem, written a year before his death, is the fragmentary 'Epithalamion'. The poem is ostensibly about marriage, but its opening scene ... features a stranger watching boys bathing and a poetic voice reveling in the erotically charged moment. Hopkins likely became in some

sense aware of the explicitly homoerotic nature of the poem because he later added both the title and an incomplete section that attempts to read the poem's sensuality in terms of heterosexual marriage.

(214)

Raymond-Jean Frontain, in Summers (2002: 343), suggested that Hopkins probably would not have considered himself homosexual despite his obsession with male beauty and discomfort with masturbatory fantasies. Frontain mentioned the poet's "crush" on Digby Dolben, speculating that Hopkins became a Jesuit partly to try to control his impulses.

EDWARD CARPENTER (1844–1929). Eve Kosofsky Sedgwick (1985: 203–13) discussed the complex relationships between Carpenter, Symonds, and Whitman, noting Carpenter's intense regard for Whitman (see also Dynes 1990 and Simes 2002), his regret that Symonds was not more openly gay, and his tendency to be happier than Symonds. Wayne Dynes, in Dynes (1990: 199–200), noted that Carpenter published books openly defending homosexuality despite attacks, promoting self-respect among gay men of his time and foreshadowing the "counterculture" of the 1960s. Charles Shively, in Malinowski 1994 (67–9), discussed Carpenter's political, religious, and sexual views; commented on his gay poetry and works promoting gay rights; and explained Carpenter's view that sexual diversity had promoted civilization's growth. Byrne Fone (1995: 147–55) surveyed Carpenter's work and related him to Whitman, Symonds, and Ulrich, noting how he rejected ideas of homosexuality as abnormal and how he pioneered gay liberation. Neil Miller (1995: 21–3) discussed Carpenter's upper-class background, his early training for the church, his generally unconventional opinions on numerous topics, and his strong response to the inspiration of Walt Whitman, especially in sexual matters. Miller explained Carpenter's view that homosexuals, both men and women, were a kind of "intermediate sex" with some possible flaws of their own but mainly with much potential to help straight men and women better understand one another and often possessing real creative gifts. Miller reported the unsolicited advice Carpenter often received from people concerned about his lifestyle, the inspiration he provided to others, and his mainly spiritual (rather than simply sexual) views of homosexuality.

Gary Simes, in Aldrich and Wotherspoon (2002: 88–9), described Carpenter's chance relationship with his long-time lover, George Merrill, and called "*Homogenic Love*" (1884) "the first openly published defence of homosexuality" by an English homosexual (88). Simes also described many of Carpenter's other pro-gay writings, commenting that although "a few others wrote privately, clandestinely, or anonymously in favour of same-sex behaviour," Carpenter alone, in England, "publicly and openly defended homosexuality and the homosexual's rightful place in society" before the First World War (88–9). Gregory Bredbeck, in Summers (2002: 134–5), mentioned Carpenter's socialism, stressed his meeting with the lower-class George Merrill, suggested that this meeting helped inspire E. M. Forster's *Maurice*, and called *Toward Democracy* Carpenter's major literary work. Bredbeck later discussed Carpenter's pro-gay nonfiction, noted his admiration for Whitman and his idea that homosexuals were often spiritually advanced, and urged that Carpenter be further studied (135). Matt Cook (2003: 133–8) argued that Carpenter, like other homosexuals of his time, found London a freeing, stimulating city and associated it with fraternity and democracy, especially in its urban parks but also in diverse other aspects of urban life.

SARAH ORNE JEWETT (1849–1909). Josephine Donovan (1980 in Bloom 1997: 84–5) discussed Jewett's stories about female couples and love between women, listing many and particularly praising "Martha's Lady" (84–5). Lillian Faderman (1981: 197–203) noted Jewett's apparent lack of romantic interest in men, her skepticism about marriage, and the ways her "Boston marriage" with Annie Adams Fields (see also Garnes 2002) made her writing happier and more optimistic. Margaret Roman (1992 in Bloom 1997: 87–8) reported Jewett's interest in sexual role reversals (87), observing that her female characters often "assume male roles" associated with achievements denied to them as women (88). Faderman 1994 (96–8) said biographers found no "trace of a heterosexual love interest" in Jewett's life, suggesting that in "Tom's Husband" Jewett "shows that heterosexual marriage can" damage women by denying them independent identities (97) and arguing that "Martha's Lady" implies "the redemptive power of female-female love" (98). Patti Capel Swartz, in Pendergasts (1998: 193–6), discussed the lesbian and even transgender aspects of *Deephaven, The Country of the Pointed Firs, A Country Doctor,* "Tom's Husband," "A White Heron," and especially "Martha's Lady" while also noting Jewett's critique of heterosexual society, her sometimes unconventional depictions of feminized men, and the often implied lesbian sensibility of many of her texts. David Garnes, in Aldrich and Wotherspoon 2002 (229–30), mentioned Jewett's lifelong financial security (229), while Marilee Lindemann, in Summers (2002: 378–9), noted her imaginative interest in other women, calling *Country of the Pointed Firs* a "classic ... of proto-lesbian literature," discussing Jewett's complex affection for Annie Adams Fields and commenting on Jewett's mentoring of Willa Cather and the gap between their attitudes toward writing openly about same-sex relationships (379).

OSCAR WILDE (1854–1900). Jeffrey Meyers (1977: 20–31), discussing *The Picture of Dorian Gray*, mentioned two gay men who provided models for its central characters and also identified the novel's Hallward with Wilde's conscience, Wotton with Wilde's id (as well as with his cynical and artistic sides), and Dorian with Wilde's ego (21). According to Meyers, if "Hallward is the masochistic creator of Dorian's aesthetic glorification, Wotton … is the sadistic catalyst of his moral degeneration" (23–4). After reviewing and commenting on the novel's plot, Meyers said it fails "because Wilde was unable to resolve the conflict between his desire for homosexual freedom and his fear of social condemnation. … the real subject of the book is the impossibility of achieving homosexual pleasure without the inevitable accompaniment of fear, guilt, and self-hatred" (31).

Elaine Showalter (1990: 149–56, 174–8) described the initial reception of Wilde's play *Salome* (149–50), saw that work as having a "gay sexual subtext" (150), reported that "Wilde himself insisted that *Salome* was the most meaningful of his works, the one in which he could most fully express himself" (151), suggested that the veiled Salome might symbolize Wilde and that her desire for the male body might symbolize his own (151), disputed some recent scholarly commentary on the play (151), defended the relevance of Aubrey Beardsley's drawings to the text of the drama (151–6), and suggested that Beardsley conflated Salome and Wilde (156). Later, Showalter suggested that Wilde, at least in *Dorian Gray* and other examples of his homoerotic art, implied "an escalating contempt for women" (176). She also suggested that Wilde's (and others') aesthetic view of homosexuality and of the beautiful male body had "to contend with such harsh realities as aging and venereal disease," so that the deterioration of Dorian's deteriorating portrait may symbolize both. According to Showalter, evidence presented at Wilde's trials "de-aestheticized homogenic love and brought it back to the level of the human, mortal, physical, and profane" (177). Nevertheless, thanks in part to Wilde, the image of the male homosexual in the twentieth century was that of the male dandy and aesthete rather than that of a progressive male such as Edward Carpenter (178).

Stephen Wayne Foster, in Dynes (1990: 1389–91), began by noting Wilde's notoriety in college "for his effeminate pose as an aesthete" (although "it appears that he was not yet homosexual"), mentioned Wilde's marriage and two sons, said that Wilde was "introduced to homosexual practices by Robert Ross," and reported his involvement with young male prostitutes. Increasingly successful as a writer, Wilde lost a famous libel suit after having been accused of being gay by the prominent father of Wilde's lover, Lord Alfred Douglas. Wilde was, Foster said, also convicted of sex with male prostitutes, saw the collapse of his marriage and career, and contracted a fatal illness while in prison. Foster called Wilde "the most famous homosexual in history as a homosexual"; evaluated various writings about Wilde; disputed the attribution of various works to Wilde; and expressed surprise that Wilde did not flee to France rather than confronting legal problems in England (1392). "Gay people," Foster concluded, "honor [Wilde] as a martyr" (1391).

Claude Summers (1990: 29–61) asserted that "[m]odern gay fiction in English begins with Oscar Wilde" (29), suggested that "The Portrait of Mr. W. H." may be "the earliest short story on a gay subject in English literature," and also highlighted the pioneering importance of *The Picture of Dorian Gray*. Summers saw Wilde's own life and experiences as enormously influential on later gay writers, noted the paradox that the writer who emphasized art for art's sake often wrote in highly personal ways, suggested that Wilde did not become a fully practicing homosexual until 1886, and indicated that it was Lord Alfred Douglas who seduced Wilde rather than the other way around. Summers stressed the ideals outlined in Wilde's little-known pamphlet *The Soul of Man Under Socialism*, observed that Wilde might easily have escaped legal difficulties by moving abroad, and suggested several reasons that he may have chosen not to do so (including stupidity, self-dramatization, and a martyr complex). According to Summers, Wilde was forced by social pressures to deal implicitly rather than openly with gay themes in "The Portrait" and *The Picture*, with the former being the more forthright and successful of those two works and the later *De Profundis* being the best of the three. "The Portrait," Summers noted, was written with great care, was greatly enlarged while being revised, may have been intended partly to mock Shakespearean scholarship, and is as much a work of fiction as a piece of criticism. This text, which deals with Shakespeare's sonnets, contains (in Summers's opinion) certain recognizably "gay" character types, explores the complexities of Neoplatonism, implies that gay persons did exist in Shakespeare's time, and accounts in various ways for the narrator's eventual repudiation of the idea that a handsome young actor named Willie Hughes inspired Shakespeare's sonnets. Ultimately, Summers concluded, the ambivalence of the book may reflect both the narrator's internal conflicts and a response to the real anti-gay attitudes of Wilde's day.

Turning to *The Picture of Dorian Gray*, Summers noted many similarities between it and "The Portrait," especially their emphasis on self-realization and their similar ambivalence about homosexuality (an ambivalence stronger and more problematic in *The Picture* than in "The Portrait"). *The Picture*, according to Summers, was widely accused of immorality in its own day, was presented by Wilde as a moral tale even though the "immoral" characters are the most compelling, implied that Gray's sexual flaws are both straight and gay, and highlighted the psychological complexities of the relatively noble Basil Hallward, who idealizes his erotic motives while also considering them flawed. Both older men who pursue Dorian objectify him, Summers claimed; both, in different ways, "project onto the young man their own unbalanced and fragmentary images" (50). The ambiguities and ambivalences embedded in this text make it, Summers felt, both genuinely intriguing and partly unsuccessful. Far more effective, Summers thought, is *De Profundis*, which stresses the importance of imagination to a worthy human life, which turns the tables both on Douglass and on Douglass's father, and which reflects the mature, ruined Wilde's new ability "to realize the injustices of his society and the meaningfulness of suffering" and therefore to "accept himself and his plight without bitterness" (58). Summers found especially "instructive" Wilde's "progress from titillating hints of decadent homosexuality in *The Picture of Dorian Gray* and the foiled coming-out story of 'The Portrait of Mr. W. H.' to the frank acceptance and defiant defense of homosexuality in *De Profundis*" (61).

Jonathan Dollimore, in 1991, discussed Wilde's relationship with (and impact on) Andre Gide (3–6), Wilde's materialist and anti-humanist thinking (6–8), his association of individualism with disobedience and nonconformity (8–10), his emphasis on the importance of art (10–12), and the ways Wilde's influence helped Gide come to terms with his own homosexuality (12–18). Dollimore later included a chapter titled "Wilde's Transgressive Aesthetic and Contemporary Cultural Politics" (64–73), in which he argued for Wilde's continuing influence and relevance. Joseph Bristow, in Bristow 1992 (44–63), situated *Dorian Gray* in the legal contexts of its time (44–5), discussed other commentators' responses to it (45–8), described specific new laws and regulations relating to "gross indecency" (53), and claimed that Wilde's book "stands at the beginning of a self-consciously homosexual literary tradition opposing the social undesirability of cross-class sexual relationships and the decadent uncleanliness associated with them" (53). According to Bristow, in *Dorian Gray* "pleasure," "property," and "proper behavior" conflict (55), "misogyny figures as a defining feature of homosexuality" (57), and Wilde "turns his hero into a figure whose life story implicitly interrogates the iniquitous effects of legislation on sex in the 1880s" (62).

Fritz Klein (1993) called Wilde a "sequential bisexual" (140)—that is, an enthusiastic heterosexual for the first roughly thirty-four years of his life and then a homosexual until his death. Mark Lilly (1993: 27–32) argued that Wilde, more than Byron, dealt with homoeroticism in a specifically English context (27), necessarily underplayed, in *Dorian Gray*, the explicitly "sexual aspect of homosexuality" (27), and felt pulled both to be truthful and to protect himself (27–8). Lilly saw *Dorian Gray* as somewhat confusing (28, 31), suggested that its criticisms of Gray should not be taken seriously (28), stressed its emphasis on "decadent hedonism" (32), and saw its key themes as recurrent ones in later gay fictions (32).

Karl Beckson, in Malinowski (1994: 400–8), recounted Wilde's life, commented on each of his major works, discussed the homoerotic aspects of some of them (especially *The Happy Prince*, "The Portrait of Mr. W. H.," and *The Portrait of Dorian Gray*), noted the contemporary attacks on *Gray*, and discussed the famous trial that led to Wilde's almost willing martyrdom. Dowling (1994: 132–54) noted Wilde's increasing prominence in English culture before his trial, suggested that during this early period English homosexuals took the homoeroticism of ancient Greece as a sanction and model, and reported that the poet Lionel Johnson praised the homoeroticism of both Wilde and Walter Pater. Wilde's trial, Dowling said, acted simultaneously to suppress English homosexuality and stimulate discussion of it (with Wilde actually feeling that he had been "corrupted" by Lord Alfred Douglas rather than the other way around). In any case, according to Dowling, the trial damaged the reputation of Victorian Hellenism, which had exercised such a strong homoerotic influence on students who had learned about the ancient Greeks while in college. Christopher Craft (1994: 106–39) focused especially on *The Importance of Being Earnest*, particularly its subtle allusions to homoeroticism (112), its rejection of simple opposites (such as gay and straight [128]), and the ways the play, for a time, was staged precisely when Wilde was being prosecuted in his famous trial (138).

Kevin Kopelson (1994: 20–48) discussed Wilde's gay treatment of the "love-death" trope, especially in fairy tales such as "The Happy Prince" (21–4) but also in his more obviously homoerotic works for adults (24–6), which "all cloud the issue of whether gay love-deaths are murders or suicides" (26). Ancient stories of gay love, Kopelson argued, rarely feature suicide but did feature murder (28–31), but Wilde was drawn to both themes, sometimes made them difficult to distinguish (37), and dealt with them in many of his most famous works (37–48).

Joseph Bristow (1995: 4–54) suggested that Victorians felt especially threatened by gay effeminacy, that gay writers of the time reacted either with pride or shame at the idea of being considered effeminate, and that ideas about effeminacy had changed over two centuries. Bristow quoted scholars who maintained that effeminacy in the late seventeenth century was associated with political instability, quoted those same scholars as suggesting that effeminate homosexuality was especially seen as pathological only after the trials of Oscar Wilde, and himself argued that responses to effeminacy in Victorian England were intriguingly diverse before the Wilde trials. Bristow noted that effeminacy has long been stigmatized by both straights and gays because it has been associated with moral and physical weakness, that Wilde's effeminacy was rejected by later gay writer such as a sometimes-misogynistic Forster, but that other writers, such as Ronald Firbank, reacted more positively to Wilde. Bristow traced Wilde's self-presentations as a happily married man before the trials, recounted the change in his reputation the trials provoked, suggested that the effeminate dandies he depicted are not always ethical (especially in the ways they treat women), and outlined the ways Wilde's effeminacy became more and more dangerous to his own career. Discussing Wilde's life and works in great detail, Bristow concluded that Wilde "established his homosexual difference in a marketplace that ultimately used him more than he could comfortably manipulate it. His adoring audience ultimately had the power that could banish him from sight" (49).

Neil Miller (1995: 43–52) discussed such matters as Wilde's first homosexual experience (probably with Robbie Ross), his involvement with Alfred Douglas, his legal problems with Douglas's father, and the way his legal conviction helped spark a flight of gay men from England to the continent. Miller quoted from Wilde's defence of ideal homosexual affection, recounted his sufferings both in and out of jail, reported Douglas's later career as a staunch opponent of gay love, and described the aftermath of the Wilde trials, including the effects on Wilde's reputation and the reputations of homosexuals in general.

David Van Leer (1995: 27–34) placed Wilde in the tradition of camp and indeed as one of its founders (27). Paul Hammond (1996: 174–83) emphasized the themes of secrecy and fear in *Dorian Gray* and suggested that Dorian's continuing youthful appearance contradicted "the nineteenth-century idea that secret sins such as masturbation and sex between men produce a deformed physical specimen" (176). Hammond noted the tale's emphasis on both art and photography (178), linking the latter to the growth of homoerotic photography at the end of the century (179), and he particularly discussed the ways Wilde revised the book to de-emphasize homoeroticism (179–81). Commenting on *The Portrait of Mr W. H.* (181–3), Hammond maintained that its "presentation of relations between men" is "elliptical and disingenuous" (182).

Robert Drake (1998: 198–207) mainly discussed Wilde's life and summarized *Dorian Gray*, concluding that both Wilde and Gray fell short of complete honesty. Hogan and Hudson 1998 (576–7) suggested that "Wilde gradually withdrew from conjugal relations with [his wife] and seems to have been exclusively homosexual from the late 1880s on, except for one transaction with a female prostitute shortly before his death" (576). They surveyed his career, emphasized his trial, and noted that he became a patron saint of later gays (577). Gregory Woods (1998: 173–6) considered Wilde's poetry weak but homoerotic from early on (173) and intriguingly suggested that "Wilde's version of homosexual literature depends entirely on the presence of the heterosexual reader or spectator" (175). Woods argued that Wilde mainly survives today "as a cultural monument rather than writer" (176). Alan Sinfield (1999: 27–42) challenged the widespread idea that references to "Bunbury" in *The Importance of Being Earnest* allude to homosexuality (27–8), argued that Wilde, at first, was not perceived as gay (28), asserted that his trial established this perception (29), showed how this perception affected later views of Wilde and of gays in general (29–32), discussed varied views of "Wildean dandies" (who were often presented as straight [32–4]), traced the growing tendency to associate homosexuality with scandalous behavior (34–42), and concluded that Wilde refused to leave England because he prized his position in "society" (42).

Commenting especially on Wilde's *Portrait of Mr. W. H.*, Richard Halpern (2002: 32–58) proposed that St. Paul's

> equation of sodomy and sublimity in Romans is elaborated by medieval theologians and given aesthetic form by Shakespeare's Sonnets. The Sonnets, in turn, powerfully influence Oscar Wilde's later 'invention' of homosexuality as both an identity and an aesthetic. The emergence of modern homosexuality does not cancel the older ties between sodomy and sublimity, however, but simply reworks them in new guises.
>
> (3–4)

Seymour Kleinberg, in Aldrich and Wotherspoon (2002: 486–8), noted that in Wilde's youth the Anglo-Catholic Oxford Movement, with which Wilde was involved, was often suspected of promoting homoeroticism (486). In addition, Kleinberg reported both Wilde's popularity and the suspicions he aroused (486–7), his early reliance on his wife's income, his growing success as an author and man about town, and his confidence of acquittal when he was eventually tried and found guilty of "gross indecency" (487). Kleinberg concluded that

> Wilde's significance is twofold, as a writer whose sensibility helped define modernism, and as a figure whose victimisation ushered into consciousness the predicament of homosexual men in a society that would tolerate closetry but never openness. His ordeal helped bring to public attention not only the injustice visited upon homosexuals, but also the reason for that vicious homophobia: Wilde brought out of the closet not only the subject of sexual deviance, but the much larger subject of the nature of sexuality, his scandal challenging many of the received notions about sexual desire and behaviour. ... he remains for the history of homosexuality perhaps the most famous example of what would later be identified as 'gay'. Wilde himself discovered that his sexuality was not only a matter of behaviour or even desire; his sexuality gave him his identity, and ultimately the meaning of his life. His is one of the stories of the transformation of sexual desire into sexual identity, perhaps the best example of the creation of the idea of the homosexual in the nineteenth century.
>
> (487)

Claude Summers, in Summers (2002: 691–6), although repeating some points he had made in 1990 (see above), also added new ones. He stressed Wilde's literary achievement and status as a major gay martyr (partly responsible for his own martyrdom), emphasized his serious general critiques of his culture, argued that Wilde both rejected society and wanted acceptance by it, and suggested that "he seems to have begun the sustained practice of homosexuality in 1886," with Robbie Ross (691). Summers asserted that although Wilde's association with Alfred Douglas was in some ways disastrous, it coincided with his "brief period of serious [literary] achievement, which began in 1888"—not long after he began consistently practicing homosexuality (691). Summers found Wilde partly guilty for his own downfall, connected this event with Wilde's masochism, noted that he was given a chance to escape imprisonment but rejected it because of the loss of social status exile would involve, and argued that Wilde's famous speech defending same-sex love was less courageous than is often assumed (692). Examining Wilde's writings, Summers suggested that "his gay texts before his fall tend to be divided against themselves" (692) and then explained this claim in ways he had partly outlined in 1990 (692–5). Summers praised both the content and phrasing of De Profundis while admitting that it sometimes verges close to self-parody (695–6).

Colm Tóibín (2002: 35–87) dealt at length with Wilde's life and career, noted Wilde's respect for his mother (51), discussed his relationship with Douglas

(58–63), commented on the contents and tone of *De Profundis* (63–8), claimed that Wilde's imprisonment led to his best work in both poetry and prose (69), and described the writer's last years (73–87). Matt Cook (2003: 56–71, 105–21) discussed the ways Wilde's visits to unexpected London locations were used against him when he was tried (56–9), the ways his own and others' physical appearances were derided in the press (59–61), the public hostility and even violence he and those associated with him faced (69), the ways he was presented in the newspapers, after his conviction, as a weak, "ageing wreck" (70), but also the existence of at least some sympathy for him (70–1). Later, Cook discussed such matters as hostile critical reactions to *Dorian Gray* (105), Wilde's possible involvement in composing the explicitly homoerotic novel *Teleny* (106), the significance of that work's geographical settings (106–7), both the resemblances and differences between *Teleny* and *Dorian Gray* (107, 116), the London settings of the latter book (107–11), and the anti-gay suspicions the book aroused (111, 114). According to Cook, Wilde increasingly became associated with decadence and effeminacy (116–18); his personality, "foreign" values, and public trials may be alluded to ambivalently in Bram Stoker's *Dracula*, whose titular figure is a sexual pervert whose final defeat reaffirms family values (118–19). Wilde's trials, Cook suggested, helped create and solidify various negative stereotypes about homosexuals, but a gay subculture continued to exist in London despite Wilde's conviction (119–21).

Morris Kaplan (2005: 224–51) tried to set the Wilde trials in various historical and biographical contexts (225–6), recounted Wilde's career as "perhaps the first modern celebrity" (227), explained the events that led to Wilde's trials (227–32), noted that he was accused of corrupting youth and reported his responses to this charge (232–6), recited the evidence used to convict Wilde (236–42), reported the hostility of the press and public (242–4), and added more details about the trials (244–51). Fenton Johnson (Canning 2009: 78–87), focusing on *De Profundis*, called it "frankly a mess," praised its final pages (79), recounted its origins and content (80–5), discussed its religious attitudes (83), and called Wilde less a "gay writer" than "an outsider" (85). Johnson ended by remarking that, having witnessed "the first decades of the AIDS pandemic, I cannot help finding in Wilde's suffering and in *De Profundis* a prefiguring and a primer for that later, vaster trauma" (87).

8

The Early Twentieth Century

A. E. HOUSMAN (1859-1936). Warren Johansson, in Dynes (1990: 563-4), noted that Housman's most famous collection of poems, *A Shropshire Lad*, was subtly homoerotic, betraying "a melancholy over male love and male beauty forever lost, but still alive in dreams" (563). Johannson reported Housman's early, unreciprocated love for another man, observed that Christian condemnation of homosexuality made Housman an atheist, saw painful ambivalence in Housman's attitude toward his homoerotic feelings, and noted that eventually Housman, on the continent, had gay relations with males and read pornography. Housman's true feelings, said Johansson, did not become fully public until roughly forty years after he died (564). William G. Holzberger, in Malinowski 1994 (188-91), discussed Housman's pessimism, the greater erotic openness of his posthumously published poems, his strong sense of society's unfairness to gays, his feeling of having been born gay, his emphasis on frustrated love, his lack of self-pity, his manly tone, his ideal of male comradeship, and his imaginative depictions of ideal male bonding. Robert Drake's comments about Housman (1998: 208-9) were brief and biographical. Hogan and Hudson 1998 (294) suggested that most of Housman's "contemporaries identified his evocations of doomed youth and unrequited love with their own personal losses, especially the tragedies of World War I." Hogan and Hudson observed that Oscar Wilde was a friend of Housman's brother, Laurence, and that Housman sent Wilde "an autographed copy of *A Shropsire Lad*."

Carol Efrati's 2002 book on Housman dealt extensively with his homosexuality and its impact on his writing, setting his works within the constraints of his era, noting how that era's homophobia forced him to be subtle and indirect, discussing his work in relation to Whitman and other predecessors, and charting previous discussion of Housman and these writers in terms of their homoeroticism. Efrati surveyed Housman's life, discussed his apparently unreciprocated desire for Moses Jackson, described the censorship (by Housman's brother) of the poet's notebooks, commented on the homoerotic implications of some of his nonsense verse, but also commented that it may be that the "verses that are most revealing and least disguise Housman's own sexual identity and attitude are found only in [his brother] Laurence Housman's memoir" (80), published years after Housman's death. Efrati explored the sometimes-somber implications of Housman's parodic verse, suggested that he preferred adult men to younger males, discussed his mature poetry in great detail (emphasizing its frequent homoeroticism), and asserted that often in his verse

> the poem shifts from dawn to sunset, from fertility to barrenness, from life to death, from happy—and heterosexual—coupling to the barrenness of homosexuality. ... The terrible aloneness of Housman's luckless lads in a world of heterosexual couples is evoked again and again, especially in poems ostensibly celebrating the spring. ... Spring is the traditional time for couples to pair off, but not for Housman's personae.
>
> (123, 131)

Efrati carefully explicated the *Shropshire* poems, noted other critics' commentaries, stressed the poet's "parody of the normative relationship between the sexes" (192), discussed but also questioned his (perhaps deliberately cultivated) reputation as a misogynist, suggested that some poems that seem poorly written may actually be parodic, and reported that he even joked about scandalized reactions to *A Shropshire Lad*. Discussing poems definitely (or in some cases perhaps) inspired by Housman's love for Moses Jackson's brother Aldabert, Efrati then explored "Housman's own attitude toward his sexual orientation before turning to the poetry of which Moses Jackson is undoubtedly the subject" (238). She argued that the "tone of the poems in which Housman commemorates the non-erotic male is charged with grief and regret for lost comrades and the persona's own youth" (240), discussed erotic imagery in verse, set some of his texts in the context of the homosexual subculture of London, and commented on Housman's ambivalence about his own orientation. Exploring at length the fine poems inspired by Housman's love for Moses Jackson, Efrati concluded that Jackson's death "was the death of Housman's poetic muse, and we have seen more than one expression of his farewell to his friend and poetry together. His abandonment of poetry after his friend's death was quite deliberate" (318). All in all, Efrati produced a book exemplary in the thoroughness of its engagements with the poet, his historical contexts, the critical tradition, and, above all, the poetry itself.

Garry Wotherspoon, in Aldrich and Wotherspoon (2002: 216–17), discussed Housman's discovery of his homosexuality, his travels abroad to act on that discovery, his acquisition of a large collection of erotica, and the status of his brother Laurence as "an early homosexual rights advocate" (217). Joseph Cady, in Summers (2002: 346–8), called the posthumous *More Poems* and *Additional Poems* "more candid" than Housman's earlier work, reported that Housman's brother was gay, asserted that Housman "is the first homosexual poet to have left an indisputable body of private homosexual work paralleling his more coded public writings," but conceded that this may also have been the case with some eighteenth-century writers (346). Cady thought Housman was the first writer to show, through his caution, the full impact of the Oscar Wilde trial (346), asserted that Housman's homosexuality remained unconfirmed until 1967, observed that the Housman-Moses Jackson correspondence was mainly destroyed, and noted Housman's anger about "homosexual suffering and persecution" (347). Cady tabulated the different kinds of love described in *A Shropshire Lad*, commented that some of the homoerotic content in that collection is implied rather than overt, and stressed the unusual explicitness of "Hell Gate," a posthumously published poem (347).

Mark Merlis (Canning 2009: 71–7) noted Housman's admiration for Matthew Arnold, said that "*A Shropshire Lad* is replete, in between tiresome mock-pastorals, with an acid mix of calfish lad-love and doting reveries about violence" (72), and said that despite Housman's upper-class manners "he also loved proles, soldiers, and farmboys, in the standard way" (73). Merlis recounted Housman's infatuation with Moses Jackson (73–4), wondered about the cause of their estrangement (74), mentioned Housman's sexual escapades in Europe (74), but emphasized the poet's enduring, adolescent devotion to the unresponsive Jackson (74–5), thus racking up a lifetime of self-shaming obsession with a man who never felt any sexual attraction to Housman (75). According to Merlis, Auden considered Housman "best read by adolescents, partly because he never really developed as a poet or a man" (75), and Merlis himself found Housman's verse only intermittently impressive while admiring a few poems very enthusiastically indeed (76).

CONSTANTINE CAVAFY (1863–1933). Wayne Dynes (in Dynes 1990: 207) noted that Cavafy's poems are often "poignant reflections on the fleeting joys of youth, especially in the homoerotic sphere," frequently presenting

> a comprehensive picture of the urban gay man's world that is easily recognizable today: street cruising, one-night stands, pressures to remain closeted, regret at growing older, ethnic and social contrasts, and nurturing friendships.
>
> (207)

Dynes praised the enduring literary quality of Cavafy's poems as well as their strong influence both in Greece and beyond.

Mark Lilly (1993: 33–52) reported evidence of Cavafy's guilt over his "relentless autoeroticism," noted the poet's careful circulation of his works, observed that pronoun usage in Cavafy's poems is sometimes ambiguous (33), and found in the poet's works an emphasis on "regret, doleful memory, occasional twinges of conscience about homosexuality, and an obsession with time and the ageing process." Lilly noted the poet's stress on imperatives and saw in his work

> a Wildean set of values: about defying the canons of conduct and taste in a loutish culture, about refusing to feel guilty about sexual pleasure, about retaining personal integrity, tenderness, a kind of softness. And about courage.
>
> (34)

Lilly thought Cavafy considered courage "the pre-eminent virtue," stressed "resignation" as a theme (35), insisted "on the supremacy of the mind and its imagination, over the sordid so-called realities of life," and examined "love in all its meanings, from selfless solicitude to casual sexual encounters, [and] from the heart's longing to the frankly erotic." According to Lilly, Cavafy's poems often concern the past and "do not celebrate present pleasure, but significant memory of it" (36). These works, Lilly thought, hang together well as a coherent group, partly because of their similar themes and similar characters, including "the unabashed sensualist, whose days of pleasure are over" (37). Lilly stressed two common Cavafian themes: "first, the seedy surroundings which give a piquancy to the sexual experiences," and, secondly, "moral uncertainty" (38, 40). He argued that "the experience of sex in Cavafy's poems is an escape from, and a kind of denial of, the poverty in which it takes place." According to Lilly, Cavafy emphasizes only casual prostitution (39) and "records both the experiences and the sensations of those who pay for sex, and those who take pride in not doing so. He also represents the lifestyle of the brothel habitué, sometimes exciting and fulfilling, sometimes desperate and empty." Some poems attack "the tired orthodoxies of sexual morality" (40) and some show that "it is not merely that the most exciting and impassioned relationships are brief; we also see that their end can be poignantly sudden" (43). Moreover, the "distressing invasion of … involuntary thoughts—producing a mournful restlessness—is a constant Cavafy theme" (46), as is a strong emphasis on "physical beauty" (48). This emphasis, Lilly thinks, may seem excessive and is thus somewhat problematic for modern readers, but Cavafy "makes a clear effort to de-romanticise relationships" (49), partly by stressing "wounds, pain, and death" (50) and by depicting sexual love as "often secretive, poignant, and brief" (51). All in all, Lilly offered an especially comprehensive overview of Cavafy's poems, with extensive quotation and analysis.

Peter Christensen, in Malinowski (1994: 71–4), offered a particularly fine overview of Cavafy's gay poetry and especially of critical responses to it. He suggested that Cavafy is most famous and prized for his non-erotic "historical" poetry but also discussed the many writers, often gay, who have been inspired by the erotic works. He reported, however, that some critics have faulted the "gay" poems on various grounds, such as their alleged sentimentality and nostalgia. Robert Drake (1998: 260–2) said that Cavafy's poems "are able to find the sexual promise in a fleeting glance, and in a sense they serve as early 'cruising' poems" that capture momentary desire rather than describing lengthy relationships (262). Hogan and Hudson (1998: 125) suggested that Cavafy and E. M. Forster may have been lovers, noted his gay poems' emphasis on "melancholy, irony, and, often, the historical settings [found in] the rest of his work," and saw the poems' characters as resembling Cavafy himself.

Gregory Woods (1998: 187–91) wrote that Cavafy chose to write as a homosexual, without compromising his poems, even if this meant that they could not be widely published (187), and contrasted Cavafy's emphasis on physical sex with T. S. Eliot's fearful revulsion and reticence. (187) "While Eliot tends to regard sex as an ineffable source of ugliness and degradation," Woods wrote, "Cavafy is more likely to treat it as both a source of immediate impressions of beauty and the inspiration for the eternal beauty of works of art" (187). According to Woods, Cavafy's difference from Eliot resulted partly from the strong influence of the Greek classics (188), and Woods also credited Cavafy for depicting gay men in various ways in urban environments (189). He wrote that the "relationships Cavafy deals with are always either sexual or missed opportunities for sex," with an emphasis on his own art as "the central motif" in a poetry rooted in actual physical experience (190) that prizes the beauty others condemn as "degenerate." Indeed, according to Woods, others' condemnation makes such beauty seem all the more beautiful to this poet (191).

Christopher Robinson, in Aldrich and Wotherspoon (2002: 91–3), called Cavafy "the foremost homosexual poet in modern European literature" (91–2), discussed his early sex life, reported that his brother Paul was blatantly gay, and noted that Cavafy himself was reticent about telling other men he was attracted to them (92). According to Robinson, some of Cavafy's

> confessional notes among his papers show that he had difficulty coming to terms with his erotic appetites, but interestingly these 'confessions' stop about

the very time that his more overtly erotic poems were beginning to be written (after 1911), as though the poems become a justification in themselves, an idea which is actually present in a poem such as 'Their beginning' (1921).

(92)

Robinson reported that little attention was paid at first to Cavafy's homoerotic poems, partly because an authority on Cavafy was a homophobe and considered these poems minor (92–3). But Robinson argued that in fact nearly every poem Cavafy ever wrote "is an expression, at some level, of issues of marginality, of the gap between individual and social persona, of cultural separation and of the need for immediacy of experience, all of which are clearly connected with his sexual identity" (93). Robinson asserted that Cavafy's

> 'political' poems reflect the transitoriness of what society regards as important and the enduring quality of individual experience; his private poems insist on the centrality of love and desire. Few poets of any age have celebrated male beauty with such fervour or placed so much emphasis on the power of transitory sexual pleasure to be the creative force behind great art. Equally, few poets have more poignantly evoked the precariousness, the sense of isolation and of loss which can haunt those who are not central to a society's power structure.

(93)

Peter Christensen, in Summers (2002: 139–41), discussed Cavafy's stature, career and sexuality, commented on editions of his poems, saw part of the poems' purpose as offering a "coming-out story," and reported on his reception by other gay writers (139–40). Christensen also discussed various homoerotic poems, saw 1893–1904 as a "breakthrough period" in Cavafy's writing of such texts, suggested the poet's love for Alexander Mavroudis, surveyed the development of Cavafy's gay poems in the early twentieth century, and reported that none of these poems "concerns a mutual love or a committed partnership" (140–1).

David Plante (Canning 2009: 127–37) recommended the translations of Cavafy's poems by Nikos Stangos (127–8), reported Auden's view that the erotic poems were "kitsch," said that Stangos agreed (128), and observed that the

> young male couples in [Cavafy's] poems are fated to separate, to die, but never to grow old together, as if two men growing old together could not have been an inspiring fantasy for him. His young lovers *are* beautiful for him to be inspired, and to make sure they remained young, he made them separate while still young; he made them die young. This is fantasy.
>
> There is no lasting love between Cavafy's lovers, but lust, as if he could not conceive of love lasting beyond lust, beyond the lustful impact of beauty.

This is fantasy. ... There is almost a sense of Cavafy's manipulation of the sex of his beautiful young men as objects of sexual fantasy, a fantasy without responsibility, because the young men are, after all, of no importance to life except as inspirations to poetry.

(128–9)

Although Plante suggested that Cavafy's verse uses few images, that his metaphors are often clichéd (129), and that his phrasing is sometimes "muddled" (130), he contended nonetheless that this poet's language is frequently beautiful, elegant, musical, and depersonalized in a way that often makes it timeless and "raise[s] it above personal fantasy" (130), with little emphasis on "overt" sex, which tends to be presented with deliberate vagueness (131) and in a way that suggests an enduring desire that transcends the merely physical (132). "In fact," Plante said, "Cavafy finds it awkward even to infer acts of sex that are too specific to be generalized" (132). Plante also emphasized Cavafy's use of irony, the "twang of longing his poetry arouses," and his emphasis on memory, stating that the "irony is that Cavafy allows the reader to indulge in sexual fantasy, and at the same time, by his undercutting, he lets the reader know that this *is* fantasy" (134) in a way that Plante finds somewhat frustrating but ultimately satisfying (136).

MARCEL PROUST (1871–1922). Jeffrey Meyers (1977: 58–75) focused on Proust's novel *Cities of the Plain*, arguing that

Proust distinguishes a great variety of homosexual types, and places this human species in the perspective of the natural order. The manoeuvre is daring, serious, sad, ironic, and comic, and the tone of the entire Introduction, with its frequent shifts in logic and mood, is determined by the amoral and fatalistic attitude of Marcel [the narrator]. ... Proust deliberately places Marcel outside homosexual society, but allows him to retain an intimate knowledge and sympathetic understanding of its habits.

(61)

Meyers noted the book's large number of homosexual characters (74), discussed its plot and topics, and concluded that the "prominent homosexual theme in Proust's novel is closely related to his attitude toward his mother and his inversion [i.e. homosexuality] as well as the discovery of his real purpose in life: his artistic vocation" (75). Warren Johansson (in Dynes 1990: 1069–71) began by praising Proust's talent as a thinker and writer, called him "the first major novelist to deal extensively with the theme of homosexuality," thereby "ending ... centuries of spoken and unspoken taboo," noted that many literary critics at first tried to avoid the topic, and suggested that when the topic *was* eventually addressed it was often treated in limited psychoanalytic terms (1070). Johansson observed that Proust created both gay and lesbian characters, stressed Proust's care in dealing with homoerotic themes, and discussed the novelist's own unrequited homoerotic attractions. Stressing the complexity and subtlety of Proust's thinking about homosexuality, Johansson concluded that he played "a central and incomparable" role in gay liberation, partly because he was so widely read by heterosexuals (1071). Douglas Alden, in Malinowski (1994: 303–9), noted that Proust's homosexuality was not dealt with by critics during his lifetime or in the decade after his death, that evidence of his homoerotic orientation emerged during the late 1930s, and that during his own life he "made every effort to stop the slightest suggestion that he was homosexual" (306). Alden discussed at length the ways Proust's biographers increasingly documented his homosexuality, assessed evidence for that orientation in *In Search of Lost Time* (Proust's massive masterwork), and dealt with that multi-volume novel's treatment of gay and lesbian characters and themes and its allegedly pessimistic theory of love.

Robert Drake (1998: 240–2) called *In Search of Lost Time* "voyeuristic" and termed it "sexually fluid, redolent of homosexual undertones that approach a modern camp sensibility" (241). Gregory Woods (1998: 193–200) commented on Proust's view of homosexuals as a despised minority and especially on his interest in gay men attracted mainly to straight men (195). By conforming to social pressure and making his narrator straight, Woods said, Proust damaged his book (195), although his focus on sexual secrets and the detection thereof gave the work interest (196–9), so that Proust turns "all his readers into inveterate gossips" (199). Woods again, in Summers (2002: 532–7), surveyed Proust's life, works, and sexual experiences and relationships (532–3), focused on *In Search of Lost Time*, especially its camp status, discussed the attraction to gays of the Moncrief translation and the negative aspects of Charlus as a gay role model, noted how frequently homosexuality is both a theme and sub-theme, and commented on the narrator's often caustic depiction of "inverts" (532–4). Woods explained Roland Barthes's approach to the novel, emphasized the narrator's obsession with secrets and with often mistaken speculations about characters' sexuality, and commented on the evidence the narrator uses to speculate and to arrive at often "reactionary" opinions in a book Woods called a "*peephole* novel" (534–7).

Terry Castle (2003: 579–81) argued that "Proust's novels represent one of the richest troves of lesbian-related material in all of nineteenth- and twentieth-century literature." Comparing and contrasting his treatment of lesbianism with those of other French writers, she said that Proust "exploited [this theme] more artfully and intuitively than any of his precursors" (580). She suggested that Proust's emphasis on lesbianism was a way to deal with homosexuality without compromising the ostensibly straight identity of the novels' central character, and she reported that some lesbian readers have disagreed about the persuasiveness of his depictions of his lesbian personae (580).

Felice Picano (Canning 2009: 116–21) first recounted his growing acquaintance with Proust's fiction (116–19) and then, turning to *Time Regained*, said that "on the face of it" this particular book seems "really radical, really queer, and really—sick" (119) as well as "depressing," partly because by the end of the volume "no one escapes the dissolution, the decay, the despair, the death's heads all about. And anyone not dead is revealed as a closeted homosexual" (120).

Emma Donoghue (2010: 131–2) briefly observed that "Proust broods over the perverse position of the man who suspects, denies, but finally cannot help knowing that his beloved's most erotic feelings are reserved for other women." According to Donoghue, "Proust's women, for all their prettiness and playfulness, are straight out of the French tradition of lesbian decadence" (131). Donoghue even suggested that Proust might have been partly responsible for the common tendency to link the colors violet, lavender, and purple with lesbian sexuality (132).

WILLA CATHER (1873–1947). Blanche Galfant (1971 in Bloom 1997: 43–4) commented on "the remarkable gallery of characters for whom Cather consistently invalidates sex." They "invest all energy elsewhere." Galfant perceived, in this respect, "the strange involuted nature of [Cather's] avoidance. She masks sexual ambivalence by certainty of manner, and displays sexual disturbance, even the macabre, with peculiar insouciance" (43). Jane Rule (1975: 74–87) described the ways Cather tried to discourage biographical interpretations of her works, reported on such interpretations, suggested that Cather was friendly with men but had no erotic interest in them, recounted her close connections with various women, and contrasted her youthful fearlessness with her later reticence and reserve. Rule, noting that many critics have seen Cather's sensibility as masculine, discussed this writer's methods of strongly identifying with her characters, commented that she was especially interested in writing about art and artists, described resemblances between Cather herself and St. Peter in *The Professor's House*, and also saw parallels, in style, lifestyle, and talent, between Cather and Henry James. Roger Austen (1977: 31–3) saw both "Paul's Case" and

"The Scultptor's Funeral" as stories relevant to the isolation felt by gay characters in small towns, especially if they were sensitive adolescents (31–2). Deborah G. Lambert (1982 in Bloom 1997: 47–8) asserted that "Cather never dealt adequately with her homosexuality in her fiction." In *Alexander's Bridge* and *The Song of the Lark* "sexuality is peripheral," although many, but not all, "of the later novels include homosexual relationships concealed in heterosexual guises" in which the male character is a disguised female and lesbian (47), but this disguise often leads to self-censorship that creates an inner emotional emptiness and may, in at least one case, reflect developments in Cather's own personal life (48). Judith Fetterley (1986; Bloom 1997: 50–2) noted how difficult it would have been for Cather to express, openly, her lesbian sensibility (50). Fetterly noted the conventionally female traits of Jim in *My Ántonia*, suggesting that since Cather couldn't show "him doing women's work," he "does virtually nothing," making him seem somewhat insubstantial (51). Fetterley saw in *My Ántonia* "a woman's voice making love to a feminine landscape," partly because she could not openly deal with human lesbian love (51), whereas the land could be "safely eroticized and safely loved" (51). Sharon O'Brien (1987 in Bloom 1997: 52–3) argued that "Cather's projection of self into male characters, her portrayal of romantic love as heterosexual, and her occasional creation of unconvincing male masks whose gender seems indeterminate or female raise interpretive difficulties" for readers (52). To assume that "all Cather's heterosexual plots are cover stories" and all her "male lovers ... [are] masks for women simplifies both text and writer" in reductive ways (52). In Cather's works, O'Brien wrote, "meaning and authorial intention" often "oscillate back and forth between the cover story and real story" (52). This "creative tension between expression and suppression produced novels that are subtle, richly symbolic, and ambiguous" and may even have given Cather herself creative pleasure, although her earlier works are less successful in creating this sort of ambiguity than her later ones (53).

Evelyn Gettone (in Dynes 1990: 205–6) noted Cather's youthful, unreciprocated interest in other women, commented on her writings about female beauty (eventually using male narrators), mentioned her enduring, passionate feelings for Isabelle McClung, and reported her eventual "Boston marriage" with Edith Lewis. "She did not," Gettone observed, "choose to become an open lesbian, though it was always women that she loved, [and] their support that made her work possible" (205). Cather destroyed her letters to McClung, but other letters survived, and, Gettone said, "her need to veil her inner emotional life did not condemn her to silence, but inspired her great writings" (206).

Claude Summers (1990: 62–77) focused especially on Cather's famous short story "Paul's Case," which he considered partly a response to the Wilde trials despite Cather's early disdain for Wilde himself because he seemed effeminate (62–4) and despite her interest in other unconventional writers (64–5). Summers argued, however, that in "Paul's Case" Cather was implicitly more sympathetic to Wilde (65–6). In general, he read the story as an account of Paul's "inability to integrate his homosexuality into real life" (68). Summers saw failures of imagination both in Paul and in Paul's society (68–71), stressing especially Paul's inability to sympathize with others, including his father (71–2). Paul, by emulating Wilde, suffers unnecessarily (75), and Cather creates a story that "vividly depicts what at first glance may seem to be the almost inevitable fate of gay people in an unsympathetic, nonpluralistic society, only to deconstruct this pessimistic assessment by subtly implying alternatives to alienation and suicide and envisioning possibilities implicit in those homilies by which the world us run," particularly homilies about the need for *agape* love (76). Summers saw in the story a "humane plea for an imaginative accommodationism—one that insists on individuality and self-acceptance" and one that is both "more attractive and far more realistic than Wilde's bitter rejection of a persecuting society" (76). Summers argued that this kind of accommodationism became increasingly common in later gay fiction.

Donald A. Barclay, in Malinowski (1994: 69–71), wrote that Cather

> always remained silent on her sexuality, partly because of the era in which she lived, partly because of her own sense of privacy. For this reason there is no first-hand evidence of Cather's lesbianism; there is, however, an abundance of circumstantial evidence. ... [Furthermore], as with her life Cather's writing gives only indirect evidence of her sexual orientation. None of Cather's female characters is overtly lesbian, though many of them might be. ... As for male characters, Cather created a number who might be gay, though as with her female characters, their homosexuality is never made explicit.
>
> (70)

Barclay noted that homosexuality is not an explicit theme in Cather's work but suggested that it is relevant to a number of her more obvious interests, such as artists, pioneers, and other unconventional characters.

Lillian Faderman (1994: 234–6) speculated that Cather may actually have seen herself "in medicalized terms as a man trapped in a woman's body," noted that in any case "her significant relationships were all with other women" (234), and commented that although none "of Cather's works deal specifically with lesbian relationships, ... many critics have pointed out that her male characters are often women in drag" (235). Faderman suggested that Cather "might have felt that nothing is lost and everything is gained by presenting as male those female characters she had anyway conceived as having a masculine identification" (235). According to Faderman, one can read "Tommy the Unsentimental" as a story in which "a lesbian plays a heterosexual woman," even though a "tacked-on ending ... suggests Tommy's interest in the opposite sex" (235). Neil Miller (1995: 61–3) noted that Cather became mentally distraught and physically ill when her close friend Isabelle McClung married and that she later destroyed all her correspondence with McClung. Miller commented on Cather's early tendency to identify as a male, on a growing social suspicion of close friendships between women, on the lack of any surviving evidence that she was physically intimate with another woman, and on her decision not to identify as a lesbian, despite her close relationships first with McClung and later with Edith Lewis. Hogan and Hudson (1998: 124–5) noted that Cather destroyed "as much of her personal correspondence as she could lay her hands on," suggested that she would have rejected lesbian views of her work, reported that early surviving letters lament "her 'unnatural' attraction and love" for Louise Pound (124), and speculated that Cather may have been responding to growing antipathy toward homosexuality in the 1890s (125).

John Anders, in his 1999 book on Cather, emphasized her interest in male friendships, surveyed earlier critics' reactions to the homoeroticism implied in her fiction, discussed the sexual implications of some of her language *about* writing, noted the suggestive indirection and silences of much of her phrasing, and connected her homoeroticism to her literary modernism and heightened romanticism. He argued that her early journalism often revealed "an indirect response to an emerging gay sensibility" (18) and implied her complex responses to gay male literary traditions. Anders showed that she was familiar with Greek and Roman homoerotic texts as well as with Whitman and with Pater, Housman (whom she admired), Wilde (whom she attacked), and other British gay writers, and he demonstrated that she admired various gay French writers, especially Pierre Loti, whose influence he examined at length. He cited indications of homoeroticism in Cather's own fiction, reviewed previous critics' comments on this aspect of her work, focused especially on "Paul's Case," and asserted that

> Cather's concern for sympathy continues as the focus of her fiction shifts from the world of art to that of human relationships. While *O Pioneers!* (1913) recognizes human differences, *My Ántonia* (1918) presents the struggle for

self-identity, and in both novels Cather's treatment of homosexuality refines the technical and thematic complexities begun in *The Troll Garden*. ... [Later, in the], homosexual paradigm in *One of Ours*, *The Professor's House*, and *Death Comes for the Archbishop* ... Cather now shifts the focus at the heart of *O Pioneers!* and *My Ántonia* to a concentration on male friendship, through which she continues to explore the spiritual potential of human relations.

(59, 71)

After discussing all these books in detail and in turn, Anders then mentioned, briefly, later works in which women rather than men were the main characters and finally concluded that "Cather's male-centered novels of the 1920s helped pave the way from the repressive 1910s to the more expressive 1930s ahead," so that when by "the end of the 1940s America's first 'gay classics' emerged," their appearance had been prepared for by Cather's earlier work (138).

William J. Spurlin, in Aldrich and Wotherspoon (2002: 89–91), commented on various works by Cather, especially *My Ántonia*, reporting that lesbian "readings suggest, for instance, the strong possibility that the novel was not a capitulation to convention in spite of Cather's lesbianism, but a *resistance* to heteronormative relations." Spurling noted, in particular, that "Judith Fetterley has argued that unlike *Ántonia*, who has traditionally been idealised as the pioneer heroine, the character of Lena Lingard, who resists marriage as restrictive to women, elicits desire in the fictional narrator and in the narrative voice (i.e. Cather's) that describes her" (90). Marilee Lindemann, in Summers (2002: 136–8), noted Cather's long-term relationship with Edith Lewis, reported her early presentation of herself as almost male, recounted her career and the reception of her works (136), and suggested that she became increasingly pessimistic about the social status of women (137). Lindemann discussed the presentation of gender in Cather's middle period, her frequent "marginalization of female characters," her embittered reaction to left-wing criticism in the 1930s, and her late efforts to destroy evidence of her lesbianism (137–8).

Terry Castle (2003: 587–8) noted the ambiguity of Cather's treatment of sexual themes (587), reported that Cather ordered much evidence about her own life to be destroyed when she died (588), but observed that "Cather's fiction is often strikingly homoerotic in atmosphere," partly because she "treats emotional relationships between characters of the same sex with sensuous intensity, even when those characters are two men" (588). According to Castle, in one story ("Tommy, the Unsentimental") Cather seems to "envision a new-style heroine— in whom virility, stoicism, and discretion combine to produce an authentic (if phlegmatic) lesbian chivalry" (588).

AMY LOWELL (1874–1925). Lillian Faderman (1981: 392–9) noted Lowell's opposition to censorship, discussed her relationship with Ada Russell, distinguished between poems using personae and those reflecting Lowell's own experiences, especially examined the latter poems, observed that in some poems the gender of the speaker is left unclear, and agreed with D. H. Lawrence that Lowell's use of personae often weakened her work. Faderman also (in Dynes 1990: 750–1) emphasized that some of Lowell's most overtly homoerotic poetry was inspired by her love for Ada Russell, who eventually became her long-time partner. Disputing various criticisms of Lowell's work, Faderman wrote that most of the poems based on her own experiences "suggest a life and a relationship that were extremely happy and productive" (751). Faderman later (1994: 460–2) observed that while Lowell's adolescent diaries "evince an early bisexuality, as she grew older she became less interested in men and finally dared to give up all pretense of heterosexuality" (460). According to Faderman, many of Lowell's "most successful poems" are about the actress Ada Dwyer Russell "and Lowell's love for her, as she freely admitted to her acquaintances if asked" (460). In fact, Faderman wrote, the "sequence of forty-three poems that comprise the section 'Two Speak Together' in *Pictures of the Floating World* (1919), arguably her best poetry, is a document of their life together" (461). Like other lesbians of her day, Lowell (according to Faderman) had to resort to encoding lesbian meanings because she typically could not state them openly (461). Nevertheless, her lesbianism was attacked by various literary critics who implied that her interests were too narrow to make her a successful writer (461–2). Faderman, however, said that Lowell wrote "some of the most inspired love poetry of the twentieth century" (462).

Sarah Holmes, in Aldrich and Wotherspoon (2002: 279), reported that Lowell was "noted for her strong, independent, dramatic and courageous personality. Among her peers she was unusual for transgressing conventions, smoking cigars and forming a 'Boston Marriage' with Ada Dwyer Russell." Carolyn Leste Law, in Summers (2002: 423–4), discussed Lowell's family, life, writings, and relationships with Ada Russell and Eleonora Duse, noting her effective imagery (423), her veiled but sometimes more obvious lesbianism, the later tenderness of some of her lesbian lyrics, and the opposition she sometimes faced from rivals and critics (424).

Terry Castle (2003: 649–50) compared Lowell's verse to that of Emily Dickinson and Christina Rossetti and called her poems "delicate, filigreed, and often piercingly erotic" (649).

W. SOMERSET MAUGHAM (1874–1965). Geoff Puterbaugh (in Dynes 1990: 783–5) noted Maugham's long-time reticence about his homosexuality, discussed his relationships with Gerald Haxton and Alan Searle, assessed his impact on the gay community as a closeted role model, and quoted Maugham's assertion that "he had wasted his life pretending that he was three quarters heterosexual and one quarter homosexual, while the reality was the other way around." Puterbaugh also disputed the reliability of Robin Maugham's published memories of his uncle (784). Fritz Klein (1993: 141–3) saw Maugham as bisexual—straight in his youth, gay later on—and stressed that bisexuals, in Maugham's day, tended to be even more closeted than gays. Robert Drake (1998: 229–31) saw, in Maugham's novel *Of Human Bondage*, "the classic homosexual dilemma that has haunted much of Western culture: the society-blessed life of the fraud heterosexual or the spirited, passionate life of the outlaw homosexual" (231). Alan Sinfield (1999: 42–7) emphasized the fear that Oscar Wilde's trial inspired in Maugham and others of his age and class (42), the "privilege" as well as "oppression" of these men, and Maugham's status as Wilde's "most obvious follower" (43). "Queerness in Maugham's plays," Sinfield continued, "emerges mainly through a preoccupation with scandal" (43). David Higdon, in Summers (2002: 436–7), quickly surveyed Maugham's life and career, commented on his intimate relationships, and ended by noting that Maugham "carefully avoided treating homosexual themes" and characters, perhaps because he recalled the Oscar Wilde trial (437).

GERTRUDE STEIN (1874–1946). Jeannette Foster (1956: 247–51), in her pioneering book on lesbian literature, summarized the plot of Stein's novel *Q.E.D.* Jane Rule (1975: 62–73) noted that *Q.E.D.* was first published after Stein's death in a limited edition, called it surprisingly clear and frank, emphasized its stress on morals in conflict with sexual yearning, reported on biographical interpretations, and observed that Stein had managed to publish parts of it early in her career by disguising the gender of certain characters. Rule then summarized and analyzed the plot, discussed Stein's life, and ended by praising Stein's honesty despite the limitations of her personal aspirations. Marianne DeKoven (1983: 116–17) noted the social pressures Stein felt to disguise her lesbianism but suggested that she rebelled against such pressures less in her subjects than in her style and structures (116). Stein, who had been depressed while living with her brother, became happy and productive as the "husband" of Alice B. Toklas, and later she even began to "feel better about her female identity" (117). Estelle C. Jellinek (1986 in Bloom 1997: 120–1), discussing *The Autobiography of Alice B. Toklas*, suggested that if "Stein had written in her own voice about Toklas's wife-like functions, her readers would probably have been shocked or disturbed." Thus she chose to write in Toklas's voice (120). Jellinek argued that physical relationships between women were not common before the twentieth century because, earlier, women "were so ignorant of their bodies that they did not often connect sexuality with anything save procreation" (121).

Evelyn Gettone (in Dynes 1990: 1245–7) discussed Stein's early affair with May Bookstaver, assessed its impact on her posthumously published book *Q.E.D.* ("the only work in which Stein wrote explicitly of a lesbian relationship"), noted her later long-term love for Alice B. Toklas, and saw reflections of that love in some of her later poetry. Gettone suggested that the famous "obscurity of much of [Stein's] writing is probably [partly] linked with her desire to advert to aspects of her lesbianism, but without openly avowing it" (1247). Kevin Kopelson (1994: 74–103) compared and contrasted Stein and Virginia Woolf, particularly Stein's *Autobiography of Alice B. Toklas* and Woolf's *Orlando* (75). According to Kopelson, love is both a key concern and a key method of the *Autobiography* (80), where "being and loving are expressly linked" (82), although in that book "the interdependence and living/loving and telling/listening is somewhat problematic for Stein" (81), and the book sometimes hides tensions in the two women's relationship (89). But Kopelson concluded that "Stein, unlike Woolf, is a devoted lover who can laugh at love as she knows it" (102).

Jayne Relaford Brown, in Malinowski (1994: 357–60), observed that although Stein wrote "some of the most unapologetic and frankly erotic accounts of lesbian lives in the early part of [the twentieth] century, … she withheld [such] work from publication and masked its lesbian content through a variety of innovative stylistic disguises" (359). Brown noted the early neglect of Stein's work in general, the growing interest in it in recent decades, the responses of particular critics to her sexuality and its impact on her style, her increasingly famous relationship with Toklas (often described in nonsexual terms by early writers), the significance of such works as *Q.E.D.* and *Lifting Belly* to a fuller understanding of her sexuality, and the enthusiasm for her work among some recent lesbian critics.

Lillian Faderman (1994: 452–5) suggested that in Stein's writing, "her lesbian material is often encoded in her hermetic style" and noted that only "with the posthumous publication in 1951 of *QED* (which Stein had hidden away in a drawer after writing it in 1903) was it understood by the more astute that much of her writing was specifically lesbian" (453). Faderman even called "lesbian love and sex" Stein's "favorite subject," but argued that Stein avoided the standard images of the lesbian as "a medical category or a carnivorous flower" (454). According to Faderman, even in Stein's early novel *QED*,

> a remarkable psychological study in the manner of Henry James, the lesbian characters are presented as struggling with moral and emotional subtleties, but their problems stem from the fact that they are complex people rather than congenitally burdened or sinful as a result of their lesbianism.
>
> (454)

But Stein knew, according to Faderman, that this sort of writing would not appeal to most readers (454). She therefore later employed "techniques of obfuscation." These "permitted her to describe graphically what no other published writer felt free to describe for another half-century—for example, orgasm in lesbian sex" (454). Her love for Alice B. Toklas meant that much of her later writing was inspired by their relationship, and her story "Miss Furr and Miss Skene" is, in Faderman's view, a "striking example of how much Stein could get away with by encoding her lesbian material" (455).

Neil Miller (1995: 146–8) focused mainly on Stein's relationship with Toklas, comparing the couple to 1960s hippies, noting that Stein was the "husband" and Toklas the "wife," stressing their individuality, their disinterest in being part of a lesbian community, and Stein's contempt for gay males. Miller also emphasized their sexual intimacy. Gregory Woods (1998: 203–4) suggested that Stein had negative views of gay male sex (203). William J. Spurlin, in Aldrich and Wotherspoon (2002: 419–21), reported Stein's belief that homosexuality was innate and immutable (419), saw Stein as one of various "modernist writers, including lesbians, gay men, heterosexual women and people of colour [who] have been misjudged, trivialised or altogether omitted from the study of modernism," linked Stein's particular form of modernism to her lesbianism, and asserted that her "experimentation with language allowed her to carefully encode lesbian desire in her reformulations of language" (420). According to Spurlin, "Stein's 'As a Wife Has a Cow: A Love Story', published in Paris in 1926, contains detailed depictions of lesbian sex, including orgasm, if the reader is able to carefully read and decode Stein's adverbial and participial style," and he also claimed that "'Miss Furr and Miss Skene' … reveals that some women who had sex with other women in the 1920s did take on a lesbian identity and often referred to themselves as 'gay', as homosexual men did" (420).

Corinne E. Blackmer (Summers 2002: 635–9) surveyed Stein's life (including early lesbian involvements), career, style, works, and developing reputation.

She especially emphasized *Q.E.D.*, *Fernhurst*, and *Three Lives*, questioning some "lesbian" interpretations of the Jeff-Melanctha story in the latter work (635–6). Blackmer later discussed the impact on Stein of Otto Weininger's *Sex and Character*, the importance of her relationship with Alice Toklas, the traits of her style and characterization, and the homoerotic significance of such works as "Miss Furr and Miss Skene," "Men," *Tender Buttons*, and various "ebullient" works reflecting her relationship with Toklas, including the popular *Autobiography* (636–8). Blackmer closed by mentioning the emphasis on male "homosocial camaraderie" in *Brewsie and Willie* (639).

Terry Castle (2003: 679–81) called Stein's manner of self-presentation "an early and striking epitome of early twentieth-century high butch style" and noted the lesbianism implied in many of her works, arguing that in some of these (such as "Lifting Belly") Stein "invents her own private language for lesbian eros: a speech at once abstract and formal, yet instantly and voluptuously comprehensible" (680). Kathryn Kent (2003: 139–65) concluded a lengthy discussion of this author by asserting that "Stein rewrites the nineteenth-century stereotype of the sterile spinster into an empowering lesbian identity, and she makes her relationship with Alice B. Toklas into the model of a new kind of domestic (re)productivity" (165).

E. M. FORSTER (1879–1970). Jeffrey Meyers (1977: 90–113) discussed at length four of Forster's books (*A Room with a View*, *Maurice*, *The Longest Journey*, and *The Life to Come*), commenting especially on the bathing scene in the first book but mostly dismissing the latter two as artistic failures. Meyers argued that the characters in *Maurice* are uninteresting, that its title character is flawed, and that its happy ending seems forced. He similarly disliked the stories in *The Life to Come*, criticizing their "arch language and prudish heartiness" and calling the tales "puerile, pathetic, sentimental, and thoroughly unimaginative fantasies" (108). Stephen Adams (1980: 106–26) noted that the posthumous homoerotic works were not initially well received (they were condemned as "narrow" and "dated") and said that for a time this negative reception damaged the standing of Forster's already-published writings (107–8). Although Adams defended *Maurice* to some degree (109), he thought the title character somewhat dull, criticized the cursory early chapters (110), noted that Clive becomes less appealing as the novel progresses, called Forster's characterization of Clive and Maurice sometimes inconsistent (111), observed that Forster himself admitted to disliking Clive, and found Clive immature (112). Although Adams praised the concluding chapters (114), he conceded that they could be seen as sentimental in implying a happy ending, but he admired Forster's credible presentation of Alec (116) and refuted various criticisms of the book (118–19). Commenting on some of Forster's posthumous gay short fiction (119–26), Adams suggested that often in these works

> a chance homosexual encounter is developed into a symbolic clash of values between a white, Christian middle class code complete with its guilts, inhibition, hypocrisy, and emphasis on self-control and those of some other ethnic or social group whose tribal, pagan, peasant, or working class code stresses impulsive action, passion, sexual pleasure and simple living.
>
> (125)

Wayne Dynes (in Dynes 1990: 417–19) noted the influence on Forster's homosexuality of his days at Cambridge ("among students and faculty the atmosphere was strongly homoerotic") as well as his Platonic friendship for another student there (417). Dynes also commented on such matters as Forster's attraction to more liberal, non-English countries, the heterosexual focus of most of his early novels, his composition, in 1914, of a "gay" novel (*Maurice*, which went unpublished until after his death), and his promotion, in England, of the poetry of Constantine Cavafy. According to Dynes, Forster became more happily involved in gay relationships beginning in 1915, opposed the banning of Radclyffe Hall's lesbian novel *The Well of Loneliness*, became attached, for years, to a straight policeman, and did not live to see the controversy caused by the posthumous publication of *Maurice* in 1971. Dynes defended the literary merits of *Maurice*, suggested that the book's conclusion was "modeled on the successful life of Edward Carpenter"), and asserted that Forster's "familiarity with the ideas of the early homosexual rights movement was actually a source of strength" in his work (419).

Claude Summers (1990: 78–111) called Forster "the most acclaimed gay writer in modern English literature" and said Forster embodied "more than any other writer of his generation a modern gay-liberation perspective" (78). Summers noted Forster's emphasis on homoerotic relationships between men of different classes and ethnicities (78), his stress on comradeship, his lack (despite some critics' views) of self-hatred for being gay, his characteristic tone of sadness (79), and his frustration at being unable to write and publish openly as a gay man during his lifetime (80). Summers explored such matters as the connections between Forster's gay and non-gay fiction (80), the genuine power of his posthumously published gay works, and the ways his gay fiction represented the range of his whole career as a writer (81), including the few works with homoerotic themes he *was* able to publish while still alive, such as "The Curate's friend" (81–3), which, in its happy ending, foreshadowed his posthumous gay novel *Maurice* (83). Summers traced the composition history of *Maurice*, noting that Forster gave an increasingly large role to Scudder and also reporting that the book, read in manuscript by D. H. Lawrence, influenced the latter's *Lady Chatterley's Lover* (84). Summers had high praise for *Maurice* and commented on its social and political dimensions (84–5), its exploration of two different ways of being gay (platonic and physical), and the ways it was influenced both by Edward Carpenter and Oscar Wilde (85). He especially extolled the book's artistry, including its structure, imagery, point of view, characterization, and themes (86–7). Discussing the novel in some detail, focusing particularly on the depiction of Clive, the significance of setting, and even the book's often-criticized, and admittedly imperfect, ending (87–101), Summers deeply admired *Maurice* and defended it on numerous grounds (102–3). He also examined Forster's posthumously published gay short fiction, which appeared in a volume titled *The Life to Come and Other Stories*, paying special attention to the title story and to "Arthur Snatchfold" and "The Other Boat," which he commended not only for their themes but for their artistry (103–11). All in all, Summers offered one of the best and most vigorous defenses of Forster's posthumous gay fiction that had ever been presented.

John Fletcher, in Bristow (1992: 64–90), cautioned that Claude Summers's reading of *Maurice* might be "anachronistic," wished the book had been published earlier, thus giving gays a positive depiction of homosexuality than they had (64), called Forster's book "more celebratory and socially radical than Radclyffe Hall's self-lacerating and deeply conservative" *The Well of Loneliness*, but regretted Forster's decision to erase intellectuals like himself from his most important piece of gay writing (65). Fletcher discussed the book in relation to the thought of John Addington Symonds and especially Edward Carpenter (65–74), commented at length on its plot and characters (74–89), and concluded that in "composing the novel's imperative happy ending as a vision of sexual sameness, of virile doubling, Forster erases himself as a sexual subject" and as an "unmanly intellectual" (90).

Mark Lilly (1993: 53–63), after noting the contrasting reactions of conservative and radical gay readers to Forster (the first "admired" him, the second "despised" him), focused on *Maurice*, mentioning its several revisions (53), his hesitation to publish it (53–4), how it explores social- and self-imposed limits on personal freedom (54–5), its "systematic" exploration of the "dead hand of uniformity" (55), and its "sinister undertone of discriminating in favour of, and overvaluing, the beautiful, *as people*, which we notice in the poems of Cavafy" (58; Lilly's italics). According to Lilly, the novel tries "indirectly to enlist the support of heterosexuals, by identifying a common enemy in the anti-sex church" (58) and shows how "the mighty institutions of church, medicine, education, and polite society all unite to deny basic human needs" (58). The two gay characters are, finally, two against the world (58), with the ending of the book, if not realistic, being a metaphorical endorsement of continuing the fight (59). Lilly conceded, however, that the "objection still remains ... that in contrast to the mundane world, Forster sets up a series of Arcadias: the greenwood, Ancient Greece (a favourite ploy with gay writers and painters), Cambridge"—a fact that some critics consider escapist (59). Lilly considered the book's treatment of sex vague (60) and laid the blame on "the inherited sexual guilt of British culture" (61). He thought the novel's narrator resembled Forster himself and found Forster conflicted in his portrayal of effeminate gay men, so that he made Maurice "a manly, sports-oriented boxer" (61). He concluded that Forster might have been "less emancipated" than he imagined and argued that the novel is somewhat "embarrassed by its advocacy of fully fledged (that is, including physical sex) homosexuality" (62). Noting that some readers have found the book sentimental, Lilly ended by saying that to him "it combines a strong, successful critique against Edwardian hypocrises" still in place in 1993 "with a spirit of defiance which exhilarates even those readers able to see the novel's many flaws" (63).

Richard Dellamore (1994: 83–97) noted the negative impact the Oscar Wilde trials had on Forster's life (83–4), commented on the way his fiction presents close relations between men as potentially dangerous (84), discussed the homoerotic aspects and triangular relationship in his story "Albergo Empedocle" (83–97), and explained why Forster, constrained by the laws and mores of his time, chose not to republish this story while he lived (96–7).

Murray S. Martin, in Malinowski (1994: 138–9), suggested the possible relationship between Forster's interests in both "colonial exploitation and homosexual repression," the homoerotic aspects of *Maurice*, *The Life to Come*, and *The Longest Journey*, the likelihood that Forster would have written more if he had not had to hide his sexuality, his interest in depicting "the glorification of relationships with men from the lower classes" (139), and the ways critics have responded, in particular, to *Maurice*.

Joseph Bristow (1995: 55–99) began by stressing Forster's ambivalence toward manly British imperialists, whose philistinism he criticized but whose masculine strength he admired. "From the outset," Bristow contended, "Forster's impulse is to make the effeminate boy into the manly man" (62). Bristow traced homoerotic elements in Forster's early fiction (including *The Longest Journey*, *A Room with a View*, *Howards End*, and *Where Angels Fear to Tread*) and emphasized the changes evident in Forster's later work, including *Maurice*, where Forster abandoned his earlier concern with "cultured masculinity" and focused instead on the ways

> two men overcome the class barriers set between them by obeying an unstoppable impulse to love the body. Here the intrusive femininity that has so far [in Forster's earlier writings] interposed itself between the male lovers is finally eradicated from the plot, and with misogynistic consequences.
>
> (80)

But Bristow argued that the ideal male love celebrated in the ending of *Maurice* could only, for Forster, remain imaginary, so that in *A Passage to India* he emphasized the very real obstacles (including imperialism) that prevented successful love between men, especially men of different cultures. "In this respect," Bristow concluded, "*A Passage to India* finishes on a loud protesting note against those forms of imperial masculine power that once promised to strengthen the effeminate man of culture" (90). Concluding by focusing on the homoerotic short fiction Forster eventually published in *The Life to Come*, Bristow saw an emphasis on frustrating age differences between males and equally frustrating oppression by heterosexual society.

Byrne Fone (1995: 169–77) discussed the homophobia of Forster's era, commented on the inspiration of *Maurice* (a visit with Edward Carpenter), and called that work

> the first homoerotic novel to inscribe in fiction Whitman's and Carpenter's awareness that a portrayal of same-sex desire must recognize that the inequities of class must be define in sexual as well as social terms, and to propose that sex between men can erase class inequality.
>
> (172)

Fone emphasized that *Maurice* concentrated not on outlandish behavior but on recognizable English society, that it traced one relatively normal young man's growing consciousness of his homoerotic desires, and that it challenged the common assumption that close relations between males should only be Platonic. According to Fone, "*Maurice* can rightly claim to be the first and best modern homosexual novel" because it foreshadows later developments both in fiction and in life (175).

Marjorie Garber (1995: 312–16) discussed standards of sexual "normality" in Forster's day, summarized the plot of *Maurice*, called Scudder the one real bisexual in the book, and ended by suggesting that Clive remains intrigued by Maurice despite their break. Robert Drake (1998: 226–8) reported that Forster, in a concluding note to *Maurice*, "looked forward to a year when homosexuality would no longer be a crime" and observed that "it was a year he never knew" (228). Neil Miller (1995: 157–9) commented that Forster "showed no interest" in women, was inspired by a visit to Edward Carpenter to write *Maurice* (although one scholar found the inspiration in the suicide of one of Forster's gay friends), and had an important gay relationship while in Egypt. Although Forster's later close friend, Bob Buckingham, claimed not to have known that Forster was gay, Miller cited scholarship suggesting the contrary but also noted Forster's concern not to hurt his mother by being openly homosexual. Paul Hammond (1996: 195–203) faulted *Maurice* for showing so little of Alec's history, sexual evolution, attitudes toward class, or dealings with women, and he also argued that Forster "repeatedly recoils from the physical expression of love" (200) as well as simply from vivid descriptions of the male body (201). Hammond thought that "a strong seam of denigration" in the novel defines "homosexual desire, and particularly its physical expression, through the language of disgust"—a language that partly reflects Forster's own attitudes (201). Hammond noted that Forster discarded a planned epilogue that depicted Maurice and Alex living happily together as rural woodcutters (203). Hogan and Hudson (1998: 217–18) noted that Forster remained closeted partly out of concern for his mother, that after 1910 he wrote some gay stories but never published them in his lifetime (217), and that the wife of his longtime-lover "came to accept" her husband's relationship with Forster (218).

Gregory Woods (1998: 218–19) noted the difficulty, in *Maurice*, of achieving "an ending that seemed happy but not mawkish or forced," so that the original conclusion was cut and Forster continuously labored on one that would seem credible (218). Woods thought the title character "intolerably boring" and mocked the "laughable implausibility" of the happy ending (218). He argued that the "more interesting homosexual man in this novel is Risley," although "his main role is to be what Maurice is not: camp, distinguished, conspicuous" (218–19). Woods thought Maurice (the character, not the novel) *had* to be boring; he found the same trait in many other gay novels that focused on "the potential respectability of homosexual love" (219). Suggesting that if Forster had simply given the book a "tragic" ending he could have published it when it was written, Woods reported that gay friends of Forster found various attempts at a happy ending hard to believe (219).

Seymour Kleinberg, in Aldrich and Wotherspoon (2002: 195–6), noted that Forster published his gay fiction posthumously, having destroyed some of his early work. During his life he was "publicly closeted" but "did what he could to help create a climate of toleration." *Maurice* was at first condemned by establishment critics as sentimental because of Forster's insistence "on a happy ending and the depiction of homosexual love as guiltless and fulfilling" (195). Claude Summers (Summers 2002: 263–7) covered much of the same ground here that he had already covered in 1990. Especially worth emphasizing here is his discussion of gay undertones in the "straight" novels for which Forster is most admired and in some of the early short stories (263–4). Also valuable is his discussion of the impact of Wilde's *De Profundis* on *Maurice* (265) and his account of Forster's impact on younger gay writers (267). Gregory Bredbeck, in Frontain (2003: 137–60), argued that Forster's posthumous story "The Life to Come" deals with two key topics of Forster's thought in general: "homosexuality and British colonialist expansion into India." Bredbeck maintained that Forster fused these two topics in his story and thus offered in many ways his "most interesting and successful attempt to come to terms with the imaginative and political powers that these themes could offer up as tools of critique" (138). Bredbeck contended that Forster's posthumous fiction, influenced by Edward Carpenter, shows Forster's desire to escape from the limitations of western prejudices (158).

RADCLYFFE HALL (1880–1943). Cyril Connolly (1928 in Bloom 1997: 56–7) considered The Well of Loneliness, her most famous novel, a piece of melodramatic propaganda, over-emphasizing tragedy, that presented lesbians both as victims and as superior beings (57). Jeanette Foster, in 1956 (279–81), recounted the plot of Hall's *The Well of Loneliness*, noted the outrage it—unlike some earlier, similar novels—provoked (because it *defended* lesbianism), and observed that forty-five prominent British writers came to the book's defense when efforts were made to ban it. Jane Rule (1975: 50–61) emphasized the importance and influence of *The Well*, discussed its roots in Hall's life, saw its protagonist as Hall's idealized alter ego, noted how the novel was influenced by the thinking of German sexologists, and stressed that Hall wanted to present the protagonist's lesbianism as innate and thus somewhat tolerable. Rule recounted early reactions to the book, wondered how it would be received in the 1970s, suggested that in retrospect it seemed less radical than its contemporaries assumed, and rejected it as a model for the lives of contemporary lesbians. Louise Benikow (1980 in Bloom 1997: 61–2) stressed the book's emphasis on self-hate resulting from homophobia and called it "monster literature" that presented "the lesbian as deviant, deformed, [and] sick" (61). In Hall's book, "lesbian lovers

... must parade their pain, express anger at heterosexual tyranny: look what you have done to me" (62). The book's protagonist "defends herself against her mother and against the world by accepting their terms and trying to put herself into the existing scheme of things" (62).

Lillian Faderman (1981: 317–23), while also discussing *The Unlit Lamp* and "Miss Ogilvy," called *The Well*, a later work, "the most famous lesbian novel that has yet been written" (318). Faderman argued that Hall defended the belief that lesbianism was congenital and therefore immutable rather than a sickness or a choice. According to Faderman, Hall wanted heterosexuals to tolerate gays and treat them with mercy rather than trying to change them. Unfortunately, "despite her efforts to create a pathetic picture of creatures who begged only for pity and understanding, those who began with a prejudice seem not to have been affected" (321–2). Faderman reported that many twentieth-century lesbians found the novel demeaning—a view Faderman shared, suggesting that the book treated lesbians as morbid freaks rather than as oppressed individuals deserving wholeness and freedom. Claudia Stillman Franks (1982 in Bloom 1997: 62–3) suggested that in *The Well*, lesbianism partly symbolizes a deeper alienation and isolation "at the root of human existence" (63). In Hall's writing, "the individual is necessarily thwarted—if not by sexual nature, then by some other condition of life" (64).

Inez Martinez, in Kellogg (1983: 127–37), reported that recent "feminist critics find piety toward Radclyffe Hall difficult and appear relieved that they can at least applaud her courage in risking sapphic subject matter. They are embarrassed by her writing style, by the suffering she portrays, and by what they deem her misogyny" (127). Martinez mentioned Lillian Faderman as one such critic (127); advocated for the "continued meaningfulness of [Halls] novels" (128); explored various of her works (128–36); and concluded, concerning Hall's heroines, that "the only ones who want them to grow are their lesbian lovers" and that in the "tension between self and other they lack the courage to choose self, and although Hall does not condemn them, she does not spare them the consequent loss of personality and love" (136). Margaret Lawrence (1986 in Bloom 1997: 58–9) thought Hall implied that lesbians are "women of out-and-out muscularity of brain" and compared the effect of the book to that of Greek tragedies (58). According to Lawrence, highly sensitive people, like homosexuals, are spiritually valuable to a culture (59).

Evelyn Gettone (in Dynes 1990: 516–17) noted that Hall, at an early age, called herself "John," lived with an admiral's wife for many years, published *The Well of Loneliness* in 1928, and decided to live abroad when the book was initially banned. Gettone regretted that the novel helped promote limited stereotypes about lesbians but nonetheless credited Hall's achievement in finally bringing lesbians to widespread public attention. Catharine R. Stimpson (1983 in Bloom 1997: 66-7) contrasted the happiness of Hall's own life with the unhappiness of her novel's protagonist (66). Stimpson called Hall's *The Unlit Lamp* "far more subversive than *The Well*" (67). Terry Castle (1993: 48–53) emphasized the theme of ghosts in *The Well of Loneliness* and suggested that virtually every "English or American lesbian novel composed since 1928 has been in one sense or another a response to, or trespass upon," Hall's most famous book (52), which she also saw as alluding (like other lesbian fiction) to Marie Antoinette (142–4). Gabrielle Griffin (1993: 16–24) noted the influence on Hall of the English sexologist Havelock Ellis; discussed the mixture of pessimism and optimism about lesbians in *The Unlit Lamp*; commented on the presentation of "inversion" in "Miss Ogilvy"; and asserted that *The Well of Loneliness* dealt with homosexuality "in a complex manner which simultaneously pays homage to and subverts the realist form in which the novel is written" (21). Although Griffin had doubts about Hall's attempt to elicit readers pity for lesbians, she noted that the sympathy shown for "inverts" in *The Well* was unusual in Hall's era.

Lillian Faderman (1994: 248–51) noted that Hall, when young, wore her hair long but that later she "presented herself, especially after the publication of *The Well of Loneliness*, as a true congenital introvert, a man trapped in a woman's body" (248). Faderman noted that her wealth allowed her to defy traditional conventions of gender (248) and reported that even in her early verse "lesbian themes are broached or at least encoded" (249). Faderman called *The Unlit Lamp* "arguably Hall's best novel" and noted its open emphasis on love between two women, even if that love is never explicitly depicted as sexual (250). According to Faderman, Hall saw *The Well of Loneliness*

> as a political piece of literature whose goal was to encourage tolerance for love between women. It is directly addressed not to Hall's lesbian readers but to heterosexuals, of whom she begs understanding and sympathy. Hall reasoned that the best way to promote tolerance was to argue that homosexuals could not help being as they were, that they were born with their 'condition'.
>
> (250)

Ironically, the ban on the book helped make it "the most famous novel about love between women ever to be written. It reflected and further promoted,"

Faderman concluded, "the stereotype of the lesbian as a man trapped in a woman's body" (251).

Neil Miller (1995: 166–75), focusing on *The Well of Loneliness*, commented that this book "became the most influential lesbian novel of the twentieth century and the subject of the most sensational literary trial since that of Oscar Wilde" (166). He noted that Hall, a conservative Roman Catholic, was a prize-winning, commercially successful novelist, wrote during a time of increasing hostility to homosexuality, and wrote *The Well* from "a deep sense of duty" to "defenceless" people (167). She considered homosexuality innate, was influenced by the ideas of Havelock Ellis, received little support from her British and American publishers, but was supported by writers such as Virginia Woolfe and E. M. Forster, who doubted *The Well's* artistic merits but defended its publication. Describing varied events leading up to the trial and the trial itself, Miller reported the judge's reasons for finding the book obscene, quoted from Hall's own statement defending the novel, commented on its brisk sales in the United States (where it was also eventually ruled obscene), and recounted its historical impact, both positive and negative (171–3).

Hogan and Hudson (1998: 262–3) surveyed Hall's life and career, reported that "600 love letters from Hall" to a young Russian nurse have survived, and suggested that *The Master of the House* is her best novel. They noted that she never became a feminist, that she felt "class prejudice and anti-Semitism," and they observed the immense impact of *The Well of Loneliness*, even though "some lesbians have criticized the book's butch-femme characterizations and its bleak, self-sacrificial ending" (263). In a separate essay on *The Well of Loneliness* (including a "Publishing History" chart), Hogan and Hudson (570–1) again emphasized the novel's impact in almost defining lesbianism, stressed the book's critique of "living a lie," suggested that the book took "an activist stance," and reported that it is sometimes viewed as "a central lesbian political contribution to homosexual resistance" (570).

Gregory Woods (1998: 205–7) called Hall's protagonist stereotypically self-hating and the book's gay male as stereotyped as well, although somewhat sympathetic (205). Annette Oxindine, in Aldrich and Wotherspoon (2002: 235–6), noted that Hall's sympathetic depiction of lesbians in *The Well of Loneliness* led to the book's banning in England (235), that supporters who sympathized with her cause were sometimes not especially impressed by the book itself (235–6), that *The Unlit Lamp* is often considered a subtler, better treatment of gay themes, and that Hall herself was not as tormented by her lesbianism as *The Well* might suggest (236). Joanne Glasgow (Summers 2002: 330–2) surveyed Hall's life and career, said she "lived her lesbianism openly and proudly, convinced her inversion was 'congenital'" (330), emphasized the importance of *The Well*, noted that many of her works contain no lesbian content, but commented on the lesbian-tinged *The Forge* and *A Saturday Life* and on "Mis Ogilvy Finds Herself" (331). Glasgow recounted the genesis of *The Well* as well as its plot and reception and Hall's defense of it as well as its continuing impact (331–2).

Terry Castle (2003: 632–4) noted that Hall was "unashamed of her lesbianism," partly because she was "able to act with relative freedom owing to her wealth and social position" (632). Castle felt that some of Hall's lesser-known works (especially *The Unlit Lamp*) attain "a degree of psychological pathos seldom found in early twentieth-century popular fiction." Commenting on *The Well*, Castle called it "not as bad as it is often made out to be," despite its melodrama, reliance on outdated sexology, and sometimes "overblown and silly" phrasing (633). *The Well*, she suggested, "has not lost its audience or its strange, even startling, power to move" (633).

Ed Madden, in Frontain (2003: 161–85), argued that many critics had either underemphasized Hall's echoes of the Bible or had seen the Bible's conservative impact as a negative influence on her fiction (162). Madden stressed the ways Hall combined Biblical phrasing with the language of contemporary sexology (163) and then traced Biblical echoes throughout her fiction (163–80). Margaret Soenser Breen, also in Frontain (2003: 187–208), argued that *The Well of Loneliness* "recalls many nineteenth-century texts, including *Frankenstein*, *David Copperfield*, and *Jude the Obscure*, but its commitment to realism is perhaps most discernible in its reliance on biblical allusions, tropes, and narrative patterns to 'place' its hero and delineate its plot" (188–9). She then explained why and how Hall drew so significantly on the Bible (189–204).

Emma Donoghue (2010: 172–4) called *The Well* "by far the most famous [lesbian] coming-out novel" (172) and observed that Hall "was not the first and would not be the last author to purchase the reader's sympathy for her protagonist by means of a noble renunciation" in which a lesbian character sacrifices her female beloved to a man (173).

VIRGINIA WOOLF (1882–1941). Jeannette Foster (1956: 273–5), in her pathbreaking book on lesbian literature, summarized the plot of Woolf's

Mrs. Dalloway. Michael Rosenthal (1979; Bloom 1997: 157–8) suggested that interpretations of Woolf's fiction as "androgynous" were not especially insightful and emphasized instead her talent as a writer (158). Evelyn Gettone (in Dynes 1990: 1404–5) commented on such matters as Woolf's involvement with the "Bloomsbury" group (which included important homosexuals), her aversion to sexual relations with men (including her husband), her close connections to other women, and the importance of her novel *Orlando*, which traces "the biography of the hero-heroine through four centuries of male and female existence" (1404). According to Gettone, although Woolf's posthumously published diaries did contain some "homophobic asides," her other writings often reveal her "deep relationships with women" (1405).

Sherron Knopp, in Bristow (1992: 111–27), set *Orlando* in the context of Woolf's relationship with Vita Sackville-West (111–14), suggested that Woolf was at least as passionate as Sackville-West (114), discouraged autobiographical or lesbian readings of the novel (119), did see the book as a celebration of "just such a personality as Vita's" (121), identified Orlando as both a man and a woman (122), and saw the book's main relationship as the one between Orlando and the Biographer (126). Lillian Faderman (1994: 489–92) discussed Woolf's same-sex interests and affairs, her marriage to Leonard Woolf, her involvement with Vita Sackville-West (490), her interest in writing about lesbianism but her reluctance to be too obvious, and her treatment of lesbian themes in *Orlando* (491). Kevin Kopelson (1994: 74–84) compared Woolf and Gertrude Stein, arguing that if "*Orlando* and *The Autobiography of Alice B. Toklas* are closet dramas about lesbian love lives, they are also closet dramas that *equate* loving and being" (75). Discussing Woolf's merger of eroticism and ontology (75–96), Kopelson concluded that Woolf believes "that maternal love (the heart) not patriarchal power (the phallus) is all the desiring subject really wants" (96).

Pamela Olano, in Malinowski (1994: 425–8), emphasized Woolf's interest in and devotion to women, "the absence of any male romantic figures in her writings" (427), her tendency to present women as victims of men, and the subtle homoeroticism in her depiction of women in such works as *Mrs. Dalloway*, *Between the Acts*, *A Room of One's Own*, *To the Lighthouse*, *Orlando*, and *The Pargiters*. Neil Miller (1995: 159–650) noted conflicting views that Woolf either found straight sex incomprehensible or resisted it for feminist reasons, recounted her complex, possibly asexual relationship with Vita Sackville-West, and quoted extensively from works by and about Woolf.

Annette Oxindine, in Aldrich and Wotherspoon (2002: 584–5), noted that Woolf coined an early phrase ("Chloe liked Olivia") associated with lesbianism, suggested that concern about censorship often led her to write about same-sex love in coded ways (584), reported that some writers attributed her same-sex interests to the early loss of her mother and male sexual abuse (584–5), but observed that more recent critics have explored Woolf's basic "lesbian consciousness" (585). Hogan and Hudson (1998: 588–9) suggested that Woolf often valued maternal romantic friends, noted that she has sometimes been accused of homophobia and anti-Semitism (588), argued that she never seems to have found a single sexual identity, but concluded that "homoeroticism, lesbian relationships, and gender nonconformity" are prominent in her writings (588).

Anne Hermann (Summers 2002: 708–12) noted, among much else, Woolf's close relations with her sister Vanessa, her "ambivalent" relationship with gay men, her tendency to become attached to older, maternal figures, and her close friendships with Madge Vaughan, Violet Dickinson, Ethel Smuth, and especially Vita Sackville-West (709). Hermann reported various descriptions of Woolf's significance, emphasized the lesbian significance of *Orlando*, commented that Woolf, when writing about dealing with the underexplored topic of same-sex female love, can be by turns mournful, erotic, or non-erotic (710). Hermann stressed the unique emphasis on "female eroticism" in *Mrs. Dalloway*, the importance of female characters in *To the Lighthouse* and the more explicit *Between the Acts* (710–11), and the significance of *Orlando* to "Woolf's reputation as a lesbian writer" (711–12).

Terry Castle (2003: 775–8) noted that "Woolf's sexual orientation remains a matter of extraordinary interest," that early sexual abuse may have inhibited her interest in straight sex, that mental "instability compounded her disinclination for passionate attachment," but that whatever "sensual feelings she did allow herself were plainly evoked by other women," especially her sister Vanessa, for whom her feelings were "powerfully erotic" (776). According to Castle, "Woolf treated the lesbian theme often in her fiction," sometimes suggesting that although men "come and go, … women's most lasting erotic feelings are inspired by one another," partly because of the frequent hypocrisy of heterosexual relationships (777).

Jane DeLynn (Canning 2009: 108–15), focusing on *Mrs. Dalloway*, recounted her own history as a lesbian (108–12), remarking that Woolf's novel "validated the world inside my head. Isolated I might be, but at least I was no longer alone" (112), partly because the title character seemed an "ordinary person" to whom DeLynn could relate (113). DeLynn admired the novel despite its "very un-PC" presentation of a "closet case"; in contrast, she said of *Orlando* that "I have never been able to read more than a few pages of that fanciful book, finding it overwrought and uninteresting" despite its enthusiastic reception by other lesbians (114).

D. H. LAWRENCE (1885–1930). Jeannette Foster, in 1956 (255–7), called attention to a lesbian subplot and anti-lesbian sentiments in Lawrence's 1915 novel *The Rainbow*. Jeffrey Meyers (1977: 131–61) discussed particular homoerotic moments in Lawrence's works *The White Peacock*, *Women in Love*, *Aaron's Rod*, and *The Plumed Serpent*, relating issues there to issues in Lawrence's own life and to his own conflicted sexuality. "To escape from the unbearable conflicts he encountered in relations with women," Meyers claimed, "Lawrence evolved the theory ... that male love could be a way toward a higher form of marriage between man and woman" (160–1). In all four books, Meyers said, "the heroes experience failure with women and are drawn to homosexual love." Therefore, although "Lawrence is usually associated with the triumphant expression of heterosexual love, this love depends on male dominance and is seriously qualified by an ambivalent longing for homosexuality" (161).

Georges-Michel Sarotte (1978: 75–8) argued that the "tropisms for homosexual sadomasochism were given classic form in D. H. Lawrence's story 'The Prussian Officer'" (75), in which the "captain's sadism is a defense against his desire to be penetrated by the soldier, by life, by homosexual love" (76), so that the "officer, by expressing his homosexual love sadistically, [and] the soldier, answering sadism with sadism, turn the soft blame of love into a devastating blaze" (77). According to Sarotte, Lawrence himself feared effeminate men but "dreamed of a strong, virile, sensual friendship, yet Lawrence wished that it never be *homosexual*" [Sarotte's emphasis] (77). This complex and even self-contradictory stance, Sarotte maintained, affected much of Lawrence's fiction (78).

Lillian Faderman (1981: 350–1) saw Lawrence's novel *The Fox* as promoting the widespread view that "Women cannot find satisfaction with each other, to try to do so is sick, and some terrible disaster will befall those who test this truth" (351). Gregory Woods (1987: 125–39) argued that

> Lawrence's main erotic preoccupation is with the possibility of love between a woman and a man; but when, in practice, this love looks doomed, he turns to the homosexual alternative, not necessarily as second best option, but as a less problematical version of the same thing. ... His most insistent, but necessarily self-contradictory, erotic grail is the passionate, physical union between two heterosexual men.
>
> (125)

According to Woods, "Lawrence's ideal men were actually bisexual"; he thought of "homosexuality as a lastingly debilitating condition"; his interest in "penetratory heterosexual intercourse is limited" (126); and he found both complete heterosexuality and complete homosexuality too limiting (133).

Wayne Dynes, in Dynes (1990: 698–9), discussed such matters as Lawrence's early gay-inflected story "The Prussian Officer," his disturbance, at first, with the "sexual nonconformity" of the "Bloomsbury" intellectuals, the impact of reading E. M. Forster's unpublished novel *Maurice* (in manuscript) on *Lady Chatterley's Lover*, and the influence, on his thinking, of the gay writers Edward Carpenter and Walt Whitman (698). Dynes noted that Lawrence described masculine affection in *Women in Love* and "male bonding" in *Kangaroo*, but he felt that Lawrence's "inability to come to terms with the strong homosexual component in his essentially bisexual makeup renders his example problematic" (699). Jonathan Dollimore (1991: 268–75) argued that Lawrence was unable to accept homosexuality except in idealized terms, that he tended to think of sexual relationships in terms of partners with greater or lesser power, that he disliked masturbation and solipsism, that his superficially confident pronouncements about sex betray his own anxieties, and that he was unable simply to ignore homosexuality as a topic and theme. Fritz Klein (1993: 150–8) emphasized the bisexual aspects of *Women in Love*.

Christopher Craft (1994: 140–91) dealt in detail with *Women in Love*, arguing that Lawrence seemed repulsed by gay sex partly because the idea fascinated him (156), that the obviously gay characters in the novel are soon superseded by a different notion of love between men (182), and that the novel presents "a chilling cathexis between homosexual desire and death" (190). Murray S. Martin, in Malinowski (1994: 213–16), commented on Lawrence's confused, confusing views about sexuality, reviewed the opinions of important critics of his work, emphasized his need for (but ambivalence about) strong male bonds, discussed his reluctance to ever allow such bonds to become too close, and stressed Lawrence's need to dominate in all his relationships. In Martin's words,

> Lawrence's conflicted personality makes it difficult to be precise about his sexual attitudes. He was probably bisexual, but sought cover in a kind of mystical friendship. His interest in men as lovers and friends flickers throughout, but rarely becomes the principal theme. When it does, as in *Kangaroo* and *Mr. Noon*, he tends to draw away and distance himself from the implications.
>
> (216)

Marjorie Garber (1995: 467–71) called Lawrence's *The Fox* one of the most intriguing novels about bisexuality, summarized its plot, commented on the

1968 film version, disputed negative reactions to Lawrence's work, and ended by terming the work "moving" (471). Paul Hammond (1996: 185-95) saw Lawrence as "passionately devoted to [an] ideal of male comradeship which included a strong homoerotic element" (184), despite his expressed revulsion for actual gay sex (185-6). Lawrence wrote a book about homosexuality (eventually destroyed), and the motif appears frequently in his fiction, particularly in such works as "The Prussian Officer" and *Women in Love* (186), the first of which presents the theme in negative terms, although elsewhere "Lawrence's creative engagement with his own homoerotic interests ... led him to more positive ways of reimagining masculinity" (187). He may once, according to Hammond, have "physically consummated" a relationship with a farmer from Cornwall (187), but "an intense and partly homoerotic fascination with the male body runs throughout Lawrence's fictional exploration of male friendship" (188), as Hammond demonstrated in detail, suggesting that this fascination may have had autobiographical roots (189-92). Discussing *Women in Love* and Lawrence's revisions of that text, Hammond concluded that the novelist, in general, was "attempting to fashion a new language for a new kind of male relationship which would stand alongside marriage between a man and a woman and have a comparable emotional intensity" and which would need "a comparable physical expression" (195). Gregory Woods (1998: 219-20) noted that in "The Prussian Officer" the "captain is broodily aware of his orderly's physicality. (There is nothing else to him: no personality, no preferences, no choice.)" (220). He is masculine and will soon "grow out of" any tender qualities: neither he nor the officer seems "queer" (220). By the end of the story, after the orderly has killed the officer, the two men lie next to each other, naked, in the mortuary. "As unhappy endings go," Woods wrote, "this is relatively happy. Lawrence seems to regard this unclothed togetherness on the mortuary slab as an appropriate culmination ... saved from sodomitical impurity and unmanliness by the profoundly pure virility of a violent death" (222).

Justin D. Edwards, in Aldrich and Wotherspoon (2002: 304-5), noted Lawrence's close relationship with his mother, his early and controversial treatment of lesbianism (which led *The Rainbow* to be banned), his later treatment of male homoeroticism in various novels, and the ways Scudder in Forster's *Maurice* (which Lawrence read in manuscript) helped inspire *Lady Chatterley's Lover* (304). Edwards also discussed Lawrence's attraction to various real men, their lack of reciprocation (304), his high regard for Whitman, and his friendships with contemporary male gay writers (305). Richard Kaye (Summers 2002: 408-10) noted Lawrence's conflicts with his wife Frieda, called *Women in Love* "perhaps the novelist's greatest exploration of homosexual subject matter," reported the autobiographical aspects of that novel, and commented on Lawrence's sexual relationship with a farmer (408). Kaye surveyed Lawrence's thoughts and writings about homosexuality, including the novel *Aaron's Rod*, the destroyed treatise "Goats and Compasses," and the "self-suppressed Prologue to *Women in Love*," which in the 1980s was finally published as part of the novel (408–9). Kaye suggested that perhaps "no other major modernist author was so continually absorbed in the subject of homosexual desire, a theme that continually informs Lawrence's work," including such texts as *The White Peacock*, *The Plumed Serpent*, *David*, and *The Rainbow* (409). "Like Forster and Gide, Lawrence was fascinated by the mystique of sexual relations with working-class men; unlike them, however, he expounded this fascination from the perspective of the working-class artist" (409). Kaye discussed Lawrence's conflicts about his own homoeroticism, his disdain for "effete" gays, his attraction to the earthier ideas of Whitman and Carpenter, and his interest in bisexuality (409–10), noting as well the author's thoughts about women as "upholders of suffocating marital convention," his exploration of homoeroticism in such later works as *Kangaroo*, "The Blind Man," and "Jimmy and the Desperate Woman" (410). Kaye ended by observing that Lawrence was unique among the Modernists in bringing "to the theme of homosexuality a genuine working-class perspective" (410).

Terry Castle (2003: 689–90) argued that homoeroticism, "male and female, is a recurrent topos in Lawrence's writings" (689) and that he sometimes treated lesbianism with "remarkable erotic frankness and emotional pertinence" (690). Emma Donoghue (2010: 101–3) noted Lawrence's persistence, despite censorship, in dealing with lesbian characters, who were often stereotypically labeled as "odd" in his era (101). According to Donoghue, Lawrence, in *The Fox*, offers an "ambivalent" ending: he "undercuts heterosexuality even as it appears to triumph" (102) and thus lifts *The Fox* "from a conventional man-wins-woman-from-woman story into an almost allegorical duel between different forms of sexuality" (103).

H. D. [HILDA DOOLITTLE] (1886–1961). Christine Downing (1989: 89–91) noted that although H. D. never called herself a lesbian, and although her daughter thought her mother and Annie Ellerman (also known as "Bryher") were "platonic lesbians," H. D.'s own works "reveal the strong erotic emotions she directed toward Bryher and earlier toward a girlhood friend, Frances Gregg" (89). According to Downing, "H. D.'s writing "communicates a … vulnerable image of a woman who felt fragmented and insecure in relationships with men and whole and affirmed in her relationships with women" (89). "But outside her fiction," Downing asserted, "H. D. seems to have been more confused by her sexual identity," and evidently "her analysis with Freud helped her to a healing acceptance of her bisexuality" (90), so that she "came to a kind of reconciliation with [her] mother longing" (91). Evelyn Gettone (in Dynes 1990: 325–6) discussed such matters as Doolittle's participation in an early lesbian affair, her eventual marriage to (and divorce from) Richard Aldington, and her long-time involvement with the lesbian Annie Ellerman (best known as "Bryher"). Diana Collecott, in Bristow (1992: 91–110), discussed H. D.'s use of imagery, her "fears about her own sexual desires and sexual ambivalence" (106), and her echoes of classical Greek poetry (106–10). Liz Yorke, also in Bristow (1992: 107–209), suggested that H. D. worked "within and against a modernist aesthetic" and used "unsatisfactory heterosexual codes that … distort lesbian realities" (195).

Lillian Faderman (1994: 498–500) noted recent scholarship on Doolittle's "extensive lesbian subject matter" (498), stressed the importance of her relationship with "Bryher" as well as Doolittle's bisexuality, commented on the ways she sometimes disguised her lesbianism in her poetry, especially by setting poems in the ancient past, and suggested that for Doolittle, "only by loving a woman could she free her creative impulses," even though she often "censored the lesbian content of her writing" (499), especially by suppressing some of her "autobiographical novels" (500).

Writing in Malinowski (1994: 109–10), Ondine E. Le Blanc noted that the work published during H. D.'s "lifetime—mostly poetry—addresses lesbian sexuality only very indirectly" but that the "largely autobiographical prose manuscripts unearthed after her death take her lesbian relationships as their main subject" (110). Le Blanc emphasized the poet's style, discussed her relationship with Frances Gregg, and briefly surveyed critical responses to her lesbian writings. Garber (1995: 59–62) reported that Freud considered H. D. a perfect bisexual specimen, considered the implications of this view, reported recent thinking about how "bisexuals" are or are not "queer," and commented on the chic enthusiasm for queerness in the 1990s. Hogan and Hudson (1998: 275) noted that Freud called H. D. "an 'all but extinct example' of a complete bisexual." They reported that she focused on her relationships with men in her poems and wrote three novels about relationships with women, and they suggested that the novels "express her lesbianism as a yearning for equality, support, inspiration, and even salvation" (275). Jennifer Wilson (Summers 2002: 186–8) discussed H. D.'s relations with men and women, her rejection of the "feminine" style of Victorian poetry (186–7), her distance from the more overtly lesbian writers of her day, and both the heteroerotic nature of her poetry and the homoerotic nature of her unpublished novels (187). Wilson observed that H. D.'s life and works often featured "erotic female-female-male" relationships, that she recoiled from the inequalities of heterosexual relationships, and that she saw lesbianism as an alternative to such inequalities (187–8).

Terry Castle (2003: 768–9) called bisexuality one of H. D.'s "abiding themes" (768), even though her style can sometimes be aggravatingly unclear (769). Sarah Holmes, in Aldrich and Wotherspoon (2002: 155), discussed Doolittle's involvements with various men and women and said she "often depicted romantic relationships between women, sometimes including oblique erotic passages."

KATHERINE MANSFIELD (1888–1923). Evelyn Gettone (in Dynes 1990: 764–5) commented on Mansfield's varied relations with both men and women, concluding that "she is probably best regarded as bisexual" (765). Lillian Faderman (1994: 470–2) wrote that

> Katherine Mansfield (pseudonym of Kathleen Beauchamp) often dealt in her work with bisexuality, although her treatment of lesbianism was subtle enough so that critics could, and frequently did, permit themselves to miss it. ... At her healthiest, Mansfield viewed bisexuality as a gift. She described it once as the ability to experience 'the whole octave of sex'. But such a fearless outlook was exceptional in her anxious life. Having internalized the prevailing notion of her day that homosexuality was sinful and abnormal, ... she considered herself divided into a night self and a day self, the former being her lesbian side and the cause of her unhappiness; the latter being the happier heterosexual expression of her personality. In reality, of course, the division of her generally discontented nature was not that clear-cut.
>
> (470)

In addition to stressing this ambivalence, Faderman also suggested that Mansfield often saw her female lovers as representing "the nurturing, loving figure that she felt her mother refused to be" (471); in some works, according to Faderman, Mansfield showed "her feelings of comfort and fulfillment through love of women" (471), despite the occasional disapproval of close family members (472).

Murry Martin, in Malinowski (1994: 246–8), noted Mansfield's "avoidance of homosexuality as a topic in her fiction" (247), discussed her lesbian affairs and need for female companionship, and stressed her feminism and discomfort with male domination. Terry Castle (2003: 628–9) commented on the "depth and delicacy" of Mansfield's "lifelong homoerotic feelings" (628). Murray Martin

(Summers 2002: 430–1) surveyed Mansfield's life, noted that although she wrote few openly lesbian texts she was always deeply concerned with women's status, and cited some of her New Zealand stories and the sketch "Leves Amores" as lesbian texts (430).

CLAUDE MCKAY (1889–1948). Gregory Woods (1998: 212–16) emphasized the bisexual as well as the racial dimensions of McKay's poem "Alfonso, Dressing to Wait at Table" (212), saw McKay's famous poem "If We Must Die" as relevant to both black and gay oppression (213), read "Courage" in similar terms (213–14), and stressed the possible homoeroticism of such poems as "Home Thoughts," "Adolescence," and "On Broadway" (215–16). Justin D. Edwards, in Aldrich and Wotherspoon (2002: 338–9), noted McKay's key role in helping create the "Harlem Renaissance" (338), observed that his novel *Home to Harlem* uses much contemporary slang to depict male and female homoeroticism and other queer behavior in that neighborhood (338–9), and partly for that reason offended more conservative black writers (339). McKay's next two novels avoided "overt homosexual themes," but he "did not hide his sexual desires for both men and women" and may possibly have "had affairs with Waldo Frank and Edward Arlington Robinson" (339).

Christa Schwarz (2003: 88–119) noted McKay's lack of inhibitions but fear of censorship (88–9), discussed the varied ways his sexuality has been defined (90), reported his involvement with Alain Locke's "gay network" (91–2), observed his interest in virile working-class men (92), reported that his friends remembered him as *not* effeminate (93), read various of his poems in terms of same-sex love (93–6), suggested that his gay voice was discreet (96), commented on same-sex elements in his novels, which tended to associate effeminacy with whites and virility with Blacks (96–103), suggested that McKay could sometimes seem tolerant of "pansies" (106), and argued that McKay treated lesbians ambivalently when he treated them at all (108–10). According to Schwarz, McKay tended to contrast Black male potency with white impotence (110), stressed the importance of male camaraderie (113–18), and explored homoeroticism more often and radically than some of his commentators have claimed (118–19).

DJUNA BARNES (1892–1982). Alan Williamson (1964; Bloom 1997: 12–14) emphasized Barnes's interest in incestuous or homosexual love, especially in her later works, arguing that for her the most perfect lovers mirror one another (12) and exhibit complementarity within a shared identity (13), but he cautioned that such relationships sometimes end "in mutual destruction" (13). Donald J. Greiner

(1975; Bloom 1997 14–16) saw in *Nightwood* "poetic generalizations about homosexual or heterosexual love in the midst of discussions about bestiality, the night, and religion" (16). Carolyn Allen (1978; Bloom 1997: 16–18) saw in Barnes's emphasis on love between women a stress on the "self-knowledge" that "comes from loving one who is different from yet resembles the self" (17). Evelyn Gettone (in Dynes 1990: 108) discussed such matters as Barnes's friendships with gay men, her relationships with lesbian women, the "bizarre" homosexual character Dr. O' Connor in her novel *Nightwood*, her descent into obscurity, and her eventual rediscovery by lesbian admirers. Sandra M. Gilbert and Susan Gubar (1989; Bloom 1997: 20–1) suggested that the old-fashioned language in *The Ladies Almanack* expresses "the expatriation of lesbian culture from contemporary literary history as well as the lure of lesbian lore" and saw in that work a delineation of "the unique problems and passions of the lesbian community and the lesbian couple," with a stress on eccentric characters (20). They saw *Nightwood* as "an anxious meditation on the problem of identity in a lesbian relationship" (21).

Terry Castle (1993: 180–3) called *Nightwood* "the greatest and most [Henry] 'Jamesian' novel of them all," which she saw as a "rewrite of *The Bostonians*" (180). Lillian Faderman (1994: 411–12) suggested that Barnes's inventive *Ladies Almanack* received less attention than Radclyffe Hall's *The Well of Loneliness* "partly because it did not conform to any of the more familiar literary approaches to love between women (e.g., romantic friends, men trapped in women's bodies, carnivorous flowers) and thus may have puzzled its readers" (411). "In other works dealing with lesbian themes," Faderman continued, "Barnes was somewhat more orthodox. She was fascinated by the Decadent French and English nineteenth-century writers, especially by their depictions of lesbianism" and showed this influence especially in a story titled "A Little Girl Tells a Story to a Lady" (411) as well as in her novel titled *Nightwood* (412).

Ondine E. Le Blanc, in Malinowski (1994: 27–30), discussed the personal and family background emphasized in various texts by Barnes (including her lesbian writings), surveyed various ways (sometimes de-sexualized) in which critics responded to her works, and closed by stressing that more recent critics have been more willing to discuss the sexual and social implications of her writings. Hogan and Hudson 1998 (67–8) commented on the autobiographical aspects of *Nightwood*, listed the "real" identities of some of the characters, and suggested that Barnes in that work saw desire as futile (68). Melissa Hardie, in Aldrich and Wotherspoon (2002: 44–5), noted that Barnes often used a "decadent" style to describe lesbianism, suggested that her *Ladies Almanack* became a scandalous success for offering "one of the best if more eclectic" portraits of a lesbian salon in Paris, and commented that *Nightwood* attracted attention in part for its "sexually explicit consideration of lesbianism" (44). Barnes, according to some critics, helped inspire a "darkly contemplative narrative within lesbian fiction," despite her own later attempts to distance herself from both lesbianism and feminism (45). Lianne Moyes (Summers 2002: 72-4) noted Barnes's early "camp" and lesbian sensibilities (72), discussed pro- and anti-gay readings of *Ladies Almanack*, stressed the symbolist, decadent elements of *Nightwood*, suggested the difficulty Barnes had in that text in representing sexual relations between women, and reported that *Nightwood* can be read as either negative or honestly realistic in depicting lesbian lives (73).

Terry Castle (2003: 832-3) reported that Barnes may have been raped by a male relative as a child and reprinted her short story "Cassation"—"a kind of sapphic *Rime of the Ancient Mariner*" which "tells of an attachment between two women that is at once binding, maternal, and inexplicably sinister" (832). Eric Karl Anderson (in Canning 2009: 138-45) noted Barnes's dislike of Gertrude Stein and *Nightwoood*'s impact on other writers, called it more than simply a "lesbian novel" (138); and assessed Dr. O' Connor as "one of the most peculiar and vivid characters in all fiction" (139). Anderson thought the book transcended any single genre; thought the love story had universal (rather than simply lesbian) implications (139); considered the two main characters incompatible; said that Barnes, in her *Book of Repulsive Women*, depicted both men *and* women in often negative terms; and expressed surprise that that book's emphasis on feminine sexuality did not attract censorship (140). Anderson especially admired the lesbian sensibility of *Ladies Almanack*; commented on Barnes's own disappointments in love (141); discussed an early complaint that *Nightwood* was anti-Semitic; and reported that Barnes was physically attacked by a former lover who resented the way the book depicted her (142). His final comments assessed the book as literature, commented on Barnes later years, and noted her resistance to being labeled a lesbian (143-5).

VITA SACKVILLE-WEST (1892-1962). Jeannette Foster, in 1956 (189-92), quoted some sexually ambiguous poetry from this writer's collection titled *King's Daughter* (1930). Jane Rule (1975: 88-104) described Sackville-West's early life and eventual marriage, emphasized her initial guilt about her lesbian affair with Violet Trefusis, detailed that affair, stressed the author's strong love for her gay or bisexual husband, and recounted the autobiographical details of much of this author's creative writing. Rule suggested that Sackville-West used her fiction "both to glorify passion and to punish it" (104) but also suggested that Sackville-West could not face up to the cruel, pettier, less virtuous aspects of her own character.

Lillian Faderman (1981: 366–8) emphasized that Sackville-West saw herself as a split personality, a kind of Dr. Jekyll and Mr. Hyde, with her darker, evil side manifested (she thought) in her lesbianism—a view Faderman strongly questioned. Evelyn Gettone (in Dynes 1990: 1141) commented on such matters as Sackville-West's convenient open marriage with a gay man, her affairs with Virginia Woolf and Violet Trefusis, the part she played in inspiring Woolf's novel *Orlando*, and her depictions of lesbianism in her novel titled *Challenge* and also in a posthumously published work. Lilian Faderman (1994: 268–70) argued that sexologists who saw lesbians as women trapped in men's bodies failed to comprehend the many reasons women had to feel "anger at the rules of male privilege—anger that would cause women to want to violate men's prerogatives through their own belligerent claims to masculinity" (268). But, Faderman continued,

> a further complexity in Vita Sackville-West's gender identification and sexual orientation is that sometimes she unquestionably internalized the sexologists' definition of the lesbian as a man trapped in a woman's body, just as she (contradictorily) internalized the notions of Decadent literature that characterized the lesbian impulse as evil.
>
> (268)

According to Faderman, the writer's journal "suggests a great struggle over her attraction to women, made more difficult because of her ambivalence and confusion about her masculine identification, which she associates with the dark side of her nature." This masculinity, Faderman noted, "appears sometimes as an amusing masquerade and sometimes as a self-consciously romantic stance" (269). Thus, "it is not always easy for the reader to determine to what extent she had true conviction about her masculinity and to what extent it was a nose-thumbing and/or drama-loving pose" (269). Faderman concluded that in Sackville-West's only novel "to present love between women in clear terms, *The Dark Island*, … neither of the women is masculine and gender identity is not seen as integral to lesbian identity" (270).

Marie Kuda, in Malinowski (1994: 337–9), discussed Sackville-West's relations with other women, her discovery that her husband was an active homosexual ("information he shared after a VD scare" [338]), her complicated connections with Trefusis, the ways those connections influenced *Challenge*; and the importance of her poems. Marjorie Garber (1995: 408–19) mainly discussed Sackville-West's life in bisexual terms, focusing especially on her posthumously published autobiography and its filmed adaptation (408–19). Hogan and Hudson (1998: 489) emphasized her marriage to Harold Nicolson (himself gay), its ups and downs, and her affairs with various women. Annette Oxindine, in Aldrich and Wotherspoon (2002: 459–60), noted that Sackville-West's novel titled *Challenge* was suppressed for being too clear about the author's lesbianism, even *after* she changed the gender of the main characters (460). Unsurprisingly, the novelist mostly avoided explicit lesbianism in later works (except in *No Signpost in the Sea*), but she did express overt feminism in *All Passion Spent*. Her "1920 secret journal, discovered after her death from cancer in 1962, is her most direct and sustained treatment of her own sexuality," about which "she was even somewhat cryptic in her letters" (460). Sherron Knopp (Summers 2002: 578–9) mentioned the author's subtle references in her letters to her lesbianism, her early involvement in lesbian relationships, her self-described Jekyll and Hyde personality, and the autobiographical aspects of *Challenge* and *Dark Island* (578). Knopp wrote that only *No Signposts in the Sea* mentions lesbianism overtly (and there Sackville-West "carefully distances herself from it") and that this writer's works show a "lesbian consciousness" beginning to form (579). Terry Castle (2003: 746–7) noted the posthumous discovery of an autobiographical work describing the author's marriage, while Carol Anshaw (in Canning 2009: 146–50) discussed the commencement and complications of Sackville-West's love affair with Woolf (147–8) as well as Vita's maternalism and aura of excitement (149).

EDNA SAINT VINCENT MILLAY (1892–1950). Evelyn Gettone (in Dynes 1990: 818–19) discussed Millay's drama *The Lamp and the Bell* (about a strong bond between two women), the sexual ambiguity of some of her sonnets, her eventual marriage, and an ultimate decline in the quality of her work—a decline perhaps due in part to "her felt need to suppress one half of her sensibility" after she married (819). Jean Edmunds, in Malinowski (1994: 264–7), commented on Millay's reticence about her private life, discussed her lesbian affairs, noted her mother's hope to have a boy rather than a girl, and suggested that Millay resisted any relationship that might interfere with her writing. Jennifer Wilson (Summers 2002: 453–5) noted Millay's bisexuality and under-explored homosexuality (453), her various "intense female friendships," her lesbian-tinged works, such as *The Lamp and the Bell* and *Fatal Interview*, and the need for fuller study of her homoeroticism (454).

WILFRED OWEN (1893–1918). Warren Johansson (in Dynes 1990: 934–5) noted that Owen died young (in the First World War), that his brother tried to suppress discussion of Wilfrid's possible homosexuality (while conceding that Owen was interested in the topic in "abstract" terms), that Owen's writings show a strong interest in "young male beauty," and that Owen's homoerotic nature was, in Dynes's opinion, central to his creativity (935). Michael Lutes, in Malinowski (1994: 287–8), said that Owen's "private life remains an enigma and is open to much speculation," noted the influence of his "domineering mother," and reported that some critics, to support their arguments that Owen was gay, "point out themes such as patriarchal blood lust, narcissism, injustice collecting, hostility [toward] and distaste of women, troop love, antagonism toward God, and masculine imagery" in addition to an "underlying current of latent homosexual symbolism." Paul Hammond (1996: 203–12) surveyed Owen's homoerotic writings, setting them in the context of other such writings from the First World War (203–6), and valuably explored unpublished manuscript drafts of poems, arguing that throughout these drafts "runs a vein of homoerotic sensibility, partly shaped by the aesthetics of late Victorian pederasty, which Owen often removed from his completed texts" (208). According to Hammond, Owen was often uncertain how, and to what degree, he could express homoeroticism in his war poems (210), although when he solved this problem he often wrote especially well, as in "'I saw his round mouth's crimson' (surely Owen's finest poem)" (211). Robert Drake (1998: 237–9) suggested that the "pointless slaughter of male beauty in war seems to have appalled" Owen and stimulated him to write poetry far better than his earlier verse (238). George Piggford, in Aldrich and Wotherspoon (2002: 397–8), mainly discussed Owen's life but did note Paul Fussell's claim that "Owen occupies … a firm place in the tradition of homoerotic war poetry" (397). Stephen Guy-Bray (2002: 500) emphasized Owen's associations with gays and his updating (with realism) of the elegiac tradition.

SYLVIA TOWNSEND WARNER (1893–1978). Evelyn Gettone (in Dynes 1990: 1383–4) discussed Warner's enduring, if unsteady, relationship with a troubled woman named Valentine Ackland. Gillian Spraggs (1990; Bloom 1997: 130–2) commented that "lesbianism as a theme is nowhere tackled directly" in Warner's fiction, although male homosexuality is sometimes touched on. The absence of lesbianism might have resulted from the reluctance of respectable British publishers to risk dealing with that theme, nor could Warner financially take the risk since she (unlike Radclyffe Hall) was not independently wealthy (131).

But Spraggs highly commended Warner's lesbian love poems (132). Terry Castle, in Bristow (1992: 128–47), discussed Warner while attempting to define "lesbian fiction" (128–9), challenged some ideas by Eve Kosofsky Sedgwick (129–34), focused on Warner's little-known novel *Summer Will Show*, saw that book as a spectacular challenge to the conventions of standard heterosexual fiction (134), related it in particular to the standard "wife-mistress situation," called it a "revisionist" work of English fiction (138–9), and concluded that this book, like many other works by lesbian novelists, oscillates between "realistic and fabulous modes" (146). "Lesbian fiction," Castle concluded, is likely to be both in fact and in intent non-canonical because it challenges the ways fiction is usually written (146).

Sarah Watstein, in Malinowski (1994: 385–8), noted both Warner's and Ackland's involvements with both men and women, reported that Warner (unlike Ackland) had little trouble accepting her lesbianism, cited their mutual involvement in radical left-wing politics, traced the theme of personal freedom in Warner's novels, and suggested that her books deserved more attention. Patricia Smith (Summers 2002: 678–9) stressed the homoerotic aspects of *Mr. Fortune's Maggot*, Warner's involvement with Valentine Ackland, and Warner's growing reputation "as an important lesbian voice of the early twentieth century" (678). Terry Castle (2003: 900–2) wrote that Warner's poetry "is of considerable interest, not least on account of its frankly sapphic nature"; in this poetry "we seem to eavesdrop on intimate voicings, at once amorous, philosophic, and subtly disquieting" (901).

ELIZABETH BOWEN (1899–1973). Jane Rule (1975: 115–25) reported that Bowen's fictional emphasis on relations between women began after her husband died, noted that in her work such relations are typically more emotional than overtly physical, recounted the plots and discussed the characters of various texts by Bowen, and ended by contending that Bowen "finds nothing unnatural in love between women" but "a great deal that is hostile in the world in which they try to survive" (125). Allison Rolls, in Malinowski (1994: 38–40), stressed Bowen's longtime preoccupation with "gender and gender roles," her "marked ambivalence about her personal and [Irish/English] cultural identity," her interest in depicting people on the margins, and her many extramarital lesbian affairs. Renée Hoogland (1997: 81–105) argued "that the 'unclassifiable' nature of Bowen's writing methods also offers the key to the disruptive sexual subtext underlying her dense and multi-layered narratives, which, on various interconnecting textual levels, attribute a critical role to the operations of female same-sex desire." Hoogland contended that *Friends and Relations*, for instance, "can be (re)appropriated as a lesbian text on several counts. First, and perhaps most straightforwardly, because of the incisive critique it presents of the established system of gender relations." Furthermore, Hoogland suggested, "a second, related motive for such (re)appropriation would be the fact that the story's emotional and intellectual focus, despite an ostensible preoccupation with the problematical aspects of male/female relationships, indisputably lies with female same-sex interaction" (83). Thomas Dukes (2002: 104) surveyed Bowen's life and career, noted her friendships with various gay men and women, observed that her characters reflect "varied sexual identities," commented on her relationship with May Sarton, and reported the homoerotic aspects of such works as *The Death of the Heart*, *The House in Paris*, *The Little Girls*, *The Hotel*, *The Last September*, and various short stories, which collectively present "a range of homosexualities." Terry Castle (2003: 839–40) listed some of Bowen's devoted female friends and reported that erotic "attraction between women (often an adolescent girl and an older woman) is a recurrent theme in Bowen's early novels—notably *The Hotel* and *The Last September*—and again in *The Little Girls* (1964) and *Eva Trout* (1969)" (838).

HART CRANE (1899–1932). Robert K. Martin (1979: 115–63) emphasized Crane's Platonism, stressed the poet's concern with ideal love and with the artist's alienation, explored his responses to Oscar Wilde, discussed various early poems, and saw in his mature work a concern with the importance but also the impossibility of attaining true love. Martin next assessed Crane's mature styles, explicated a wide range of homoerotic poems, and examined Crane's complex responses to Whitman, particularly the latter poet's influence on various texts, including *The Bridge*. According to Martin,

> Whitman had always been for Crane a source of confidence in his own homosexuality and in the expression of his love in his poetry. ... Whitman called for a poet who would be American—as Crane was—and who would be the poet of the new adhesive order—as Crane wished, but did not quite dare, to be.
>
> (163)

Gregory Woods (1987: 140–67) noted that many early critics neglected even to mention Crane's homosexuality (140), observed that his first published poem alluded to Oscar Wilde (141), called *White Buildings* "a more personal volume than *The Bridge*," partly because it contains gay love poems (144), disputed some critics' emphasis on Crane's supposed bisexuality (144–5), emphasized the importance of such poems as "Garden Abstract" and "Posessions" as gay works (145), discussed Crane's use of phallic imagery in the latter poem (146), and argued that all "but the first poem in the 'Voyages' sequence were influenced by Crane's love affair with Emil Opffer" (149). Woods highlighted Crane's emphasis on "the difficulty of love" (151), discussed numerous poems in detail (151–65), argued that his suicide might have resulted from the complications of a *heterosexual* relationship (165), and stressed Crane's need for gay love (166).

Wayne Dynes (in Dynes 1990: 278–9) linked the complexity of Crane's poetry to his sense of sexual alienation; ascribed his general success, in *The Bridge*, to his happiness in a love relationship (after previous frustrations); and noted the strong influence of Walt Whitman on his writing. Paul Christensen, in Malinowski (1994: 93–6), discussed various influences on Crane's "absolutist" poetry, emphasized the sensuality in *White Buildings*, stressed the sensuality of the poet's imagery, and suggested that poems addressed to women were often inspired by men. Fone (1995: 257–61) called Crane America's best gay poet after Whitman, recommended Thomas Yingling's book *Hart Crane and the Homosexual Text*, reviewed other critics' responses to Crane; quoted at length from "Episode of Hands," and concluded that "Crane presents the dilemma of the American homosexual poet, being unable to clearly express ... what he still felt impelled and yet forbidden to say" (261). Robert Drake (1998: 251–60) mainly reviewed Crane's life and death. Hogan and Hudson (1998: 157–8) noted that some critics think Crane "wrote in an opaque style to conceal his homosexuality"; that his extended relationship with Emil Opffer helped inspire "Voyages"; that some earlier and even recent biographers either ignored his homosexuality, saw it as Platonic, or considered him "yet another 'doomed homosexual'"; and reported that more recent scholars have acknowledged a gay identity that Crane was one of the first to accept (157) and have seen him, after Whitman, as "the second great gay American poet" (158).

A. M. Wentink, in Aldrich and Wotherspoon (2002: 128–30), discussed Crane's sexual relationships (129), his open homosexuality while living in New York, his mother's tacit understanding of his orientation but Crane's fear that his father might learn of it, his strong interest in sailors, conflicting explanations of his suicide, and his mother's efforts, despite their estrangement, to promote his reputation (130). Wentink reported one critic's claim that "much of the imagery in his poetry" unites "gay love-making and Christian Science 'transmemberment'" and argued that "Crane's dense imagery is replete with homoerotic themes couched in traditional poetic forms, as in 'Voyages', inspired by his intense love affair with Emil Opffer" (130). Meg Schoerke (Summers 2002: 167–8) discussed Crane's complex relations with his parents, his late (and first) "heterosexual love affair" (167), and relations between his style and his sensibility (168).

9

The Later Twentieth Century

LANGSTON HUGHES (1902–67). Jim Kepner, in Malinowski (1994: 191–4), noted that Hughes's sexuality has not been pinned down, that his biographers have sometimes claimed and sometimes denied that he was gay, that he himself left almost no hard evidence of his actual preferences, and that the evidence that does exist is usually ambiguous. Drake (1998: 343–5), noting the uncertainty about Hughes's sexual orientation, argued that

> ... in the end the strongest argument for Hughes's homosexuality is that no one, really, seems able to argue otherwise—convincingly. He is canonical [in Drake's gay canon], however, for the way African-American queers ... have mined his poetry for their own purposes. Hughes's work has become, rightly or wrongly, the bedrock of black gay poetry in America.
>
> (344)

Hogan and Hudson (1998: 296–7) noted evidence of at least one same-sex encounter by Hughes, observed that he is often considered asexual ("or at least not interested in sex with men or women"), cited "Café: 3 A.M." as a poem that has been read as gay-oriented, and observed that the film *Looking for Langston* "was in part inspired by the enigma of Hughes's sexuality" (297).

Gregory Woods (1998: 210–12) noted that Hughes described both men and women as beautiful, thought he was "particularly good on sailors" (210), commented that his poems show "Hughes's clear attraction to young black men and his concern at their plight" (211), and asserted that "there is, surely, a gay element to the poet's attitude to his male subjects" (212)—an attitude he saw implied even in such an apparently "straight" poem as "Joy" (214–15) and far more explicit in a lyric titled "Café: 3 A.M." (216). Woods credited Hughes (in contrast to Claude McKay and Countee Cullen) with having achieved a "sassy and incisive voice," influenced both by Walt Whitman and the Blues, which often sounds like "camp" (216). Scott Bravmann, in Aldrich and Wotherspoon (2001: 199–200), observed that

> Hughes never had a significant love-relationship, though the poem "F. S." (1921) suggests otherwise, and his autobiographical writings briefly mention sex with men. … During the latter years of his life, as rumours about his homosexuality circulated freely, Hughes guarded his privacy—perhaps to retain the respect and support of black churches and organisations, certainly to avoid exacerbating his precarious financial situation.
>
> (200)

Bravmann noted that Hughes's biographers disagree about his sexuality and suggested that "Hughes's evasiveness on the topic troubles the certainty of contemporary categories of identity" (200).

Carbado et al. (2002: 56–7) noted that Hughes's sexuality was still a matter of controversy, that some remembered him as "asexual," that his works sometimes dealt with overtly gay issues, and that his story "Blessed Assurance" is one example (57). Alden Reimonenq (Summers 2002: 349–50) assumed Hughes *was* gay, reported controversies about such assumptions (349), cited conflicting views of biographers, noted his reasons for thinking Hughes was homosexual, and suggested that many "of Hughes's poems invite gay readings," including "Joy," "Desire," "Waterfront Streets," "Young Sailor," "Trumpet Player," "Tell Me," and many poems in *Montage of a Dream Deferred* (350).

Christa Schwarz (2003: 68–87) noted that critics who claim that Hughes was gay "challenge the [common] assumption that he was 'asexual'" (69), reported that his biographer could find no solid evidence that he was gay, conceded that "there seem to be no indications that Hughes was a self-identifying gay man" (70), observed that attitudes toward "gay" readings of his works "vary decisively" (71), discussed the possibility that he engaged in self-censorship (72), suggested that "there are several instances in Hughes's [Harlem] Renaissance writings in which, however ambiguously, same-sex desire is presented" (72), explored such writings (72–6), focused especially on his work depicting "sailors and sea journeys" as especially relevant to gay themes (76–83), admitted that Hughes rarely describes openly "homosexual" characters (83), challenged Anne Borden's claims that Hughes often resists racial/sexual stereotypes (83–6), and noted his disdain for effeminacy (85) and lesbianism (86) and particularly for "fairies" and "mannish women" (87). Schwarz concluded that

> Hughes's literary gay voice appears to have changed over the years, yet it seems that critics, presuming a gay identity for Hughes, falsely claim his

all-encompassing tolerance and empathy for gay men and lesbians, thereby creating an image incompatible with Hughes' life and work.

(87)

COUNTEE CULLEN (1903–46). Alden Reimonenq, in Nelson (1993, *Critical*: 143–63), emphasized the importance of studying Cullen's poetry in light of his gay sexuality (143–5), stressed the significance of his friendships with Alain Locke, a key Black intellectual who was also gay, as well as with other gay men (145–55), discussed his failed marriage (155–7), and reported on his literary activities (155–9) and his later love life (159–63). Deborah Turner, in Pendergasts (1998: 99–101), surveyed Cullen's poetic works and closeted life, noted the possible homoerotic implications of various particular texts (such as "The Black Christ" and "Tableau"), and reported how recent critics have begun to read Cullen more and more in light of such implications.

Hogan and Hudson (1998: 163–4) noted mixed reactions to Cullen's "Keatsian" poetry, reported that he was inspired both by Alain Locke and by Edward Carpenter, and observed that Cullen himself taught James Baldwin (164). Gregory Woods (1998: 212–14) stressed Cullen's double oppression (as Black *and* gay), observed that Cullen could deal openly only with one of these problems (213), and noted the homoerotic aspects of "The Black Christ" (212), "From the Dark Tower" (213), and "Tableau" (214). Woods cautioned, however, that Cullen's sexuality was not this poet's major theme despite its implied appearance in various poems (216). Scott Bravmann, in Aldrich and Wotherspoon (2002: 134–5), noted "The Black Christ" and "Tableau" as poems open to homoerotic readings, suggested Cullen's romantic interest in Langston Hughes, reported his "long-term relationship with Harold Jackman" (134), and observed increasing recent interest in his sexuality (135). Alden Reimonenq (Summers 2002: 173–4) noted Cullen's productivity and his inner conflicts (173) and various poems that seem homoerotic, including "The Shroud of Color," "Fruit of the Flower," "For a Poet," "spring Remiscence," "Uncle Jim," "Colors," and "More Than a Fool's Song" (174).

A. B. Christa Schwarz (2003: 47–67) noted Cullen's high literary status during the Harlem Renaissance (48), discussed Cullen's homosexuality (which at least one scholar has denied [49–50]), reported Cullen's fear of being identified as gay in general and effeminate in particular (50–2), observed that Cullen nevertheless dealt, sometimes ambiguously, with gay themes in his work (52), offered gay readings of several of his works (such as "Heritage," "The Black Christ"; and "Judas Iscariot" [52–7]), stressed the "carpe diem" theme in his poetry (57–9) as well as the themes of love, doom, and death (59–61) and of courage and hope

(62–7). Cullen, she concluded, "interwove religion, race, gay contemporary discourse, sexuality, and romantic literary form, thereby appealing to overlapping audiences" (67).

HARLEM RENAISSANCE (1920s). Ward Houser (in Dynes 1990: 518–19) discussed such matters as the sexuality of prominent Renaissance writers Countee Cullen, Langston Hughes, Bruce Nugent, and Wallace Thurman; Nugent's story "smoke, Lilies, and Jade (1926)"—perhaps "the first fictional account of American black homosexuality" (518); the popularity of bisexual and lesbian Harlem entertainers, including among white visitors; and the generally more open acceptance of gays and lesbians in this part of New York City. Neil Miller (1995: 135–44) discussed such figures as Langston Hughes, Gladys Bentley, Bruce Nugent, Ruby Walker, Bessie Smith, Ma Rainey, Ethel Walters, Alberta Hunter, "Moms" Mabley, Josephine Baker, Lilian Simpson, Countee Cullen, Alaine Locke, Wallace Thurman, and others, emphasizing not just gay writers but gay artists of all sorts. He paid special attention to the mysteries of Hughes and Cullens's sexual identities and stressed Nugent's relative openness and his importance as a pioneer in black gay literature.

Hogan and Hudson (1998: 269–70) described how low rents and persecution in the South made Harlem an attractive area for Blacks after 1905 and suggested that "[m]any, if not a majority, of the most famous and accomplished people associated with the Harlem Renaissance were bisexual, gay, or lesbian." Hogan and Hudson briefly described gay social life in the area; noted its decline in the 1930s; and commented that only in the 1970s did the homoerotic aspects of the Renaissance begin to be discussed (269). Gregory Woods (1998: 209–16) discussed various authors, noting that a "characteristic which all these writers share with gay white writers, but which is given a doubled intensity by the context of racism, is their interest in the related themes of oppressed beauty and love under threat" (212). Thoughts about miscegenation resembled thoughts about other kinds of "forbidden love" (213), although Woods cautioned that white gay readers should "not be tempted to believe that their homosexuality necessarily gives them much of an insight into the oppression experienced by black people" (214). Carbado et al. (2002: 88–9) noted Cullen's collaboration with the gay composer Virgil Thompson (89).

Christa Schwarz (2003: 6–24) noted the reluctance of many scholars to explore the possible homosexuality of prominent writers of the Renaissance (2–3), reported that many people of that time and place identified as exclusively neither gay nor straight (3), indicated her own focus on possible gay readings of writings by Claude McKay, Countee Cullen, Langston Hughes, and Richard Bruce Nugent (3), provided social and historical background information (6-12), discussed Alain Locke's "gay network" (12-14), reported on the hostility toward gays and lesbians (especially lesbians [39]) of Harlem's black middle class (14-22), observed that homosexuality among Blacks was often blamed on negative white influences (21-2, 42), and suggested that gay males in Harlem were slightly better tolerated than gay females (23). Schwarz argued that while gay lifestyles might enjoy some tolerance in Harlem, openly gay writings enjoyed far less acceptance (25), noted that many Black leaders wanted to present positive images of African Americans (26-32, 36-8), reported that attitudes about this goal among Black "gay" writers could be mixed (33), and maintained that young Black writers, especially "modernists," often rejected middle-class sexual mores (42-7).

CHRISTOPHER ISHERWOOD (1904-86). Stephen Adams (1980: 131-55) discussed Isherwood in connection with similar writers, focusing especially on those who emphasized school or college settings as well as travel. Adams argued that in Isherwood's works, "the individual who ventures like a tourist into other lives comes to be seen as more of a parasite than a pioneer" (142) and contended that Isherwood's "perennial themes of aloneness and separation, of the multiplicity of self, and the individual's search for a homeland, develop out of the homosexual experience" (143). Adams called Stephen Monk in *The World in the Evening* Isherwood's least appealing narrator, partly because of his sense of privilege and self-centeredness (143). He thought *Down There on a Visit* an example of "Quaker camp" (145) but considered the private self presented in *Christopher and His Kind* "at once more human and more genuinely heroic" than the weak men depicted in his earlier works (148). Adams discussed *A Single Man* at length (149-54), emphasizing the complexity of George, the central character (149), commenting on the novel's comic touches (150), stressing the theme of different kinds of minority existences (151-2), and concluding that George "is heroic in the sheer ordinariness and common humanity of his homosexuality, and in his courageous determination to embrace and live out *all his selves*" (154; Adam's emphasis).

Geoff Puterbaugh (in Dynes 1990: 614-15) discussed Isherwood's increasingly open life as a gay man and recorder of gay life and also credited him with "what may be the first satisfactory explanation of camp" in his 1954 book *The World in the Evening* (615). Claude Summers (1990: 195-214) surveyed gay themes in the whole range of Isherwood's work, noting their unapologetic treatment in the early writings and stressing the author's resistance to homophobia in the later works (196). Summers called Bob Wood, from *The World in the Evening*, "one of the earliest sympathetic portraits of a gay militant in Anglo-American literature" (197) but especially praised *A Single Man*, asserting that its protagonist is "the most fully human of all Isherwood's gay characters" (199). Praising its tight construction (200) and "masterful control of narrative technique" (201), Summers admired the ways the book induces readers to identify and sympathize with the main character (201–2). "Unlike most gay fictions of its day," Summers wrote, "*A Single Man* is not a *Bildungsroman* focused on the protagonist's acceptance of his sexuality," a sexuality "which is simply a given, not the source of agonizing self-examination" (203). Summers stressed the ways Isherwood depicted gays as one minority group among many in a country made up of numerous such groups (203–4) and noted the political implications of this theme (204). After dealing in detail with the novel's plot while also setting the book in its various historical and philosophical contexts, Summers concluded that

> *A Single Man* has far more than historical or sociological interest. A tour de force in which every nuance is deftly controlled, it is both Isherwood's finest novel and a masterpiece of gay fiction. It movingly conveys the resentment of homosexuals at their mistreatment by the larger community, yet its anger is leavened by humor and its minority consciousness is qualified by its transcendent vision.
>
> (214)

Summers repeated many of these arguments in Nelson (*Contemporary*, 1993: 211–19), arguing that Isherwood "sees the homosexual as a faithful mirror of the human condition, a symbol of individuality and uniqueness and also of the variousness of human possibilities" (214). Summers also discussed the homophobia and pigeonholing that for a time affected Isherwood's reputation (218).

Mark Lilly (1993: 180–9) argued that *A Single Man* affirms "the value and validity—indeed, the essential decency, if not actual superiority—of [its] gay hero" (180). In this character, not "only is there no sense of sexual guilt or neurotic self-loathing, or suicidal tendencies," traits often found in other "gay" novels, but the normality and even benefits of gay life are stressed (181). In this book, the oppressors, not the oppressed, seem pathological (182), and the oppressed central character is not "angelic or forgiving" but sometimes full of hate (184). According to Lilly, this "cold, well-adjusted, pleasant but by no means perfect protagonist is more threatening to the prejudiced reader than a victim" (184). Although Lilly did not consider *A Single Man* unusually "distinguished" as a work of literature, he did call it "the work of a gentle and perceptive social critic, written in a relatively conventional mode, with good sense and considerable feeling" and said it deserved attention as "one of the very earliest novels to give an emphatically positive face to the gay experience" (189).

Claude Summers, in Malinowski (1994: 195–8), discussed such matters as Isherwood's interest in "isolation, sexuality, and spirituality" (196), his ability to "depict the homosexual as a faithful mirror of the human condition" (197), and the importance of his relationships with his father, other writers, and various partners. According to Summers, Isherwood's writings reveal "his fascination with the anti-heroic hero; his rebellion against bourgeois respectability; his empathy with 'The Lost' (his code name for the alienated and the excluded); and his ironic perspective, [which] are all related to his awareness of himself as a homosexual" (197). In his early works, Summers wrote, Isherwood "presents homosexuality unapologetically and naturally. He domesticated aspects of gay life that lesser writers sensationalized, and he reveals considerable insights into the dynamics of gay relationships" (197). Summers examined such works as the early writings from Isherwood's time in Berlin, his later writings from his time in California, his ability to be an advocate for gay liberation without becoming a mere propagandist, and the high quality of his prose, calling him "one of the best writers of his generation" (198).

Robert Drake (1998: 266–8) said that in Isherwood's *Berlin Stories*, homosexuals "are neither played up to nor repressed"; when they appear, they "are for the most part dealt with candidly by Isherwood and often share the same fatalistic sensibility as many of the work's heterosexual protagonists" (266–7). According the Drake, Isherwood waited until 1971 (after his parents' deaths) to "come out" fully as gay. Reed Woodhouse (1998: 155–69) focused especially on *A Single Man*, arguing that the "urgency of the novel comes not from the invention of improbably melodramatic events, but from Isherwood's clear view of the forces that lie just under the surface of George's life" (156). After summarizing the plot, Woodhouse called the novel a "far more uncompromisingly gay book, [and] a far more liberating one" (168) than David Leavitt's much-later work *The Lost Language of Cranes*, which Woodhouse considered variously disappointing. Gregory Woods (1998: 336–8, 350–1) saw many of Isherwood's early protagonists as "the same emasculated simulacrum of their author" who had to engage in self-censorship, although Woods contrasted the reticence of *Goodbye to Berlin* with the much later openness of *Christopher and His Kind* (337) and pointed to a particular instance of suppressed gay details in the earlier book (338). Seymour Kleinberg, in Aldrich and Wotherspoon (2001: 206–7), cited four novels by Isherwood that deal with homosexuality, noted that the author was "one of the first writers of international reputation to champion gay rights as minority rights," suggested that by "the late 1970s he had become a champion, if not a cult figure, among gay men for his insistence that sexual preference needed no apology, no stance of contrition or remorse," and argued that Isherwood's "own dignity, his egalitarianism and good humour, and his domestic happiness made him a post-Stonewall role model" (207). Claude Summers (Summers 2002: 361–4) surveyed Isherwood's life and career, noted his growing distrust of "communism" and "left-wing rhetoric," and commented on his use of various archetypal figures (the Truly Weak Man, the Truly Strong Man, and the Evil Mother) and recurring themes ("the test, the struggle toward maturity, and the search for a father" [362]). Summers thought Isherwood's homosexuality helped make him sympathetic to other minorities, noted that his early gay characters share with straights a "soul sickness that denies life and distorts reality" (362), and emphasized how, in the later novels, gay characters try to achieve community without sacrificing their individuality (363). Summers discussed such works as *The World in the Evening*, *Down There on a Visit*, and "Isherwood's masterpiece," *A Single Man*, which presents "the most fully human of all Isherwood's gay characters" (363). Summers stressed the political implications of Isherwood's work, an unattractive bisexual character in a late novel, Isherwood's Whitmanesque view of gay love, and Isherwood's emphatic embrace of gay liberation (363–4).

Patrick Ryan (in Canning 2009: 210–17) called *A Single Man* not only "highly economic and compulsively readable" (210) but also "loaded with compassion and charm, devoid of sentimentality" (211). He praised its intimate tone, its sophisticated use of perspective (211), its unapologetic treatment of homosexuality (212), its pioneering depiction of a "bromance" involving "one of the most charming and erotic flirtations in contemporary fiction" (215), and its effective treatment of wide-ranging emotions (216).

MARY RENAULT [PEN NAME OF MARY CHALLANS] (1905–83). Discussing *The Charioteer*, Stephen Adams (1980: 138–9) wrote that it has "all the hallmarks of a sentimental homosexual fantasy" (138) and claimed that the novel "overworks its attempt to show … clean, responsible, *manly* loves," especially by mocking its effeminate characters and also by presenting homosexuality as a kind of minor handicap (138–19). Geoff Puterbaugh (in Dynes 1990: 1106–7) wrote admiringly of Renault's fiction, which often featured gay male characters, calling *The Last of the Wine* "one of the few classic novels of male homosexual love" and praising this book, as well as *The Charioteer* and *The Persian Boy*, as especially successful. Claude Summers (1990: 156–71) compared and contrasted *The Charioteer* with Gore Vidal's *The City and the Pillar*, often to Renault's disadvantage, partly because her book displays a "depth of homophobia internalized by its gay characters and [an] utter disdain for the homosexual subculture that it depicts" (157, 164). Summers regretted these flaws but also attributed them, in part, to the virulently anti-gay era in which the novel was written (157–8). He found the main characters almost implausibly good (160) but also saw them "portrayed as emotionally as well as physically crippled" (162). Nonetheless, Summers praised the book's intentions and its impact (164–5) and showed real sympathy for its main characters (166). He admired the optimistic ending (170), even if he found the book as a whole less impressive than Gore Vidal's *The City and the Pillar* (171). Pamela Bigelow, in Malinowski (1994: 323–4), wrote that Renault

> is one of only a handful of authors published by mainstream publishers [before 1994] to have openly homosexual characters in her works. More remarkable still is that she published these works in the 1950s through the 1970s, when homosexual characters typically ended up either dead or profoundly unhappy. … Yet another unusual facet of Renault's writing was that she was barely fictionalizing history in the historical novels for which she is most well known.
>
> (323)

According to Bigelow, for many readers, "*The Persian Boy* provided their first inkling that homosexuality was tolerated and even encouraged in ancient times" (324).

Kevin Kopelson (1994: 104–28) argued that Renault believed "that lovers should be equals who know one another very well" (105) and explored in detail the ways Renault presented the complex relationships between love and sex (128). Paul Hammond (1996: 228–34) compared and contrasted *The Charioteer* with *Despised and Rejected*, by Rose Laure Allatini, another impressively direct novel by a woman about gay men in a wartime setting (228–9). "Romance and realism," Hammond wrote, "meet in a way which is quite different from Forster's vision in *Maurice*" (233), and he argued that *The Charioteer* actually ends with "all three [main] characters realizing their own versions of the Platonic ideal" (234). Hogan and Hudson (1998: 474–5) surveyed Renault's life and career, noted that she rejected the label "feminist" because she thought her "inner persona occupied two sexes too indiscriminately to take part in a sex war," and reported that she "was largely unaware of her status in gay circles" (475). Michael Stanton

(Summers 2002: 547–8) suggested that all Renault's novels "deal at some level of explicitness with homosexuality," that her first five subtly imply lesbianism, that she eventually changed her focus from the present to the past, from women to men, and from third- to first-person narration. Stanton discussed the male bisexuality implied in many of her books, the features of some of her best volumes, and her general excellence in characterizing people from past cultures (548).

Terry Castle (2003: 995–7) noted the "idealization of sexual relationships between men" in Renault's novels set in ancient times (996), the extent to which the classical settings allowed her to treat topics she could not have dealt with in modern settings (996), and her ability in the "classical" novels to imbue "once-taboo sexual topics with moral sophistication, historical complexity, and a colorful, empathic romance" (996). According to Castle, "*The Friendly Young Ladies* (1944), published under the title *The Middle Mist* in the United States, is Renault's most 'lesbian' work of fiction," although Renault herself admitted the "silliness" of its implausible heterosexual conclusion (996). Jim Grimsley (in Canning 2009: 249–52) recounted the impact of Renault's work on his own life (249–51), praised Renault's skill as a historical novelist (251), discussed her own life and times (251–2), suggested that as a lesbian she found, in her novels about gay men, a distanced way to explore her own concerns, noted the popularity of her books, and praised their "impeccable prose" and "immense integrity" (252).

W. H. AUDEN (1907–73). Gregory Woods (1987: 168–94) emphasized Auden's homosexuality, noted that Auden discouraged readers from interpreting his love poems in these terms (168), observed that he kept his orientation largely hidden except from friends (168–9), discussed the technical challenges his orientation created for him when writing love poems (which often leave the beloved's gender unspecified [170]), and asserted that Auden "never completely outgrew the sniggery vicar-and-choirboy version of gay relationships" (171). According to Woods, Auden disapproved of the oppression of gays, stressed, in his early poems, an "atmosphere of suspicion, and of political and social subterfuge" (171), and wrote of homosexuality in especially interesting ways in *The Orators* (which Clive James, Woods thought, had helpfully explicated in especially valuable ways [172]). Woods noted that critics have varied in their identifications of Auden's "gay" poems (175–6), reported that very few of those poems appear "in the 1976 *Collected Poems*, which stretches over 673 pages," observed Auden's interest in working-class men (176), and discussed many individual poems (176–94).

Wayne Dynes (in Dynes 1990: 91–2) discussed such matters as the evolution (and perhaps decline) of Auden's style, his youthful admiration for "hearty" young men, his long love affair with Chester Kallman, his unpublished piece called "The Queen's Masque," and his very explicit "piece of doggerel called 'The Platonic Lay.'" Dynes also commented on the discomfort some critics felt with Auden's homosexuality. Richard Johnson, in Malinowski (1994: 16–22), dealt with varied issues, including the relative silence by critics (at least before 1994) about Auden's homosexuality, his own de-emphasis on this subject, his growing commitment to Christianity after his radical youth, his initial sense of betrayal when his long-time lover strayed, and the frequent theme of loneliness in many of his "gay" poems (which he usually left unpublished). According to Johnson, Auden often disguised the genders of people in his poems, was interested in divided psyches, typically treated gay themes with reticence, occasionally wrote openly gay poems, and was influenced, in numerous ways, by a homoeroticism he never advertised but could never deny. Alan Sinfield (1994: 60–4) used Auden's poem "The Truest Poetry" to discuss, in general, the confining, reticent behavior commonly expected of gay writers and readers by straight critics. Hogan and Hudson (1998: 49–50) suggested that Auden returned to Christianity partly in "response to the pain of Kallman's infidelities," "knew he was gay, although blatant homoeroticism" never featured in work he acknowledged, wrote "sexually explicit poems in German in the 1920s," and wrote the gay poem "Pleasure Island." They called his quite explicit poem "A Day for a Lay" his "most unique contribution to gay male culture" (50).

Seymour Kleinberg, in Aldrich and Wotherspoon (2002: 38), noted Auden's "stormy" but long-term relationship with Chester Kallman and then observed that

> Auden said that a writer's private life 'is, or should be, of no concern to anybody except he himself, his family, and his friends'. He never wrote about his homosexuality except for a few poems which he did not publicly acknowledge, and he was conservative about issues related to gay politics, but he was not closeted in his life outside the public sphere. Auden was a poet, a great poet, who happened to be homosexual rather than a gay writer.

Claude Summers (Summers 2002: 57–8) emphasized Auden's love poetry, love relationships, eventual view of his own sexuality as liberating, awareness of "the limitations of eroticism," and belief that ideally eros and agape should be balanced. Summers noted Kallman's impact on Auden's life and texts, the poet's "camp wit," and his influence on later gay writers (58).

STEPHEN SPENDER (1909–95). Robert Marks Ridinger, in Malinowski (1994: 352–5), noted Spender's discovery, at sixteen, that his family was Jewish (information they had hidden), his college friendships with W. H. Auden and Christopher Isherwood, his bisexuality, his defense of that orientation; and his responses to such other writers as Shakespeare and E. M. Forster. Marjorie Garber (1995: 355–64) recounted the legal controversy provoked when American novelist David Leavitt based one of his own works on Spender's autobiography. She suggested that Leavitt saw bisexuality as a kind of treason, reviewed the details of Spender's life, reported critical commentary on Spender and the controversy, and expressed her own sympathy for Spender, whose era denied him any chance to be absolutely, freely homosexual, even if that had been his desire. Roger Bowen, in Aldrich and Wotherspoon (2002: 492–3), mentioned Spender's long-suppressed novel *The Temple* as particularly revealing about Spender's "sexual ambivalence," cited the memoir *World Within World* as especially relevant to his homoerotic feelings, noted the writer's "ultimate belief in the 'wholeness' of heterosexual love" (492), reported Thom Gunn's criticism of Spender's ambivalence, suggested the value of Spender's nonfiction, and reported his "copyright infringement suit" against the gay novelist David Leavitt (493). G. Patton Wright (Summers 2002: 627–9) noted Spender's relative emphasis on politics over sexuality (627), his ideal of male friendship of all sorts (including bisexual), his involvement with Rony Hyndman, his marriages and the ways they have been interpreted, and his early involvement with a German named Helmut (628).

ELIZABETH BISHOP (1911–79). Sue Russell, in Pendergasts (1998: 31–4), discussed Bishop's mostly closeted life, her involvement with various women, her subtle allusions to lesbianism, her impact on various other lesbian and gay poets, her small body of work, but also the esteem in which she is held. Meg Schoerke (Summers 2002: 98–100) surveyed Bishop's life, career, and lesbian relationships, mentioned some lesbian love poems (98–9) and noted her often indirect language (99). Colm Tóibín (2002: 172–94) commented mainly on Bishop's life, style, loneliness, and letters, noting that no letter refers to her lesbianism (183), but he did discuss her happiest lesbian relationship (189). Kathryn Kent (2003: 167–234), exploring Bishop's relationship with her mentor Marianne Moore, argued that "conflicts in Moore's and Bishop's work and in their intimacy were not simply moments of maternal prohibition or prudery or filial rebellion but instead complex disagreements over the ways in which gender and sexual identities should be represented in language" (18). Kent sought to examine how "both Bishop *and* Moore's subjectivities were formed and reformed in part out of their intense, sometimes tense, sometimes erotic, relationship of power and nurture." Kent maintained "that their interactions pose a challenge to the use by feminist literary critics of the mother/daughter relationship as the dominant model for female-female 'literary influence' and for understandings of the emergence of female gender and sexual identity" (169). Terry Castle (2003: 980-1) noted that Bishop rejected being called a feminist poet and would probably would have objected to being called a lesbian poet, although (in part) she was (981).

TENNESSEE WILLIAMS (1911-83). Georges-Michel Sarotte (1978: 107-21) argued that from the beginning "mental transvestism" was "a major key to Williams's art and one of the homosexual artist's principal stratagems for achieving universality." According to Sarotte, "Williams never treats heterosexuality without embodying himself in the heroine," and if "he happens to identify with one of his male characters, it is with some victim of American social mores" (108). In Williams's drama, Sarotte asserted, the "homosexual never appears on stage" (an opinion he later qualified [110, 120]), and he claimed that in *A Streetcar Named Desire*, "Williams introduces the homosexual theme with enormous caution" (108). The gay character (resembling Williams himself) has died before the play begins. Meanwhile, "Blanche's nymphomania recalls the homosexual's obsessive cruising, and her taste for young adolescents is a homosexual taste. She is a female projection of Tennessee Williams, just as her [dead] husband is a male projection" (109). In Sarotte's opinion, the

> fact that it is easy to categorize Williams's characters in play after play as the aging, frustrated nymphomaniac, the pure *and* oversexed young man, or the handsome brute suggest that all three correspond to aspects of the author's personality, or that they are embodiments of a fantasy. ... Stanley Kowalski [in *Streetcar*] is the Other; he is what Williams is not but would have liked to be.
>
> (110)

One gay character by Williams who *does* appear briefly onstage (Baron de Charlus, the masochist in *Camino Royale*) is given, Sarotte said, "a symbolic role, as a decadent, as the habitué of a Dantesque hell of which this play is a modern version" (110), and is juxtaposed with the pure, apparently manly, but also emasculated Kilroy (110-11).

Sarotte reported that four gay men are mentioned (but never displayed) in *Cat on a Hot Tin Roof*, argued that Maggie symbolizes William's ideal woman, partly because of her tolerance of homosexuals (112–13), and claimed that "Maggie, Big Daddy, and the author all agree ... [that] Brick and Skipper's friendship [came] to a tragic end because of the world's intolerance" (113). In Sarotte's view, Brick's "psychological problems cause him to suffer not at Skipper's death but at Skipper's confession which revealed to him their feelings for each other" (113). In Sarotte's opinion, Williams admires Brick in some ways but dislikes his refusal to pursue or discover his true self (114). Williams often, according to Sarotte, "seems to identify principally with the off-stage homosexuals" because they "are American society's true victims who are given a posthumous absolution by a virile, kind, and loving father—the unrealizable homosexual fantasy" (114). Sarotte maintained that Brick, in particular, provoked highly ambiguous feelings in Williams, and Sarotte also argued that although Williams often depicted openly gay heroes in his short fiction, he could not do so in his plays (114–15). In the latter works, said Sarotte, Williams depicts *foreign* (or foreign-seeming) macho men (like Stanley Kowalski) with real admiration because he did not find them threatening, as he would have if they were Americans.

Sarotte also suggested that Williams was "able to describe the anguish of a middle-aged nymphomaniac more poignantly than others: he need only write about himself, changing the gender of his pronouns" (116). He compared many of Williams's ideal heroes to Melville's Billy Budd: "the personification of Innocence, Purity, desexualized Masculinity" (117) and, commenting on *Suddenly Last Summer*, he noted its various resemblances to earlier plays by Williams but also stressed its emphasis "on scandal, a common obsession among American homosexuals" (118) and "the author's own guilt complex: his inability to show himself on stage as he truly is" (119). Finally, in discussing *Small Craft Warnings* (1972), Sarotte noted that "Quentin is the first homosexual to appear in the flesh in a Williams play," and he claimed that

> in *Small Craft Warnings* we encounter face to face all of the characters who have populated Tennessee Williams's dramatic work: the pure, delicate (often homosexual or asexual) man; the stud, with his enraptured clientele; nymphomaniac or frustrated women; antipathetic heterosexuals. Williams, who publicly admitted his own homosexuality, has indulged himself by playing [sic] the role of Quentin, his first homosexual, on stage.
>
> (120)

Rodney Simard, in Dynes (1990: 1392–3), discussed such matters as Williams's devastation over the death, in 1963, of his long-time partner Frank Merlo; the publication of his "sexually explicit *Memoirs* in 1975" (1393), his tendency to disguise his gay identity in earlier decades, the more open treatment of gay themes in his later work, the homoeroticism of his poems, and the sensitive, if alienated, nature of many of his characters. David Bergman (1991: 153–7) dealt with Williams's *Suddenly Last Summer* as part of a larger chapter on "Cannibals and Queers," discussing Simon's death as a kind of apotheosis, depicting his life as crossing social and class barriers by imitating "Christ's love for the poor" (155), and seeing his murder as a sort of eucharist. Commenting also on a story titled "Desire and the Black Masseur," Bergman again saw a Christ-like protagonist willing to die for gay love.

Claude Summers (1990: 130–55) claimed that Williams, like Truman Capote, "fills his fiction with grotesque characters and situations," saying that the work of both writers "often reeks of decadence" (133). But Summers saw Williams's writings as "altogether more various and affirmative" than Capote's and he especially praised *One Arm and Other Stories* and *Hard Candy and Other Stories* (133). Summers discussed, in detail, the title stories of both collections and argued, for instance, that "'One Arm' celebrates the power of sexuality—quite specifically including homosexuality—to express the spiritual and thereby to invest life with meaning" (137). Commenting also on "The Black Masseur" (Williams's "most notorious" short story [137]), Summers defended the work against critics, emphasized its comic, allegorical, and parodic dimensions (138–9), and praised it aesthetically and as a thoughtful exploration of human nature (140). Summers also discussed such other Williams stories as "The Angel in the Alcove" and "The Night of the Iguana," briefly stressing how the former defends homosexuality by attacking cruelty (140) and examining the second in detail, emphasizing its various ironies (140–4). Assessing a later story called "The Mysteries of the Joy Rio," Summers called it "an extraordinarily moving love story" (145) which, despite its occasional Gothic flaws (146), effectively explores "grief and loneliness" (147). But Summers was even more impressed by a comparable tale, "Hard Candy" (147–50), calling it less affecting but more artistically successful than "The Mysteries" because it "avoids the sentimentality and Gothic trappings of the earlier story" and concluding that the "earlier tale is a gay love story, focusing on issues of love and grief, while 'Hard Candy' is preoccupied with age and the defiance of death. Its dissolute protagonist achieves a kind of heroism precisely because he refuses to surrender to old age" (150). But the Williams story to which Summers devoted most attention was "Two on a Party" (150–4), which he praised especially for its characterization (150), calling it "a masterfully wrought narrative in which humor intensifies pathos" and in which "despair is leavened by a brave pluckiness" (154). Summing up Williams's achievements in short fiction, Summers wrote:

> Peopled by a wide variety of social outcasts, from "dirty old men" to hustlers, from timid masochists to flamboyant queens, Williams's stories explore universal themes of loneliness and isolation that are poignantly localized and made concrete in the dilemmas of their characters.
>
> (154)

Those characters, Summers felt, transcended stereotypes and often achieved true heroism by exhibiting "surprising strength and dignity" (154). Emphasizing the implied politics of Williams's work, Summers also stressed his humane sympathy for outcasts and his disdain for "cruelty and mendacity" (155), concluding that precisely "because [Williams] views homosexuality as a fully human variation, he writes about it with a naturalness, a freedom from self-consciousness, that is highly unusual in the 1940s and 1950s" (155).

John Clum (1992: 149–66) argued that Williams

> was much more successful at dramatizing the closet than at presenting a coherent, affirming view of gayness. Yet homosexuality in Williams' plays forces the protagonist into a complex relationship with traditional images of masculinity, extending and to some extent subverting those images.
>
> (149)

Clum discussed Williams's elliptical allusions to homosexuality in *A Streetcar Named Desire*, Blanche's disgust at Allan's gayness (which provokes his suicide), and Blanche's own role as (paradoxically) "the quintessential gay character in American closet drama" (150), so that Williams protects his "homosexual subtext … by hiding it within the actions of a heterosexual female" (150–1). Clum suggested that "Blanche chooses sanity, which means, for the homosexual, choosing camp, a theatricality that is a protective covering and defensive stance toward the hostile, straight world" (153–4). Williams, Clum said, also links Blanche with pederasty and promiscuity—two standard charges straights leveled against gays. In *Suddenly Last Summer*, Clum noted, Williams again presented another dead gay male (Sebastian), while in *Cat on a Hot Tin Roof* homosexuality "is linked to an inability to grow up into any kind of relationship" (156), so that the homophobic Brick lives in fear of being exposed as gay. In later works, Clum contended, Williams dealt more explicitly—but still defensively—with homosexual themes: "Williams was compelled to write about homosexuality, but equally impelled to rely on the language of indirection and heterosexist discourse" (166).

Nicholas de Jongh (1991: 66–82) briefly mentioned British censorship of a gay allusion in *Streetcar*, noted the controversy the play provoked when first staged in London, commented that this work made young males objects of sexual desire, and suggested that Williams's homosexuality made him a natural ally of other nonconformists and freedom-seekers, not only in *Streetcar* but also in the homoerotic *Cat on a Hot Tin Roof*. Quoting Williams on his status as an outsider and bohemian, de Jongh defended the playwright against charges that his heroines are mere drag queens, conceded that Williams often felt guilt and ambivalence about his own gay orientation, recounted the playwright's promiscuity and inability to commit to a single sexual relationship, and emphasized his fear of aging. In *Cat* and in *Suddenly Last Summer*, according to de Jongh, Williams depicted contemporary America's fear of homosexuality, partly because he often hated gays while being gay himself. De Jongh called *Cat* "the first truly modern play about homosexual desire and the most important one" (74), particularly in the way it characterizes Brick, his fear of being considered a "sissy," his insistence that his relationship with Skipper is just manly friendship, and his dread of growing older and leaving his youthful glory behind him. De Jongh assessed various productions of the play, from the 50s to the 80s, as well as reviewers' initial refusal to come to grips with the work's sexual implications. Turning to *Suddenly*, DeJongh noted that both in New York and in London it was first staged in small theaters, reported that reviewers approved its apparent criticism of homosexuality, commented that Sebastian in the play seems both masochistic and narcissistic, related the work to Williams's own life, and concluded by asserting that this text is Williams's "one play that resists liberation, or finds in liberation that depravity which the orthodox of the 1950s believed was synonymous with homosexuality" (82).

Mark Lilly (1993: 105–26) focused especially on *The Glass Menagerie* and *A Streetcar Named Desire* before moving on to other plays (105). He saw Laura's lameness, in the first play, as "a metaphor for Williams's view of homosexuality" (105), suggested how Williams tries to make homosexuality, in this play, unproblematic (107), suggested Tom's desire for an "all-male community" of sailors (108), and discussed how Williams depicts conventional life (110–11). Commenting on *Streetcar*, Lilly noted how Williams implies a "connection between sexuality and social ostracism" (112), seems pessimistic about "the chances of alternative sexuality," holds out little hope for "coming out of the closet," and stresses the theme of hiding (114). Even in later plays, according to Lilly, Williams's "presentation of homosexuality continues" to be "self-pityingly bleak," emphasizing the need for forgiveness for sin (114). Lilly thought that in

Small Craft Warnings, for instance, Williams depicted a "gay man who cannot relate sexually to other gay men" and who "actually *wants* to pay for sex to ensure its impersonality" (115; Lilly's italics). For Lilly, Williams's negative presentations of gay life were rooted in Williams's own biography (115). Lilly argued that Williams often displays a "preoccupation with ... male figures as sexually attractive rather than loving or lovable." In fact, "their sexual desirability is largely built of their not being lovable or solicitous," as is true of such characters as "Stanley Kowalski, Brick, Val, and Chance Wayne" (116). But Lilly contended that the "idea of a pure male friendship is at the heart of *Cat on a Hot Tin Roof*" (117), and he cautioned against the tendency of some gay readers to rely on the argument that homosexuality is more common than it is (117). Lilly ended his chapter on Williams by surveying the plots of *The Rose Tattoo* (121–4) and *Sweet Bird of Youth* (124–6).

Jim Kepner, in Malinowski (1994: 408–15), surveyed Williams's works and career, noted his frequent reticence about gay themes but his growing public comfort with his own orientation, recounted attacks on him by various critics (often homosexuals) for being too indirect in dealing with homoeroticism, defended Williams against such charges, called attention to works (especially poetry) in which gay themes are more explicit (including his *Memoirs*), and discussed the ways in which Williams often dealt with gay issues even when depicting heterosexuals. Robert Drake (1998: 288–90) called *The Glass Menagerie* the richest of Williams's plays from a gay point of view, particularly in its portrait of Tom. Neil Miller (1995: 280–4) noted Williams's "strong identification with women," his talent for creating effective female characters, and the way his character Stanley Kowalski "gripped audiences and completely transformed how America viewed male sexuality" (282). Miller also stressed the genuine mutual love between Williams and Frank Merlo and discussed the lasting negative impact of Merlo's death on Williams's own life.

Sarah Schulman (1998: 62–4) called *Suddenly Last Summer* "a work that really allows us to look at the complex position of women who survive gay men" (62) and also called it a play about "the dialogic relationship between women and gay men. Like many fag hags and lesbians who pal around with gay men, Catherine had a relationship with Sebastian of mutual appreciation and mutual use" (63). Finally, Schulman emphasized the "racial issues at the core" of the work, arguing that Sebastian "bought sex from the starving dark young boys who end up murdering him" (64).

Reed Woodhouse (1998: 35–50) focused especially on Williams's "gay" short fiction, which he considered "more, not less liberated (and liberating)" than

James Baldwin's novel *Giovanni's Room*. He emphasized the stories' sensuality, eroticism, and rejection of self-examination (36) as well as their stress on comic "self-division" (37): "By ridiculing what the 'squares' take seriously—family and children, female moral nobility, religious virtue, the sublimity of 'love'—[Williams] subverts our notions of seriousness itself" (37). According to Woodhouse, "Williams's great conceptual advance in writing about gay men lies precisely in a refusal to justify homosexuality" and in an absence of "special pleading" (37). The stories emphasize desire for men, make their "gay" characters appealing, and often feature "wounded" men (38); they satirize mainstream values in ways not always obvious and are thus more political than is often assumed, even by pro-gay critics such as John Clum (whom Woodhouse repeatedly refutes [41–50]). Woodhouse concluded that the "characteristic most typical of Williams, and most typical by its absence in Baldwin, is wit," so that although Williams "writes *about* nightmares and obsessions, his tone is light" and features "a saving streak of vulgarity which will always make it vulnerable to high-minded dismay" (50).

Gregory Woods (1998: 298–9) dismissed *Suddenly Last Summer* as a "preposterous ... exercise in voyeuristic cod-Freudianism and overblown emotion" (298) in which "two women fight over the sexuality of a man who had no sexual interest in women" (299). According to Woods, "Williams never shows any sign of believing that a homosexual man could be happy other than in fits of momentary pleasure for which the inevitable come-uppance would be swift and brutal": gay men in Williams are fated by their sexuality to live tragic lives (299). Hogan and Hudson (1998: 578–9) noted Williams's attachment to his mother, his regret that she had taught him to expect the world to be too loving, his relationship with Frank Merlo, and his "severe nervous breakdown" in 1969 (578). They reported that

> Williams has received a mixed critical reception from gay critics, who have sometimes found his characterizations of gay men depressing and negative. Williams defended his negative depictions as honest accounts of gay life as he had experienced it. He characterized his approach to gayness as 'Chekhovian', because, like the wistful characters in Chekhov's plays, gay people of his era 'were living for a future that would happen after they were dead'.
>
> (578)

Hogan and Hudson noted that Williams also defended himself from accusations by gay critics that he created gay male characters in drag; he saw that accusation as similar to the kind of abuse he received from straight critics. Hogan and

Hudson ended by citing Gore Vidal's high praise for Williams's short stories, which Vidal considered far superior to the playwright's *Memoirs* (579).

Alan Sinfield (1999: 186–204) noted that "Williams flourished in the 1950s, when the idea of a female soul in a male body persisted" (187) and noted as well that Williams's heroines often found gay male admirers (188). Sinfield claimed that Williams, in creating Stanley Kowalski, invented the modern queer macho man but warned that someone like Stanley would probably not welcome gay advances (189). Sinfield then commented on several plays by Williams, calling *Suddenly Last Summer* this author's "most homophobic" work (192) and then commenting on Williams's discomfort with his own sexuality (despite his relatively successful love life). Sinfield remarked that "an unusual determination to set queerness on stage led Williams to risk his career by alluding to it at all" (193). "The plays are oblique," Sinfield asserted, "not because Williams couldn't [personally] handle gayness, but because he had to negotiate prevailing theatre institutions," which made it hard for him to treat the topic openly (194). According to Sinfield, "Williams adopted demeaning Freudian notions about gayness," underwent analysis, and was influenced by Freud in the ways he depicted women (195). In Williams's later plays, Sinfield suggested, gayness is dealt with in a "scarcely-veiled autobiographical manner," and although the "gay characters are no more lonely or dissipated than the straights," they are associated with the pain of "coarseness" (196). Discussing a number of Williams's most famous plays (especially *Streetcar*, *Cat*, and *A Period*), Sinfield called them "radical in their dwelling upon the faultlines of the sex/gender system" (202). He thought Williams's success was surprising in view of his radical ideas (202) and concluded that in a sense Williams satisfied the American need in the 1950s for a "major" playwright (204).

Seymour Kleinberg, in Aldrich and Wotherspoon (2001: 447–8), noted Williams's tensions with his parents, the prominence of homosexuality in his *Collected Short Stories*, and the straightforward (rather than anxious or closeted) presentation of gay desire in those works. According to Kleinberg, Gore Vidal accused Williams, in his later years, of making a "circus" of his life, and Kleinberg himself suggested that Williams's conflicts about his orientation made *Small Craft Warnings* a dark play and made Williams unable to "utter the words 'gay' or 'homosexual' in his literary works, thereby creating a contrast between his serious writings and his public persona" (448). John Clum (Summers 2002: 698–700) noted Williams's complex relations with his father, mother, and sister; said his "gayness" was for most of his life "an open secret"; commented that Williams sometimes presented himself as a pathetic gay; and emphasized his stories and poems for providing insights into his homosexuality (698). Gays in the playwright's dramas were usually "dead, closeted safely in the exposition but never appearing on stage" and in the "post-Stonewall plays, in which openly homosexual characters appear," they mainly "dramatize Williams's negative feelings about his own homosexuality," and in general even in his stories "homoeroticism is always linked to death. Only in his lyric poetry does one find positive expression of homoerotic desire" (698). Clum noted debates about the possibility of Williams's own internalized homophobia, commenting that Williams often linked homoeroticism with the "transient joy ... of aging, ugly people coming into contact with youth and beauty." The stories link "sodomy with malignancy of the bowels" and gay sex with beauty and death, emphasize "young, dark, down-and-out hustler[s]" "and associate 'homosexual desire' with 'disease and death'" (699). Clum praised the poem "Life Story," noted how Williams's darker vision of gay life appears in *Cat on a Hot Tin Roof*, suggested that that play "comes as close to valorizing homosexuality as Williams got in his plays," contrasted that play with the even darker *Suddenly Last Summer*, and commented that only "Baron de Charlus in ... *Camino Real*" is a gay character in the earlier plays who actually appears on stage. Gays do appear in later plays, such as *Small Craft Warnings*, which depicts a "self-hating homosexual artist"; but Clum ended by emphasizing, more positively, Williams's talent for camp and the ways some of his best plays can be read as gay in coded ways (700).

Annette J. Saddik, in Nelson (2009: 646–51), noted that Williams's homosexuality was "an open secret throughout his life" (646), recounted his lengthy involvement as a young man with Frank Merlo, observed that Williams often treated gay themes by exploring the lives of straight women, and commented on the open importance of homoeroticism in his later works, especially his short fiction. She suggested that these works often deal directly with such matters as polysexuality, sadism, masochism, "unrestricted desire," and "literal, physical fragmentation." This included a cannibalism to which only gay men are subjected, both figuratively and literally (647). Discussing Williams's most famous plays of the 1940s and 1950s, she reported how they often implied rather than openly stated gay themes, how even gay themes treated subtly sometimes had to be eliminated from filmed versions of the plays, and how even Williams said he was unsure whether Brick in *Cat on a Hot Tin Roof* was actually gay (648). Saddick commented on the growing overtness of Williams's treatment of homosexuality in plays of the late 1950s and 1960s, his increasing tendency to abandon simple realism, and the ways critics often objected to the more open exploration of homosexuality in his later works, often finding them "too much, too personal, too 'gay'" (648). She related some of his late works to "pop art, camp, and vaudeville" and to a deliberate theatrical ridiculousness (648–9), and she reported that in twelve of his later plays, nine "either mention or deal explicitly with homosexual themes" (649). She ended by noting that critics have debated whether Williams's drama features women designed as stand-ins for gay men, by reporting that his later plays are more overtly political, especially in treating gay themes, and by observing that some readers consider his sexually honest *Memoirs* too explicit (650).

Christopher Bram (2012: 13–24) discussed the significance of Williams's decision to change his name from "Tom" to "Tennessee" (14), stressed his emotional self-expression in his early works (15), recounted his early life and friendship with Gore Vidal (15–17), and suggested that Williams began to try to use his homosexuality to inspire his writings (19). Bram discussed Americans' views of gays in the late 1940s and early 1950s (19–20), detailed the genesis of *Cat on a Hot Tin Roof*, which began as a short story (20), and expressed his personal dislike for Williams's openly "gay" play, *Suddenly Last Summer* (22).

ANGUS WILSON (1913–91). Stephen Adams (1980: 156–66, 170–5) stressed the depiction of middle-class gays within ordinary, conventional contexts, emphasized that Wilson steered clear of propaganda, and praised the diversity of his characters and the ways he often presented homosexuality as a comical problem for liberals (156–7). According to Adams,

> Wilson's delight in the surfaces and styles of behavior, in poses, mannerisms, affectations, in the revealing detail and expressive function of dress, décor, and material surroundings, in placing people by drawing attention to their attempts to place themselves ... betrays an abiding fascination for the comedy of camp.
> (160)

Adams contended that Wilson was especially interested in themes of "immaturity, insincerity, play-acting, and self-deception" as well as in "artifice in human relations," citing *Hemlock and After* as especially relevant to this claim (160). In that novel as in *The Bell*, Adams wrote, the protagonist's homosexuality is "more of an intellectual construction, an ironic test devised for pompous idealists, than a deeply felt and integral aspect of character" (170). Wilson does not, Adams claimed, treat "homosexual men as easy targets for dismissive laughter" but instead shows how their "common human weaknesses ... prevent them [from] fulfilling themselves *in terms of their own sexuality*" (181; Adams's emphasis).

Robert Drake (1998: 312–14) praised Wilson for publishing *Hemlock and After* "fifteen years before homosexuality would be decriminalized in England, giving Wilson the balls that Forster should have had and in the process earning Wilson the admiration of Forster himself and other queer luminaries such as Auden" (314). Gregory Woods (1998: 294–7) suggested the realistic but also "loosely didactic, even political, aims" of Wilson's fiction, which often teaches readers about the place of gays in English society at the time (294) and how this place might be improved (295). Calling attention to the bisexual aspects of *Hemlock and After*, Woods noted that Wilson tried "to demonstrate that not all homosexual men conform to the camp, effeminate stereotype," even if many do. Instead, he showed that gay men "constitute a range of types, and come from all social classes" and are therefore appropriate characters in "traditionalist English fiction, with its heavy concentration on character and class" (295). Woods argued that although Wilson emphasizes the dangers of blackmail, he also shows the existence of a "homosexual *community* from which the individual may derive strength and support," thanks especially to the "solidarity of camp men," whose "campness is a sign of strength, mutuality, exclusivity, self-identification as homosexual, and co-identification with other homosexuals" (296). Woods refused to exaggerate *Hemlock*'s political intentions or effectiveness; instead, he suggested that "Wilson's third novel, *The Middle Age of Mrs Eliot* (1958), contains one of the period's most affirmative representations of the stable possibilities of homosexual coupledom" (296) and stressed that Wilson is often strongly interested in the ways straights react to gays (297). David Higdon (Summers 2002: 700–1) admired Wilson's unpredictability, noted his various gay characters and his "nonapologetic gay viewpoint," reported that his birth name was "Frank Johnstone" (700), and observed Wilson's recurring interest in problems of authority as well as the ways his "wit and satire join with Wilson's general pessimism and rigorous depiction" of "self-delusion" and "enlightenment" (701).

JANE AUER BOWLES (1917–73). Evelyn Gettone (in Dynes 1990: 161) discussed such matters as Bowles's marriage to the bisexual writer Paul Bowles, her various lesbian relationships, the couple's years in Morocco, their habit of hosting visiting gay writers there, and her "powerful sense of women's independence from men." Thomas Wiloch, in Malinowski (1994: 40–1), commented on Bowles's emphasis on alienated characters, her interest in women's liberation, her depictions of sexual experimentation, her openness about her own lesbianism, and her emotional and psychological instability.

JAMES BALDWIN (1924–87). Roger Austen (1977: 201–4) defended Baldwin's work *Another Country*, calling it a "powerful, almost allegorical novel, [in which] the sex and race themes are tightly interwoven" (201), describing its persuasiveness and status as a "problem novel," and admiring Baldwin for presenting homosexuality more as "an existential answer" than as "a kinky perversion" (202). Austen thought both its straight and gay characters are "all victims of urban blight, with little hope of escape to any sort of pastoral refuge" (202), saw the novel as a book implying that if you're going to be gay in New York, you're going to have to steel yourself to cope with seediness, frustration, and despair" (203), and reported both the attacks and defenses the novel provoked (203–4).

Georges-Michel Sarotte (1978: 27–9, 54–60, 96–103, 170–3) noted that Baldwin's *Giovanni's Room* was one of the first American novels to show two men cohabiting, although their joy (partly because David is mentally insecure) is short-lived, and the novel's conclusion is "brutal and fatal" (27). The European setting may suggest at first that the characters have a chance at stability, but the rest of the book subverts this possibility (27–8). In *Another Country*, Sarotte claimed, Baldwin depicted two gay men—one conventionally "masculine," the other conventionally "feminine," whose relationship becomes unusually explicit in a work Sarotte calls a true "love story," featuring an atmosphere of "purity, peace, and mystic union" (28). "Baldwin's purpose," wrote Sarotte, is to make the love between these characters "acceptable to the reader, to make the reader feel sympathy for this male couple by creating situations that are traditionally associated with the love between men and women. He seems to be saying, 'They're just like you: they do as you do, therefore they are you'" (29). But Sarotte claims that in this novel by Baldwin,

> *There can be no virile homosexual.* Neither Vidal nor Baldwin really believes it possible. It can appear true only at special moments, brief as they are vivid, at times of adolescent ambivalence, or in pederastic situations à la Greek, playing on the sexual ambiguity of the sex object and on the pseudo virility—a relative virility, maturity, rather—of the sexual protagonist.
>
> (29)

According to Sarotte, Baldwin concludes this "'bisexual' novel on a note of homosexual hope" (29). Later, Sarotte discussed the sexual complications presented in Baldwin's *Go Tell It on the Mountain* (1953), which features an insecure youth, ashamed of his appearance, who fantasizes about more obviously attractive and virile young men in ways that recall the writings of other

American authors of this period (54–6) and who, as so often in American fiction of this period, is attracted to a young heterosexual of his own age (55–6). Similar characters and themes, Sarotte observed, appeared in Baldwin's short story "The Outing" (1951), which in various ways foreshadowed *Giovanni's Room* (1956). In that novel, Sarotte said, David experiences repeated fear when he feels sexually attracted to other men: "like Vidal's protagonists, David is trapped between his horror of homosexuality and his frantic desire for masculine embraces" (58). For both novelists, according to Sarotte, "the sexually confused stage of adolescence is the chosen ground on which homosexuality ... can briefly flourish and appear to be accepted as healthy, virile, and normal" (58). Discussing *Another Country* (1962), Sarotte compared and contrasted it with other homoerotic works by Baldwin, suggesting that various works present various sexual combinations of characters of different races (or of the same race), with sometimes a Black character or sometimes a white character taking the sexual initiative (59). Sarotte argued that "many young, virile, black rebels" often haunted "Baldwin's imagination" (59), as did the theme of "self-acceptance" (60). Commenting on *Tell Me How Long the Train's Been Gone* (1968), Sarotte observed that the "novel's circular structure (aside from the many flashbacks it contains) is an attempt to unite the ecstatic moment of initiation with the more lucid, less tumultuous, but also enduring moment of the discovery of love, which is, for Baldwin, homosexual happiness" (60).

Stephen Adams (1980: 35–55) argued that *Giovanni's Room* had received the "least attention" of Baldwin's novels (37), argued that if the book's "gay underworld seems squalid and shameful, this is not depicted as any exclusive concomitant of homosexuality," argued that "lovelessness" appears in both the novel's straight and gay characters (41), contrasted the duplicitous David with the appealing Giovanni, and saw the room of the title as a positive, not a negative, symbol (42). Adams saw this book, like Vidal's *The City and the Pillar*, as emphasizing "the unrealized possibilities of homosexual love" and argued that in both novels "a homosexual Eden, briefly glimpsed, is destroyed by the combined action of a rigid masculine code and a puritan legacy of guilt" (44). But Adams considered Baldwin's book "far more powerful" than Vidal's since it "presents a genuinely tragic love affair between two men whose characters are vividly imagined and whose passion and suffering engage our sympathy in a way that [Vidal's] Jim Willard, who seems insipid by comparison, never could" (45). Adams also explored in detail Baldwin's gay-inflected *Another Country* (45–54), often defending it against its critics.

Wayne Dynes (in Dynes 1990: 104) emphasized the strengths of *Giovanni's Room* (1961) and argued that his later works never quite matched his early ones either in their literary quality or their widespread appeal. Pamela S. Shelton, in Malinowski (1994: 23–6), mentioned such matters as Baldwin's bisexuality, his long-time love for a European white man, the ways he explored prejudice both against Blacks and against gays, attacks upon his homoeroticism from other Black writers, and also the ways that his prominence as a champion of African American rights may actually have shielded him from criticism for being gay.

Claude Summers (1990: 172–94), after emphasizing Baldwin's double interest in liberation for Blacks and gays (172), explored *Giovanni's Room* in detail, deemphasizing any autobiographical aspects, suggesting its potentially ambiguous interpretations (173), situating it in its historical contexts, and calling it essentially "a novel of the divided and deceitful self" (174). He stressed its two-part structure (174), its unappealing but fairly sophisticated presentation of the gay subculture in Paris (175–7), its morally flawed narrator (177–81), its stress on the symbolism implied by its title (181), and the way "David's fear of homosexuality is presented as an aspect of his American identity" (184). Summers argued that David's "valorization of innocence and his evasion of experience are related to his obsession with cleanliness," suggesting that this obsession "underlines his emotional isolation, his fear of contamination by involvement with others" (186). Summers appreciated the novel's implication that "homosexual love need not be sordid" (193) and ended by calling the book "a greater artistic achievement than either [Gore Vidal's] *The City and the Pillar* or [Mary Renault's] *The Charioteer*" (194).

David Bergman (1991: 163–87) noted Eldridge Cleaver's attack on Baldwin's homosexuality as anti-Black, suggested Cleaver's own sexual uncertainties, reported that some white critics also reacted negatively to Baldwin as gay, observed that in fact Baldwin typically depicts bisexuals, and quoted Baldwin's own discomfort with "gay" as a self-description. Bergman saw *Giovanni's Room* as dealing with gay self-hatred, praised it for its realism and historical accuracy, reported that Baldwin had suffered more from treating gay themes than from dealing with racial issues (including actually losing a publisher), and quoted Baldwin's view that Blacks were less likely to engage in "fag-baiting" than whites (166). According to Bergman, Baldwin tried to keep his homosexuality private, noting that his essays rarely deal openly with homoeroticism, reported his ambivalent responses to Gide, and examined Baldwin's story "The Outing." Bergman next explored the reactions of Black culture in general (including in Africa) to homosexuality, discussed (at length) Baldwin's complicated relations with Protestantism, and concluded by assessing the inhibiting impact Cleaver's attack had on Baldwin's writing.

David Bergman, in Bristow (1992: 148–63), explored Baldwin's tense relationship with Eldridge Cleaver, saw Cleaver's hostility toward homosexuality as not uncommon in the Black community, suggested that Baldwin re-examined "his own situation" in light of Cleaver's attacks (148), asserted that all of Baldwin's "gay" characters are in fact bisexuals, maintained that Baldwin discouraged exclusively gay readings of his works (150), attempted to explain Baldwin's "resistance to calling himself gay" as well as his occasional heterosexism (151), and stressed Baldwin's view (especially after Cleaver's attack) of sexuality as a private matter (152). Bergman also discussed Baldwin's critical view of André Gide (153), commented on various works by Baldwin (154–6), and suggested that after Cleaver's attack he saw Aimé Césaire as an intellectual and cultural role model (168–9).

Mark Lilly (1993: 144–67) noted that Baldwin's writings often imply or express a comparison between Europe and the United States (144, 156), stated that he was "generally secretive or closeted about his sexual life in public, and took no part in gay rights campaigns (144), compared and contrasted *Giovanni's Room* and *Another Country* (144), and emphasized, in discussing the latter book, the characters'" existential alienation (145) and the influence of European fiction (147–8). Lilly highlighted that novel's stress on the instability and anguish of love and on the variety of possible sexual relationships (149), and he also disputed various critics' interpretations of Baldwin's fiction (150–1). In *Another Country*, Lilly asserted,

> Baldwin describes love exhaustively, sometimes tediously, in order to describe feeling generally; what it is like to have emotions; the feeling of feeling. And the descriptions are not tidily discrete. Love is intimately linked to jealousy, lust, ambition, failure, racism, hate.
>
> (151)

Baldwin felt, according to Lilly, that "cultures rather than innate human characteristics ... put a stop to human flourishing" (156), which is why he preferred France to the United States and why he often combined the themes of racism and homophobia (158). All in all, Lilly offered an unusually lengthy and appreciative discussion of *Another Country* (144–62), which he called a "masterpiece" (163). In contrast, he found *Giovanni's Room* less courageous, partly because that work reflects a "buddy-machismo" ethic with deep roots in American culture (163). According to Lilly, in this book Baldwin is guilty of an "especially repellant kind … of homophobia" against people Baldwin called "effeminate fairies" (164). Lilly considered David's "bisexuality" the "central dilemma at the heart of the novel": he can love and value Giovanni but "longs for the settled, sedate confinement" of heterosexual marriage (165). To its credit, the book rejects "a cosy view of love" (165) and also rejects "the idea of people being fixed in any set of dispositions or traits" (167).

Emmanuel Nelson (Nelson 1993, *Contemporary*: 6–24) discussed Baldwin's unhappy youth (6–7), his relocation to France (7–8), the ways critics have downplayed his sexual themes, and his growing involvement in the civil rights movement (8). Commenting on "Major Works and Themes," Nelson stressed Baldwin's sharp break with early African American fiction in his willingness to deal with homosexuality (9), discussed the importance of that issue in *Go Tell It on the Mountain* (10–11), in the courageous, bittersweet novel *Giovanni's Room* (11), in the refreshingly uncliched *Another Country* (12–13), and in *Tell Me How Long the Time's Been Gone*, where a gay character plays a redemptive role (13–14). Gay issues do not appear in *If Beale Street Could Talk* (14) but are well-integrated and treated unsensationally in *Just Above My Head* (14). A major section of Nelson's article surveys and condemns the often homophobic reactions Baldwin's fiction has provoked (15–20), whether taking the form of embarrassment (16), discomfort (17), distaste (17–18), hysterical prejudice (18–19), or polite silence (19–20).

Shelton Waldrep, in Nelson (1993, *Critical*: 167–80), first discussed Eldridge Cleaver's homophobic misunderstandings of Baldwin (167–75) and then emphasized that Baldwin, although gay, was "a strong supporter of communication between women and men" (176). Marjorie Garber (1995: 125–34) discussed the bisexuality or homosexuality of various important Black writers, the problems Baldwin's homosexuality caused him with the "Black power" movement, the explicit treatment of bisexuality in *Giovanni's Room*, the plot and structure of that book, and the way the book "resonates with the language of many of today's bisexuals, who insist that they fall in love with a person, not a gender" (128). But bisexuality in this book, she thought, was more a device than a reality since "David, the novel's paradigmatic bisexual, seems in fact—and this is very conspicuous once you notice it—not to like women, or sex with women, at all" (128). Nevertheless, Garber considered the book worth reading as a text *about* bisexuality even if David was not a true bisexual or good bisexual role model.

Neil Miller (1995: 284–9) discussed the importance to Baldwin of the suicide of a friend named Eugene Worth, whose death helped prompt Baldwin to become an exile, emphasized the significance of *Giovanni's Room* as a pioneering gay novel, commented on Baldwin's early ambivalence about his homosexuality, and noted Baldwin's skepticism that better and more frequent orgasms led to "psychic and sexual health" (285-6). According to Miller, Baldwin "expressed discomfort with a gay identity and with gay life and culture," felt that each person must "go the way your blood beats," and denied that *Giovanni's Room* was about homosexuality per se ("It's about what happens if you're afraid to love anybody" [287]).

Robert Drake (1998: 319-26) focused mainly on *Giovanni's Room*, emphasizing David's dishonesty and cowardice and calling the book "a perfect novel of shame and deceit, the nails inevitably holding together the wood of the closet. [This book] is perfect because it does not flinch, it does not spare itself any grim candor" (325). Hogan and Hudson (1998: 64-6) noted Baldwin's early pro-gay essay "Preservation of Innocence," observed that civil rights leaders kept their distance from him because he was gay, and reported that he objected to being defined as simply a "homosexual" or as "gay" (65). Reed Woodhouse (1998: 17-35) saw the same novel as both complex and chaotic, called it a "muted narrative of betrayal, confusion, self-deception, and despair" (18), considered it "deeply ambiguous … about the nature of its subject, about its protagonist, and about the purpose for telling the tale" (20), noted that book's "various shadings of anxiety, doubt, and guilt," considered the symbolism of the titular "room" (23), observed defects both in David and in the narrative method (27), saw "fear of smothering" as "David's defining characteristic" (28), and stressed David's obsession with innocence—a trait Woodhouse considered typical of whites (31). Woodhouse concluded that the book was neither pro- nor anti-gay, calling its "apology for homosexuality" mainly "negative" (35).

Gregory Woods (1998: 292-4) examined *Go Tell It on the Mountain* as a gay novel, noting how Baldwin toned down a homoeroticism he would explore more openly in *Giovanni's Room* (292-3), which he called "a sophisticated study" of "internalized homophobia" while reminding readers not to confuse David with Baldwin himself (293). Woods found Giovanni more sympathetic than David but "not much better" morally and called both "effeminophobic" (293). Woods regretted the book's reticence about actual sexual behavior, found its ending both happy and unhappy, suggested that the final tone could be read as optimistic, and was glad that David never ruined Hella's life through marriage (294). Seymour Kleinberg, in Aldrich and Wotherspoon (2001: 27-8), suggested that Baldwin's "lasting fame" derives from his non-fiction, reported that the author's publisher warned him that *Giovanni's Room* "would damage him among the black community and among white liberals" as a spokesman for civil rights (27), noted that he was "excluded from the list of speakers" from the 1963 March on Washington "because civil rights leaders were so uneasy about his outspokenness on the subject of homosexuality," and contended that even for Baldwin gay rights were less important than issues of race (28).

Carbado et al. (2002: 148–9) noted that Baldwin wrote an open defense of homosexuality ("The Preservation of Innocence") after moving to France (148), that *Giovanni's Room* was the first "explicitly gay novel" by an African American, that Baldwin claimed the book was really about "the fear to love," that Baldwin did not openly identify as gay and in fact had planned to marry, that nonetheless his "most intimate relationships were with men," and that his novel *Another Country* is unusual in its open, honest depiction of Black gay life (149).

Emmanuel Nelson (Summers 2002: 68–70) mentioned Baldwin's "troubled" early years resulting from family tensions and from racial prejudice and homophobia, his later focus on connections between both kinds of prejudice, the importance of his early essay "The Preservation of Innocence," and an early story titled "Outing" (69). Nelson traced gay themes in Baldwin's fiction (69–70) and noted that his "open and honest explorations of gay and bisexual themes" represented "a sharp break from the established African-American literary conventions" (70).

Colm Tóibín (2002: 195–226) mainly surveyed Baldwin's life but did comment on his depiction of sexual politics (202), the problems his homosexuality created for publishers (209), his strong interest in love between siblings (213–14), the Civil Rights movement's hostility toward gays (217–20), Eldridge Cleaver's distaste for Baldwin's sexuality (221–3), and the special insights Baldwin brought to his writings thanks to being discriminated against both as a black and a homosexual (225). Douglas A. Martin (in Canning 2009: 189–95) noted Baldwin's rejection of modern sexual categories (189), discussed the relevance of Baldwin's own life (and love life) to *Giovanni's Room* (189–90), outlined the novel's reception, including harsh criticism from Norman Mailer (190–2), returned to the relevance of Baldwin's love life (192–4), and then discussed his own (194–5). Emmanuel Nelson, in Nelson (2009: 57–64), discussed such matters as Baldwin's abusive stepfather, the writer's early involvement in the church and knowledge of Christianity (58), his "growing racial, sexual, and artistic" alienation, and the way emigrating to France helped free him from such pressures (58). Nelson stressed Baldwin's non-violent approach to racial tensions (58), praised the universality of *Go Tell It on the Mountain*, and stressed the sexual aspects of that book (59). Discussing *Giovanni's Room*, Nelson praised Baldwin's "courage and defiance," compared it to works by Henry James, called it a "bittersweet remembrance of a gay romance," and observed how it conflicted with cultural standards of its day (60). Commenting on *Another Country*, Nelson stressed its exploration of the "inability to love authentically," noted how it combined both racial and sexual protest, and suggested that it envisaged a "new Jerusalem—an imaginary America—free of repressive racial boundaries and sexual categories" (60). Nelson discussed the book's complex structure, diverse characters, and innovative, non-pathological presentation of gay persons and themes, suggesting that this novel shows the "redemptive potential" of gay suffering (61). He argued that *Another Country* is "one of the very few pre-Stonewall novels in which gay romance does not terminate in murder or suicide," implying, at the end, "at least tentative signs of wholeness and durability" in gay relationships (61). Nelson contended that the possibility that "homosexuality may contain redemptive possibilities is developed even more vigorously in Baldwin's fourth novel," *Tell Me How Long the Train's Been Gone*, which is thematically typical of his work but which also suggests that gay identity and Black militancy need not conflict (61). According to Nelson, in Baldwin's final novel (*Just Above My Head*), where homosexuality is a key concern, "Baldwin reveals a relaxed and more sophisticated attitude" toward the topic: "Baldwin treats it less self-consciously, less polemically, and less stridently," integrating it "smoothly" into the plot (62). Nelson closed by assessing Baldwin's entire career, noting how Baldwin was often sharply criticized (and occasionally defended) by other Blacks, including Black feminists, for treating gay male sexuality among African Americans (63).

Christopher Bram (2012: 39–53, 96–100) stressed the value of seeing Baldwin as a gay (not simply black) writer (39), noted that he had sex with both men and women but considered himself gay "by the time he was twenty" (40), maintained that Baldwin's youthful writings are often angry (41), called attention to an early but little-known essay on homosexuality (43), suggested that "mainstream critics prefer [*Go Tell It on the Mountain*] simply because there are fewer gay elements" (45), discussed the difficulties of publishing gay fiction in the 1950s (47), called *Giovanni's Room* "*the* classic coming-out novel" (50), maintained that fear of love is the key theme of this book (and a prominent theme in much of Baldwin's later fiction [51]), and praised *Giovanni's Room* for being more "intimate" and "real" than *Go Tell It* (51). Later, Bram disputed claims that *Another Country*, a second "gay" novel, fails after its first eighty pages (96).

TRUMAN CAPOTE (1924–84). Roger Austen (1977: 114–16) admired Capote's ability to avoid, through his versatility, being "pigeonholed as a gay writer," nevertheless saw "gay overtones" in many of his works, and suggested that Capote deliberately made the main character of *Other Voices, Other Rooms* too young to be obviously gay (114). Austen agreed with another critic (William Nance) who saw Randolph in that book "as a generalized symbol of all humanity in its need for love" (115), and stressed the stylistic appeal Capote's writings hold for gay readers (116).

Georges-Michel Sarotte (1978: 46–50), although noting that Joel in *Other Voices, Other Rooms* fits the "sissy" stereotype found in some previous American novels, argued that "his emotional development is so meticulously described that he takes on an allegorical quality," so that "Capote's novel treats the renunciation of virility and the conditions that favor it" (46). Sarotte argued that Joel, like his fictional predecessors, is an outsider full of sexual fantasies, and that his only virile role models are, ironically, a tomboy and memories of Pepe Alvarez (46-7). "Capote's novel," Sarotte wrote, "deals with the perilous moment of passage from childhood to adolescence when everything can be lost or won. Yet the chances of Joel's becoming heterosexual are slim indeed" (48). Sarotte called the book "a novel of self-recognition, particularly homosexual recognition," and said that from "an allegorical viewpoint, its moral is to follow one's basic nature against the ideals of a hostile society." According to Sarotte, "Joel's refuge in homosexuality is the only solution to the anxiety plaguing anyone who adopts his nature against the sexual mores of society" (48).

Stephen Adams (1980: 57-60) argued that Capote's *Other Voices, Other Rooms* creates a world "animated by characteristics popularly attributed to the homosexual male: freakishness, affectation and effeminacy" (57), arguing that the novel "remains very much on the level of a peepshow" and that it implies that "homosexuality is a failure of manliness" (58). Adams saw Randolph in this book as "simply a grown-up version of the 'sissy' stereotype," called Capote's characters "consistently bizarre," and saw its language as "multi-layered, ornate, [and] weighed down with decoration and gaudy effect" (59). Adams thought that in this book Capote presented "the homosexual's initiation into adult life" as "an act of resignation to a deathly, ghost-ridden existence" (60) and, in general, contrasted his work with that of Carson McCullers (60).

An anonymous article in Dynes (1990: 198-9) took a generally dim view of Capote's writing (except some of his earlier works) and suggested that in public life "he often served the function (rivaled only by Liberace) of reinforcing for a mass audience their stereotype" of effeminate homosexuality. Claude Summers (1990: 130-3) argued that Capote saw homosexuality as "less a social problem that a manifestation of love's essential irrationality" and argued that he explored "the universal human need for love" (130). He considered Capote's *Other Voices, Other Rooms* less philosophically serious than similar work by Carson McCullers (131) and noted the book's flaws in style, characterization, symbolism, and plot (132). Summers also faulted the book's unappealing, stereotypical presentation of homosexuality (132–3), arguing that Capote reduces it to "the status of an affliction" and links it to a "death wish" (133). Peter G. Christensen, in Malinowski 1994 (64–7), commented on the atmospheric nature of Capote's fiction, the eventual damage he did to his own reputation, and his general avoidance of openly gay themes, especially any featuring "healthy mutual relationships between men," although "Unspoiled Monsters" is "full of gay name-dropping and bits of gossip." Christensen called *Other Voices, Other Rooms* the "one 'gay' book for which Capote will be remembered," thanks, in part, to its relatively straightforward eighth chapter, despite the view of some critics that the book reinforces "stereotypes of gay male grotesqueness, effeminacy, and escapism," although Christensen himself commends its general "complexity." He argued that homosexuality "emerges as a difficult-to-assess subtext in *In Cold Blood*," asserted that the "nonfiction collection *The Dogs Bark: Public People and Private Places* contains several journalistic pieces that feature gay and lesbian bisexual personalities that are not presented as such," and contended that "Capote wanted to be seen in the tradition of French gay writing, often comparing himself to … Marcel Proust." According to Christensen, "Capote's failure—perhaps cowardice—in confronting the gay potential in [his nonfiction] constitutes the opposite pole of his later obsession with writing tell-all stories of what really happened in the world of the jet-set." He concluded that Capote's habit of "locating homosexuality between addiction and genius contrasts strongly with the view of homosexuality in *Answered Prayers*, where it is much closer to everyday vulgarity and social climbing" (66).

Hogan and Hudson (1998: 120–1) noted that a magazine called 1966 the "year of Capote," that he drew on scandalous confessions both in *In Cold Blood* and in *Answered Prayers*, that he was "out" almost from the start, that John Cheever called him "'a conspicuous male coquette' who seemed 'to excite more curiosity than intolerance,'" and that others "cringed at his public manner, believing he reinforced the stereotype of the gay man as 'bitchy queen' and, especially in his later years," "tragic homosexual" (121). Shelton Waldrep, in Aldrich and Wotherspoon (2001: 75), called Capote "one of the most photographed gay men of his generation," noted that the narrator of *Answered Prayers* is bisexual, praised his late work *Music for Chameleons*, and regretted that *Answered Prayers* remained unfinished.

Thomas Dukes (Summers 2002: 132–3) noted some characteristic thematic emphases (on sensitivity, emotions, older women) and personality traits ("wit, barbs, and outright insults"), commented that perhaps "the clearest example of Capote's homosexual sensitivity is in *Breakfast at Tiffany's* (132), suggested that Holly's progress seemed to reflect gay males" desire to find freedom in big cities, and argued that Capote's combined early feminism and concern with oppression of gays led to "seriously underappreciated" art (133). Dukes regretted the misogyny and cruelty of *Answered Prayers*, argued that prejudice and a gay identity shaped Capote's career, suggested that Capote sometimes used his gay persona to charm straights and convince them to let down their guards, and opined that even if Capote failed as a major novelist, his strength in the face of social hostility toward gays was admirable and may result in a positive reevaluation of his writings (133).

Christopher Bram (2012: 4–11, 64–8, 91–6) set Capote's early career in its gay contexts (4–11), noted that one editor called *Other Voices, Other Rooms* "'the faggots' *Huckleberry Finn*" (8), and reported that Capote, "disappointed with the reception of his book, ... did not write directly about homosexuality again for almost thirty years" (11). Later, Bram discussed Capote's love-life (65), accused some of his reviewers of "fag-baiting" (66), called *Breakfast at Tiffany's* "a romantic friendship between a straight woman and a gay man" that can never be sexual (67), reported that Gore Vidal accused Capote of stealing the main character from Christopher Isherwood's *Berlin Stories* (67), and suggested that *In Cold Blood* had a gay subtext (94).

GORE VIDAL (1925–2012). Roger Austen (1977: 118–25) credited Vidal with creating, in *The City and the Pillar*, the first gay character in American fiction whose "gayness was not camouflaged" in various ways, noted that Vidal had written an earlier, unpublished work with a main gay character, saw gay aspects in yet another Vidal work titled *In a Yellow Wood* (118), speculated that Vidal delayed publication of *The City* in order to first build his reputation as a serious writer (119), reported both positive and negative reactions to that novel (121–2), argued that "Vidal succeeds in showing the utter naturalness of homosexual relations only in the campfire scene" (122), and faulted the novel for presenting most of its gay characters, and gay life in general, as less than wholly appealing (123).

Georges-Michel Sarotte (1978: 23–8, 51–4) said that *The City* "opened the door for the explicitly homosexual novel" (23), reported the hostility of some early critics (26), called it "the first wholly homosexual novel to reach a wide public" (26), discussed Vidal's somewhat flawed "attempt to break the stereotype of the effeminate, contemptible homosexual" (52), and noted that Vidal's next novel, *The Season of Comfort* (1949), "deals with the ambiguous world of adolescence where sex between virile, healthy boys is 'normal', part of the accepted morality, and thus does not produce in them incapacitating neuroses of lead them to take refuge in a special reassuring but sordid milieu" (52). Sarotte discussed similar characters and themes in Vidal's 1956 story "The Zenner Trophy," where a shy, insecure adult is given the uncomfortable task of rebuking and punishing an athletic, self-confident gay youth (53–4). Sarotte commented that although a gay utopia might be possible in the short fiction of this period, a "happy homosexual rebel" was far less likely to be found in this era's novels (54). He also noted that "the sun and water and showers are pivotal in *The City and the Pillar* and *The Season of Comfort*, where sexual awakening similarly occurs under the aegis of bodily cleanliness" (58).

Stephen Adams (1980: 15–34) recounted the initially negative critical reception of *The City and the Pillar* (15), compared and contrasted that novel with other, similar works of its era (16), noted that Vidal's book was pathbreaking because it focused on a "clean-cut, all American," masculine protagonist (17) similar to ancient Greek heroes (18), and emphasized the importance of the book's "circular form" (18). Adams argued, however, that in "his eagerness to counter the equation of homosexuality with effeminacy," Vidal reinforces "crude stereotypes he reproves elsewhere" (20). Adams emphasized the inability of Jim, the novel's main character, to "enter deeply into any relationship," so that the book functions as "a study of self-deception" (21) in which Jim can seem "predictable, even dull" (23). Adams saw echoes of this novel's themes in later works by Vidal, such as "several of the stories from the collection *A Thirsty Evil* (1956) and, most notably, in the novel *Myra Breckinridge* (1968)" (25), arguing that in the latter book the "earnest moralizing of *The City and the Pillar* is translated into outrageous comedy; its prosaic realism is exchanged for a high camp travesty of artistic forms" (27) that "satirizes Hollywood's cultural stranglehold on sexual identity" (28). Adams argued that although "Myra is the grotesque product of the society Vidal satirizes, she is brought to attack those same values" (31), so that the "homosexual male, the woman, and eventually the lesbian, join forces within the person of Myra Breckinridge to overthrow" sexual tyranny (31–2). Adams saw in Vidal's work in general a view of homosexuality as "a normal, healthy, human response that has been distorted by society's narrow prescription of the *right* sexual equation" (33).

Claude Summers (1990: 112–29) noted that *The City and the Pillar* "was one of the first explicitly gay fictions to reach a large audience" (112), stressing its emphasis on an inflexible homosexuality rather than a bisexual orientation (113), its lack of sentimentality, its exploration of gay subcultures, its refusal to moralize, and its "hard-edged irony" (113). According to Summers, among the central points of the book are that "repression distorts the expression of homosexuality and creates a subculture that itself contributes to that distortion" (114). He added that perhaps the book's "most revolutionary gesture" was its suggestion (unusual at the time) that "the homosexual experience itself is valuable" since it may "lead to healthy introspection and valuable social criticism" (115). Summers defended much of the book's style, praised its mythic dimensions, admitted its occasional melodrama, and explored its two-part structure (116). Discussing the book's plot and design, Summers stressed its interest in the coming-out process, its skepticism about "false idealization" and romanticism (118), its allusions to classic (and classical) gay texts, such as Plato's *Symposium* (119), and its ironic treatment of seemingly idyllic sexual initiation (120). In Summer's view, Jim, Ronald, and Paul

> can be seen as cases of arrested development not because they are gay, but because they so idealize the past and so manufacture illusions that they are unable either to live fully in the present or to accept the imperfections of reality. All of the central characters are emotionally immature. Trapped by distorting dreams, haunted by their pasts, seeking the recovery of a lost wholeness, they live in a world of illusion.
>
> (120–1)

Summers found these characters relatively uninteresting and saw many of the minor characters as stereotypes in ways not true of Jim Willard (121). Discussing the book's plot, Summers noted its hostility toward effeminacy (122), its exploration of sexual role-reversals (125), the relative failure of the novel's "stagnant" second part (125), and the "unconvincing and melodramatic" original conclusion—an ending Vidal eventually revised and improved (127). Summers ended by praising the novel, especially given Vidal's youth when he wrote it (128–9).

James Levin, in Malinowski (1994: 379–82), traced the development of Vidal's use of gay themes and characters in such works as *In a Yellow Wood*, the important and innovative *The City and the Pillar*, various writings for Hollywood, a historical novel titled *Julian*, the campy *Myra Breckenridge*, and *Live from Golgotha*. Drake (1998: 355–62) saw *Myra* as a comic rumination on the limitations of conventional sexual identities and called it "a testament to the power of the gay imagination, perhaps its manifesto" (361). Hogan and

Hudson (1998: 559-60) wrote that Vidal, [s]exually attracted to both men and women,

> has consistently rejected the very concept of homosexuality, believing terms like 'heterosexual', 'homosexual', and 'gay' have no real meaning other than as descriptors of types of sex acts. Nevertheless, ... two years before Stonewall, he was one of the few positive voices on a 1967 *CBS Reports* program on 'homosexuals'.
>
> (560)

Reed Woodhouse (1998: 53-62) focused mainly on *Myra Breckinridge*, summarizing the plot and stressing Myra's "shamelessness" (60). Seymour Kleinberg, in Aldrich and Wotherspoon (2001: 421-2), noted that Vidal was a friend of Tennessee Williams and an enemy of Truman Capote (421), observed that in *The City and the Pillar* Vidal challenged standard views of gays as "effeminate, neurotic, [and] unnatural," commented on the *New York Times*'s attack on the book and its long hostility toward Vidal's later work, and reported that Vidal felt this episode had damaged his whole career (422). According to Kleinberg, *Myra Breckinridge* was Vidal's own favorite work, and Kleinberg quoted Vidal's own comments about his deeply cold personality (422).

Edmund Miller (Summers 2002: 665-7) noted Vidal's straightforward treatment of gay themes, his depiction of gays who do not fit gay stereotypes (665), his assumption that "everyone is bisexual," his frequent use of gay characters, and his efforts to "mainstream" gay issues (666). Miller observed that *Myron* failed with critics and the public, called *Two Sisters* especially successful as a gay work, stressed Vidal's unusual frankness about his own sexuality, and praised the early collection *A Thirsty Evil* for its treatment of gay issues (666).

Paul Reidinger (in Canning 2009: 318-24) discussed the relevance of Vidal's *Palimpsest* to his own love life (318-19), praised the book's effective irony, surveyed Vidal's career (320-2), commended the book for its range of interesting material (322), and discussed how the events the book discusses were relevant to Vidal's entire life as a writer (322-4). Martin Kich, in Nelson (2009: 623-7), noted Vidal's criticism, in the 1960s, of both "the forces of institutional reaction and the radical movements that seemed, paradoxically, all too ready to adapt their own versions of cant and conformity" and called Vidal "[a]ristocratically disdainful of American mass politics and mass culture" (623). Commenting on the early reception of *The City and the Pillar*, Kich observed that the book not only was a bestseller but was also widely condemned both by the public and by elite critics (624). He discussed Vidal's revision of the book (624-5), the greater acceptance of the revised version

(625), the nature and reception of the books that followed this novel, and the importance of the "seven stories collected in *A Thirsty Evil* (1956)," which "address a broad range of gay themes" (625). Kich commented on Vidal's growing interest in historical fiction (625–6), his exploration of sex and gender in *Myra Breckinridge*, and the differences between that book and its sequel, *Myron* (626).

Christopher Bram (2012: 3–13, 117–28) set Vidal in the contexts of homosexual society in the post-war period (3–5), discussed his uneasy friendship with Truman Capote (whom he considered too flamboyant [5]), recounted the genesis of *The City and the Pillar* (5–6), noted the almost simultaneous publication of this book and Capote's *Other Voices, Other Rooms* (6), explained how Vidal later revised his novel (especially its ending [6]), and called most of the book "often tartly matter-of-fact" (7). After recounting its plot, Bram detailed its mixed critical reception (8–9), noted that it nonetheless became a best-seller (9), said that Vidal would falsely claim, years later, that it had "destroyed his career," suggested that Vidal's later prose style was influenced by Capote's, called *Myra Breckinridge* a "wonderfully mad fantasy about camp, gender, and the movies," and reported that Vidal seemed enduringly hurt by some of the reaction to *The City and the Pillar* (10). Later, Bram discussed Vidal's career in the 1960s (117–28), and focused on his infamous dispute with the conservative writer William F. Buckley, Jr., in which Buckley angrily called Vidal a "queer" on national television (121–8).

FRANK O'HARA (1926–66). Ward Houser, in Dynes (1990: 914–15), mainly discussed the traits and origins of O'Hara's style, especially the influence of everyday gay banter of the time. Hogan and Hudson (1998: 421) mentioned O'Hara's friendship with John Ashbery, his unusual openness, in the 1950s, about his homosexuality, his interest (which sometimes led to violence) in pursuing straight men, and his general interest in cruising (421). Gregory Woods (1998: 300–01) emphasized O'Hara's use of gay (even camp) slang, which he sometimes mixed with "'high' cultural languages such as those of Surrealism" (301). Wood interestingly observed that camp

> is a social and sociable mode of behavior and speech: to use it, you have to know it; to know it, you have to have learned it from someone else; to practice it satisfactorily, you have to feel in need of some kind of audience. Camp signals the existence of a gay subculture.
>
> (301)

ALLEN GINSBERG (1926–97). Roger Austen (1977: 184–6) thought that even in *Howl* Ginsberg "took care to swathe gay sex in mystical wrappings" and allude to straight sex as well, noting that many commentators "have preferred to sidestep" the issue of homosexuality in Ginsberg's writings (185). Robert K. Martin (1979: 165–70) discussed Ginsberg's invocations of Whitman, his less apparent debts to Genet, his alleged failure to develop as a writer, his eventual loss of magic and humor, and the numerous paralyzing contradictions in his later poetry. Gregory Woods (1987: 195–211) argued that Ginsberg works "within a gay tradition", suggested that *Howl* is less insistently gay than is often assumed (196–7), thought Ginsberg linked sexual and political freedom (203–4), cast doubt on Ginsberg's occasional proclamations of interest in women (206), called "Journal Night Thoughts" one of Ginsberg's best love poems (208), and, throughout, offered many readings of numerous individual poems.

Paul Christensen, in Malinowski (1994: 159–62), discussed Ginsberg's early but initially hidden homoerotic yearnings, his friendships with such other writers as Jack Kerouac and William Burroughs, his slow development as a writer, his eventual "coming out," the importance of his homosexuality to his liberated style of writing, and especially the importance of his famously shocking poem titled *Howl*. According to Christensen, Ginsberg's erotic poems become less plaintive and more celebratory after he met his long-term partner Peter Orlovsky in 1954. Robert Drake (1998: 329–30) credited Ginsberg with having created "a startlingly sexy, spiritual body of work that redefined the potential of the gay poetic imagination" (330). Hogan and Hudson (1998: 250) commented that *Howl* "openly celebrated the joys of rough gay male sex" and, after surveying his career, observed that Ginsberg defended the controversial North American Man-Boy Love Association.

Adam Carr, in Aldrich and Wotherspoon (2001: 160–1), noted Ginsberg's early familiarity with Whitman's works, reported that *Howl* "made him one of the first openly gay celebrities" in the United States (160), and observed that he considered himself a poet-prophet. Carr claimed that Ginsberg's long-time lover Peter Orlovsky "became increasingly heterosexual" and that Ginsberg himself was masochistic (161). Scott McLemee (Summers 2002: 307–8) noted Ginsberg's fame, emphasis in *Howl* on eroticism, eventual acceptance of his homosexuality thanks to psychotherapy, resemblance in style to Walt Whitman (307), and important 1974 interview with *Gay Sunshine* (308). Ernest Smith (Nelson 2003: 178–87) called Ginsberg the most famous American post-war poet (178), emphasized the poet's complicated relationship with his mother (178–9), discussed his developing homosexuality, especially after meeting and reading other unconventional writers (179–80), and mentioned his growing commitment to gay rights and other "radical" causes (180–1). Noting Ginsberg's often explicit language (184), Smith also surveyed (sometimes negative) critical reactions to his work (184–5) but ended by emphasizing his links to Whitman as a gay poet (185).

David Bergman (in Canning 2009: 183–8) noted Ginsberg's ability to combine spirituality and blunt physicality, partly by employing a "sweet campy zaniness that gains pathos from boyish vulnerability" (185). Bergman knew of no poem before *Howl* "that spoke so straightforwardly and rapturously about anal sex" in a way that expressed Ginsberg's comfort—or attempted comfort—with his own body (186). Commenting on the poem's machismo and focus on Ginsberg's mother (186–7), Bergman found the poem's last two-thirds as queer as the first, with Blake a key influence on the middle section and Whitman a key influence on the third (187). Michele Erfer, in Nelson (2009: 258–61), noted that Ginsberg was influenced by left-wing politics, Walt Whitman, William Blake, and his mother's mental illness (258), then surveyed his life, career, and friendships (259–60), and finally commented on his support for gay rights, for "nonmonogamous free love," and for love in general (261).

Christopher Bram (2012: 24–38) noted that after the Second World War, gay poets began to write about their sexuality in quiet but obvious ways (24), suggested that Ginsberg's sexual relations with straight men were designed more for *their* pleasure than his (26), called *Howl* a "coming-out poem" (31), said that Ginsberg's openness in this work about his own sex life encouraged its openness in many other ways, said that most of the poem's "energy is sexual" (32), noted that many negative critics considered the text less disgusting than boring (34), recounted its commercial success (36), and suggested that recent commentators have downplayed both the poem's and Ginsberg's homosexual aspects (37).

JOHN ASHBERY (1927–2017). David Bergman (1991: 52–9) discussed Ashbery's response to Whitman (especially the latter's imaginativeness and emphasis on innocence), commented on Ashbery's poetic self-portraits, suggested that some of his poems reveal sexual anxiety, dealt at length with "self-Portrait in a Convex Mirror," and concluded by asserting that this poet's acceptance of his "weak ego identity" is central to his impressive literary achievement. Charles Shively, in Malinowski (1994: 14–17), discussed Ashbery's early interest in LGB writers, the development of his styles, and the relative reticence of poetry that might sometimes seem homoerotic. Gregory Woods (1998: 387–8) commented especially on "Qualm," stressing how that poem, like much of Ashbery's work, offers a perspective "from which the ordinary looks extraordinary and the mundane sublime" (388). Terrence Johnson (Summers 2002: 53-4) mainly discussed Ashbery's style and friendships, noting that "there have been few attempts to read Ashbery as a gay poet" (54). Christopher Schmidt, in Nelson (2009: 39-41), discussed such matters as the strong praise for Ashbery among critics and other writers (39), his early obscurity (39-40), and his style, techniques, and the development of his career (40). Schmidt reported that some critics have linked the poet's early obscure style to a need to hide his homosexuality and observed that by the 1970s he had become freer in dealing with gay subject matter (41).

EDWARD ALBEE (1928-). Sarotte 1978 (134-49) reported on various "gay" interpretations of Albee's works (134-6), observed that Albee had rejected them, suggested that the plays *were* often gay whatever Albee's intentions (136), and commented on the gay aspects of such works as *Who's Afraid of Virginia Woolf?*, *The Zoo Story*, *The Sandbox*, *The American Dream*, and *The Death of Bessie Smith* (137-9). According to Sarotte, Albee's "handsome youths and good-looking blond boys appear with a monotonous and revealing regularity," including Nick in *Who's Afraid* (139), and all four characters in that play can be seen as disguised gay men or at least as relevant to gay family situations, including an oppressive mother (Martha) and weak father (George [140]). Sarotte traced the play's anti-gay stereotypes to such writers as Edmund Bergler, Irving Bieber, and Ernest Hemingway in *To Have and Have Not* (140), and he argued that Albee felt forced to deal with straight characters and, partly for that reason, took revenge on them in his plays, especially when depicting parents (141-2). He called *Who's Afraid* "a homosexual play from every point of view, in all it situations and all its symbols" (142), doubted that homosexuality was relevant to *Tiny Alice* (142), noted disagreements with this claim (143), and reported Albee's rejection of any such interpretation (144). Sarotte saw touches of gay issues in *A Delicate Balance* (144-5), many in *The Ballad of the Sad Café* (145-8), and some in *Malcolm* (148-9).

John Clum (1992: 174-89) compared and contrasted Albee with Tennessee Williams and William Inge, particularly in their receptions by homophobic critics (174-6), quoting extensively from those critics while disputing their arguments (176-81), including arguments from the "artistic left" (178) and even from gay critics themselves (181-3). "Albee," Clum wrote, "has been attacked from all sides," both for "being closeted and, therefore, distorting the truth of heterosexual relationships, women, and homosexual relationships," despite Albee's relatively little interest in sexuality *per se* (183). Critics helped confine

Albee to a rigid closet, refusing to take his ideas seriously *as* ideas (183), despite the real power his gay interests contributed to his play's frequent effectiveness (1984). Clum discussed several plays in particular, noting the way gay life is sometimes depicted (implicitly or overtly) in negative ways, especially in *Zoo Story* and *Who's Afraid of Virginia Woolf* (184–8). Clum conceded that Albee was less successful than Williams and Inge at creating women (186) and that his tone is often nihilistic, empty, and superficial (188), but he valued *Who's Afraid* partly for its camp sensibility (188) and for its ability to present heterosexuality "from the 'other side'" in a way that was often more effective that "inside" views created by straights (189).

Michael Bronski (Malinowski 1994: 4–5) surveyed the ups and downs of Albee's career (4), emphasized the impact of homophobic criticism, cited numerous examples of such criticism, noted that some critics accused Albee of exploring gay themes using straight characters, and observed that Albee and his writings were often attacked either for being closeted or for being too overtly gay (5). John Clum (Haggerty 2000: 42–3) repeated many arguments from his 1994 book, noted the misogynistic aspects of Albee's early work (42), and commented on various examples of Albee's themes, including "the often denied but omnipresent homoerotic dimension of relations between men" (42–3). Hogan and Hudson (1998: 23–4) noted that some early critics accused Albee of using straight characters to explore gay themes, that the lead characters in *Who's Afraid* were sometimes seen as "a gay couple in disguise," that Albee has defended himself by claiming to be proudly gay but resistant to "ghettoization," and that he has sometimes written openly about gay people and gay issues (24). John Clum (Summers 2002: 18–19) traced Albee's career, said his "place in the history of gay drama is ambiguous," commented that his early "Off-Broadway work was, for its time, daring" in treating gay themes (18), and suggested that his women often resemble drag queens and that "there is always a hint of the homoerotic in his male-male confrontations" (19). Thomas Dukes (Nelson 2003: 1–10) mentioned Albee's birth name (Edward Harvey), his tensions with the parents who adopted him (1), his first homosexual experience as a teenager, his later romantic involvement with the composer William Flannagan (2), and the ups and downs of his personal and professional lives (2–4). Dukes emphasized Albee's themes of connections, family life, confrontation, alienation, oppressive bourgeois values, and attacks on facile optimism (4–5) as well as his frequent absurdism, "verbal games" in realistic contexts, and ability to create empathy even for unattractive characters (6). He surveyed critical reactions to Albee's work (8–9) but in general paid relatively little attention to gay issues.

Christopher Bram (2012: 75–87) discussed Albee's tensions with his adoptive parents, his first gay sexual experience (75), his relationship with William Flanagan (each shared a "weakness of alcohol and melancholy"), an early Albee play on gay themes (*Ye Watchers and Ye Lonely Ones*), and positive response to *The Zoo Story* among New York gay artists (76). Bram mentioned gay elements in that play (77), Albee's break-up with Flanagan, echoes of their frequent arguments in *Who's Afraid*, the quarreling in that play "as a kind of love-making," and the play's memorable language (78). Bram reported the early popularity of *Who's Afraid*, especially as a treatment of marriage (79), but then some later attacks on the work as word began to circulate that Albee was gay (80). Similar attacks, for the same reason, affected *Tiny Alice* (81) and became prominent in later attacks on *Who's Afraid* (81–2), which were sometimes "poisonous" (82). Susan Sontag's famous essay on "camp" had recently appeared and may have helped inadvertently trigger these homophobic criticisms of Albee and other gay playwrights (83–5)—criticisms which especially affected *Who's Afraid* but which also had a more general effect: if gay writers wrote about gay life, they weren't [considered] universal. But if they wrote about straight life they were distorting what they despised or "didn't understand" (85). Bram suggested that the movie version of *Who's Afraid*—starring the famously heterosexual Richard Burton and Elizabeth Taylor—helped minimize further claims that the play's characters were gays in disguise (85–6).

THOM GUNN (1929–2004). Robert K. Martin (1979: 179–90) contrasted Gunn's lean, cool, sculpted style with the exuberant writing of Robert Duncan, claimed that Gunn avoided describing actual love-making, stressed the early poems' sadness and focus on the impossible, and asserted that "Gunn feels guilty about his homosexuality ... [and] cannot reconcile the needs of the body with the claims of the mind" (180). Martin noted Gunn's fascination with male motorcyclists, his potential drift into misogyny, his frequently macho tone, his interest in sadomasochism, and his focus on anonymous sex. According to Martin, Gunn's later poems, however, suggested that the poet had now "acquired a faith in the restorative powers of love and sees a possibility for the reconciliation of all opposites in the moment of orgasmic or mystic perception" (189). Gregory Woods (1987: 212–31) emphasized the martial imagery and concerns with virility and power in Gunn's early poems (213–14), stressed his focus on "posing tough guy[s]" (214) and their narcissism (217), thought the violence implied by some of Gunn's poems was superficial (220), highlighted the variety of poetic forms and modes and sexual identities Gunn often explored (221), claimed that Gunn saw love and sex as "metamorphic forces" (222), especially in *Moly* (223), quoted Gunn about the freeing effect that his coming out had had upon his writing (229), and concluded that Gunn's career exemplifies the general progress of the gay liberation movement (230).

Michael Bronski, in Malinowski (1994: 171-3), recounted Gunn's youth in Britain, his emigration to the United States, the profound impact on his writing of his early relationship with Mike Kitay, his increasingly open writings about his homosexuality, and the evidence of that topic in such books as *Moly*, *My Sad Captains*, and *The Man with Night Sweats*—the latter a moving response to the AIDS epidemic. Roger Bowen, in Aldrich and Wotherspoon (2001: 173-4), quoted Gregory Wood's view of Gunn as a "model of the contemporary gay poet in transition," noted that Gunn identified as Anglo-American (173), reported various influences and poetic affiliations, saw an "occluded sexual identity" in some early poems, and praised the later Gunn for embracing "the familial strengths of gay culture" and the "authenticity of choice and allegiance" (174).

Colm Tóibín (2002: 227-41) commented on Gunn's special importance for gay readers (229), the disguised sexuality in his early works (230-1), the different ways gay and straight readers might respond to his *Collected Poems* (231-2), his manner as a public reader of his poems (233), his interests as a critic of poetry (234-5), his differences from other poets of his generation (236), his long fascination with the poetry of Sir Thomas Wyatt (237-8), and the role his homosexuality played in the creation of his own best poems (240-1). Douglas Chambers (Summers 2002: 328-9) observed that "Gunn's poetry has a popular reputation for sex and drugs and leather," that *Fighting Terms* and *The Sense of Movement* favor "a heroic masculine posing" over "the dull passivity of conformity" (328); that "Jack Straw's Castle" may be Gunn's "greatest poem"; that from 1967 onwards his poems seem more appealingly relaxed; that the poems in *The Man With Night Sweats* may be "some of the finest gay elegies ever written"; and that Gunn has influenced other significant gay poets (329). George Klawitter (Nelson 2003: 188-97) offered a substantive response to Gunn as a gay poet, emphasizing his early lack of religion, his mother's feminism and communism, his happy childhood but his parents' divorce (188), his mother's death when Gunn was 15, and the positive impact of his army service (189). Klawitter stressed the key importance of Gunn's relationship with Mike Kitay; their time in San Francisco and Texas; (189); Gunn's positive view of drugs; and the great success of *The Man with Night Sweats* (190). According to Klawitter, the younger Gunn admired motorcycle culture and action rather than stagnation (190); wrote originally in ways that disguised the gender of his erotically involved characters (191); but gradually became more open about the poems' homoeroticism (192) and eventually began writing openly about AIDS and explicit gay sex (193–4). Klawitter commented in detail on several poems and ended with a solid survey of critics' reactions to the gay aspects of Gunn's work (195–6).

Gregory Woods, in Nelson (2009: 281–4), noted Gunn's range of moods, poetic development, "sexual discretion" during the 1950s, and lessening interest in "aggressive masculinity" (282). Woods discussed Gunn's meditations on his own early suppressed homoeroticism, the less restrictive style of his later poems (282), and his growing interest in varied sensual pleasures (282–3). Woods also commented on Gunn's later combinations of varied styles, the decline in his British reputation after he left for the United States, the respect he won on both sides of the Atlantic for his "serious" poems in *The Man with Night Sweats*, and the ways that book engages not just with AIDS but with many of his typical themes (283). Woods called *Boss Cupid* in some ways "Gunn's most sexual book," suggested that "he took the pleasures and pains that came with gayness as being signs of a commonality of human experience" (283), and suggested Gunn's unusual interest, for a gay poet, "in community, more than in the individualist pursuit of pleasure" (284).

Christopher Bram (2012: 230–2) said that Gunn wrote some of "the strongest poems about AIDS" (230), calling *The Man with Night Sweats* "lean, tough poems, with no emotional fat" (232).

ADRIENNE RICH (1929–2012). Gabriele Griffin (1993: 55–9) charted Rich's initial emphasis on feminism and her later stress on lesbianism. Paulina Palmer (1993: 18–20) discussed Richa's influential concepts of "compulsory heterosexuality" and the "lesbian continuum" (of woman-centered thought), noting the criticism the latter idea evoked from lesbians who thought it de-emphasized sex itself—criticism Griffin disputed. Andrea Cumpston, in Malinowski (1994: 324–7), began by commenting that during "the more than 40 years of her literary career, Adrienne Rich ... evolved from a dutiful poet following the masculine poetic tradition ... to a radical, lesbian feminist with a commitment to a global perspective" (325–6). Cumpston traced Rich's development as a writer, woman, lesbian, and political thinker, noting the poet's interest in theory, essay-writing, and cultural critique, including critique of the stereotypes people have about lesbians and the stereotypes lesbians have sometimes had about themselves. Rich, Comston noted, has argued for the relevance of a "lesbian continuum" to all women, citing her *Twenty-One Love Poems* as an especially important lesbian text. Lillian Faderman (1994: 569–70) suggested that Rich's "post-1970s work … focused somewhat less on lesbian-feminism and more on various other abiding personal and political concerns" (570). William J. Spurlin, in Aldrich and Wotherspoon (2001: 351–2), suggested the intersection of art and politics in Rich's work, mentioned her idea of a lesbian spectrum, and reported both criticism and defenses of this concept (351). Spurlin also commented on Rich's own responses to these reactions, stressed the lesbian aspects of her "Twenty-One Love Poems," and discussed in particular that sequence's "floating" poem (352). Martha Smith (Summers 2002: 549–52) emphasized Rich's stress on political themes, not merely artistic form, noted her long relationship with Michelle Cliff (549), listed her many awards (550), surveyed her career and reputation, including her growing fame as a lesbian (550), discussed the effects of that identity on her works (550–1), and proclaimed Rich both "a seer and sayer" (551).

Anne Gebhard (Nelson 2009: 530–5) surveyed Rich's life and career (530–1), noted her growing "bitterness and anger" about women's victimization, and reported her particular anger at her father and husband (531). Gebhard observed that Rich's divorce coincided with her increasingly open lesbian writing, commented on her use of poetry to oppose patriarchy, and emphasized her interests both in empowerment through self-discovery and in strong, redemptive women (532). Gebhard commented that

> *Twenty-One Love Poems* is a passionate tribute to Rich's lover. Critics have compared the sequence with Shakespeare's sonnets. With her typical effective use of oxymoron, the poet contrasts the warmth and beauty of the lovers' relationship with vivid images of torture, urban decay, and environmental degradation. The relationship ended in distrust and estrangement.
>
> (533)

Rich thought the lesbian "sense of community would replace the abusive institutions of patriarchy and contribute to a cultural transformation to benefit all humanity"—ideas expressed both in her poetry and her prose, especially in her ideas of "compulsory heterosexuality" and a lesbian continuum ranging from actual lesbianism to simply a sense of fellowship with other women (533). According to Gebhard, in the 1980s Rich's "poetry became somewhat less polemic and more philosophic" (533), becoming more forgiving of her father and husband, more open about the ways arthritis has affected her life, and "more subtle and elusive than in most of her earlier work." Gebhard ended by emphatically praising Rich's positive impact on the lives of lesbians and others (534).

MAUREEN DUFFY (1933–). Jane Rule (1975: 175–82) emphasized Duffy's early fiction by describing its plots, characters, and themes but concluded by warning against Duffy's emphasis on lesbian guilt. Michael Bronski, in Malinowski (1994: 112–14), discussed such matters as the importance of Duffy's "personal history and political commitments" (113), her feminist worldview, the significance of homosexuality in such works as *The Single Eye* (1964) and *The Microcosm* (1966), and her interest in the connections between eroticism and economics.

AUDRE LORDE (1934–1992). Bonnie Zimmerman (1990: 191–4) suggested that in *Zami*, the female orientation "may be so deeply erotic that in loving the mother, the daughter learns to look for love from other women" (193). AnnLouise Keating (in Nelson 1993, *Critical*, 88–92), emphasized Lorde's non-Western approaches to thinking and writing (88–9), saying that Lorde rejected efforts to silence women, especially women of the third world (91). Shelton Waldrep (also in Nelson 1993 *Critical* 177–9) compared and contrasted Lorde with James Baldwin and Eldridge Cleaver, suggesting that Lorde would say "that Baldwin is too brotherly and leaves the unique experiences of women out of the picture" (179). Lillian Faderman (1994: 560) noted that "Lorde's poetry and prose deal with her own battles against racism, sexism, and homophobia" and commented on Lorde's insistence, "against the denials of the African American heterosexual community at the time," that "'there have always been Black dykes around—in the sense of powerful and women-oriented women,'" even if those women would not have openly called themselves lesbians. Robert Marks Ridinger, in Malinowski (1994: 232–4), discussed Lorde's importance as a pioneering Black lesbian feminist, noted her early marriage to a man, reviewed her career, and stressed the importance of her poetry. William J. Spurlin, in Aldrich and Wotherspoon (2001: 250–1), quoted Lorde's refusal to choose just one of her multiple identities and her desire to integrate them all. He noted her interest in using different identities to promote social change, her regret that "American leftists of the 1950s remained suspicious of homosexuality" as politically dangerous, and her similar regret that homosexuals were often unwelcome among Blacks (250).

Carbado et al. (2002: 176–7) called Lorde the "most revered African American lesbian writer of her time," especially among lesbian feminists, noted her "openness" and "outspokenness" about sexuality and race (176), observed her influence on later Black lesbian poets, commented that Lorde challenged white feminists' limited understanding of black lesbian lives, and asserted that *Zami* "is remarkable for its rare and authentic rendering of 1950s lesbian culture from the point of view of a black lesbian feminist" (177). Elena Martínez (Summers 2002: 422–3) surveyed Lorde's life and career, noted Lorde's belief in "the need for women to organize across sexualities," outlined her broad definition of "lesbianism" (not necessarily involving sex [422]), commented on her political activism and her stress on love and equality of all kinds, and emphasized her opposition to all kinds of oppression (423).

Tania Katan (Canning 2009: 267–71) described Lorde's positive impact, particularly through *The Cancer Journals*, on Katan's own life and writing. Colleen Kattau, (Nelson 2009: 389–92), first discussed Lorde's life and career (389–90), argued that Lorde recognized "that to be a black lesbian poet in the 1960s was to endure a triple kind of invisibility," observed Lorde's interest in combinations of the spiritual, political, emotional, and erotic (390), and argued that Lorde "aligned her struggle against cancer with struggles against racism, capitalism, and homophobia" (391). According to Kattau, for Lorde "differences of class, race, gender, sexuality, and ethnicity make interdependence all the more necessary" (391).

EDMUND WHITE (1940–). Richard Dellamore (1994: 154–72) discussed the relevance of AIDS to White's short story "An Oracle," called this work "a cruising narrative within the subgenre of sexual tourist fiction" (156), and thought the story showed that "White is interested in the possibility that around erotics gay men may devise new modes of sociality" (172). Kevin Ray, in Malinowski (1994: 396–8), surveyed the development of White's style from the ornate to something plainer and more direct, discussed each of his books and his increasingly prominent role as a gay writer, assessed the ways his works reflected changes in American society, and closed by emphasizing his relation to the AIDS crisis as well as his subtle humor rather than any harsh satire. Hogan and Hudson (1998: 571–2) called White a pioneering gay writer who sought both to explain and excite (572).

Reed Woodhouse (1998: 263–95) called White, "by common consent, the most distinguished American gay writer" of recent years (263). After surveying White's achievements in various genres (especially the memoir), Woodhouse maintained that White's more recent works explore such emotions as "pity, forgiveness, and good humor," whereas the "old White, pre-AIDS, was furious at everyone, most of all himself" (285). Woodhouse sensed in the new work "a new tone, as of someone walking very softly among ruins, careful to see and remember and not to knock anything down" (286). Moreover, in White's writing, beneath "the elegant prose and raconteur's charm," Woodhouse said that he always heard "a haunted nervousness amounting to terror" (290). Woodhouse concluded that "White's fiction, despite his reputation for aestheticism and playfulness," seems "fundamentally serious" in ways that sometimes frustrated this critic (294). Seymour Kleinberg, in Aldrich and Wotherspoon (2001: 440), noted that a major magazine had called White "America's foremost gay novelist," that White had defined himself explicitly as a gay writer, that in his early life he had struggled with his sexuality, and that White's works are "a chronicle of gay lifestyles and society's changing attitudes toward homosexuality" (440). Randal Woodland (Summers 2002: 682–3) surveyed White's life and career (682), treating him as fiction-writer, reporter, social critic, and spokesman for gay culture and noting both the praise and criticism (especially of promiscuity depicted in *States of Desire*) he has received and his early role in writing about the AIDS crisis (683).

Robert Glück (in Canning 2009: 277–84) praised *A Boy's Own Story* for its "grandeur" despite its brevity (277), commended its treatment of time as a theme (278), stressed the importance of the father in the book (278–9), and recounted the novel's initial reception as a symbol of changes in publishing (279–81). He outlined its unexpected, in some ways, unattractive complexities, including amorality (281), saw the central character as manipulative and power-hungry (282–3), and stressed the book's darker aspects, including its emphasis on betrayal (283–4). Stephanie Youngblood, in Nelson (2009: 639–42), noted the often autobiographical nature of White's fiction, his frequent use of first-person narration, his openly gay nonfiction, and the special early prominence of *A Boy's Own Story* (640). She discussed the varied appeal of his early writings to young gay readers, the elegiac nature of his work *The Farewell Symphony*, and the continued autobiographical nature of his later fiction, including his exploration of both gay and non-gay themes. She reported that White was criticized by some for leaving the United States in the 1980s, his work then on his biography of Jean Genet, and his continuing interest in the 1980s in the AIDS crisis (641), an interest that resulted in several important works (642). Youngblood concluded by noting White's growing interest in writing about Paris and in creating historical fiction, including one work dealing with a supposed gay encounter by Stephen Crane in the 1890s (642).

Christopher Bram (2012: 175–82, 195–201, 282–91) equated White's importance to that of Gore Vidal (175), recounted his early life and career (175–82), stressed the erotic nature of his book *The Joy of Gay Sex* (180), discussed his involvement with the "Violet Quill" writer's group (196–7), suggested that this group was less innovative than is often assumed, since the members tended to write about "unhappy homosexuals," noted the popularity of White's *States of Desire* (197), called that work a "playful satire" that "makes fun of both straight and gay life," and located it in the travel book tradition (199). Later, Bram noted the popularity of White's autobiographical works (282), discussed *The Beautiful Room Is Empty* (282–4), called this book better than its predecessor, *A Boy's Story* (284), and judged the prose of a later work, *The Farewell Symphony*, "the best White has ever written" (286), although he considered the book as a whole too long (291).

GLORIA ANZALDUA (1942–2004). AnnLouise Keating, in Emmanuel Nelson (1993: 81–90), emphasized the mythic/political and autobiographical nature of Anzaldua's work (81–2), discussed various works, themes, and techniques (82–7), and concluded that her "words incite us to actively create a complex mixed-breed coalition of 'queers'—the outsiders who, because of race, gender, sexual orientation, or class position, refuse to conform to the dominant cultural inscriptions" (88). Jacquelyn Marie, in Malinowski (1994: 10–12), discussed Anzaldua's ethnically mixed background, interest in both writing and painting, emphasis on feminism for women of color, and complex descriptions of her own lesbianism and androgyny. AnaLouise Keating, in Nelson (2009: 33–6), emphasized the deliberate complexity of Anzaldua's intersecting identities as a "queer Chicana," surveyed her life and political involvements, and emphasized her preference for the word "queer" and Spanish equivalents (34). Keating argued that Anzaldua "offers one of the earliest and most complex articulations of intersectional identity," explained Anzaldua's explicit theoretical interest in such identity, and said that Anzaldua's "theory of El Mundo Zurdo represents inclusionary identity-formation and alliance-building based on affinity, self-selection, and a relational approach to difference" (35).

ALICE WALKER (1944–). Alyson Buckman, in Pendergasts (1998: 371–3), drew on other critics' ideas while also offering her own when surveying the feminist and lesbian aspects of Walker's writings. Carbado et al. (2002: 230–1) praised Walker for her "groundbreaking" exploration of Black lesbianism and her affirmation of "lesbianism as a source of liberation for black women" (230). They noted that she openly declared her own bisexuality in 1996 (231). Dorothy H. Lee (Summers 2002: 673) listed many of Walker's characteristic themes, usually centered around opposition to oppression and stressing the crucial idea that "healthy self-definition stems from self-knowledge and self-love"—goals to which lesbianism can contribute (as in *The Color Purple*) because Walker thinks there are "no forbidden loves." Mark Behr (in Canning 2009: 272–6), in a highly autobiographical essay, discussed the positive impact of *The Color Purple* on his own life.

HANIF KUREISHI (1954–). Elliott McEldowney, in Pendergasts (1998: 217–19), emphasized Kureishi's mixed Pakistani-British background, his frequent concern with that topic, and his distrust of simple, "pure" identities. In Kureishi's works, sex (McEldowney observed) "is almost always farcically comic, and almost always serves to subvert racial, national, or sexual norms, however provisionally."

TONY KUSHNER (1956–). Michael Broder, in Malinowski (1994: 210–11), said that by the early 1990s Kushner's play *Angels in America* had gone "farther than any other gay literary work in its use of gay characters and traditionally gay themes to examine a complex political, cultural, and historical reality that transcends gay ghettos and embraces all of American society" (210). Broder noted the play's treatment of such topics as "denial, hypocrisy, repression, self-loathing, self-acceptance, and self-love" and especially praised the playwright's decision to include a real historical character (the closeted attorney Roy Cohn) in this text (211). Robert Drake (1998: 452–5) called *Angels in America* "an audacious act of bravery, perhaps the most insistent product of the gay imagination to date" (453). David Frantzen (1998: 278–92) argued that Kushner, in *Angels*, "correlates sexual relations with racial stereotypes and national heritage and makes revealing use of Anglo-Saxon culture that is seldom noticed by the play's admirers." This play, according to Frantzen, "rewrites the social history of England (and America) in order to enable a new era in which same-sex relations thrive while heterosexual relations wither" (278). Frantzen saw an Anglo-Saxon "subtext" in both parts of the play (279); saw the Anglo-Saxons in the plays as oppressors (284); and argued that the

> promised land in *Angels in America* is a multicultural, tolerant world in which biological descent counts for little (there are no successful marriages in the play) and cultural inheritance imparts defining characteristics to people without imposing barriers among them.
>
> (289)

But Frantzen expressed disappointment with Kushner's treatment of the play's WASPs and even with its limited, mostly sexual depiction of contemporary gay life (290–1). Hogan and Hudson (1998: 334–6) mainly surveyed Kushner's career but emphasized his skill, in *Angels*, in integrating various socio-political themes relevant to the 1980s (336). Alan Sinfield (1998: 193) argued that "Kushner sets it up so that refusal of gay identity correlates with political and judicial corruption." Sinfield (1999: 205–7), noting that *Angels* is now considered an American "classic" (205), called it "strong, subtle, and demanding" but also regretted that it sometimes "slides into the cloudiness of irony, symbolism and profundity at moments where clear elucidation would be valuable" (207). Mark Edwards, in Aldrich and Wotherspoon (2001: 236–7), called *Angels* "the first AIDS-related art form to receive widespread mainstream acceptance and acclaim" (236). Thomas Long (Summers 2002: 393–4) noted Kushner's status as a "celebrity spokesman for gay politics and AIDS activism," the influence of Melville on *Angels in America* (393), his "fabulous realism" in that play, and its many strengths, including complexity of structure, characterization and thought and its "accessible and poetic language." Long also listed Kushner's typical themes, including liberalism, socialism, communitarianism, spirituality, and eroticism (394).

Karen Blansfield, in Nelson (2009: 26–30), discussed the differences between the two parts of *Angels* (26), saw Belize as the play's key moral voice, and reported that Kushner views the second part as a comedy (27). She commented on various themes, including "gender politics" (28), praised the play's theatrical effectiveness, and observed that it has been "credited with opening the doors for gay drama that reaches beyond the domestic realm that had been its primary territory" (29). Stephanie Youngblood, in Nelson (2009: 350–3), mainly surveyed Kushner's life and career but ended, unusually, by emphasizing his nonfiction prose related to "AIDS activism and political justice" (352).

Christopher Bram (2012: 261–76) outlined Kushner's early career (261–4), discussed the development, plot, and reception of the first part of *Angels in America* (264–9), described its diverse style and intriguing villains (266–7), and suggested that gay writers "are often more self-critical than straight male authors," particularly in presenting unappealing characters who resemble themselves (267). Bram recalled his own intense enthusiasm for an early staging of the play (268), explored its moral and prophetic aspects (269–70), described both its immense success and the controversy it provoked, even among some gay critics (271–5), and concluded by mentioning more recent developments in Kushner's career (275–6).

Conclusion

If this book had been written forty years ago, it would have been much shorter and much easier to write. However, since the 1980s, interest in both the writing and the scholarly study of "queer" literature has exploded. Tolerance for—and even hearty acceptance of—"queer" people has also grown exponentially over those decades. In the United States, support for firing known homosexual teachers fell steadily from 51.5 percent in 1987 to 21 percent in 2012 and has almost certainly fallen even further since then (Becker 2014). The proportion of people in America who found homosexual relations "morally acceptable" rose from 40 percent in 2001 to 54 percent in 2012, with corresponding falls in the proportion of people who found such relations morally unacceptable (Saad 2012). From 2004 to 2012, support for gay marriage rose from 42 percent to 50 percent in the United States and was even higher in many other "Western" countries (Saad 2012). In Britain, the number of people who considered homosexual relations "always wrong" fell from 50 percent in 1983 to 39 percent in 1998, while the number of people who considered such relations "not wrong at all" rose from 17 percent to 23 percent over the same period ("Homosexuality" [1998]). In 2019, the percentages of people who thought that homosexuality "*should* be accepted by society" stood at 94 percent in Sweden, 92 percent in The Netherlands, 89 percent in Spain, 86 percent in Germany, 86 percent in the UK, 86 percent in France, 85 percent in Canada, 81 percent in Australia, 75 percent in Italy, and 72 percent in the United States. In Eastern and Southern Europe, however, such attitudes were far less common, amounting to 59 percent in the Czech Republic, 49 percent in Hungary, 47 percent in Poland, 44 percent in Slovakia, 48 percent in Greece, 32 percent in Bulgaria, 25 percent in Turkey, 14 percent in Ukraine, and 14 percent in Russia. In Israel the figure stood at 47 percent, and in Lebanon it stood at 13 percent, with figures available for no other Middle Eastern countries. The figures for the few African countries for which data were provided were 54 percent for South Africa, 14 percent in Kenya, 9 percent in Tunisia, and 7 percent in Nigeria. In India, the figure stood at 37 percent, while in various Asian countries for which figures were available the percentages were 68 percent for Japan, 73 percent for The Philippines, 44 percent for South Korea, and 9 percent for Indonesia. In Central and South America, the figures were 76 percent in Argentina, 69 percent in Mexico, and 67 percent in Brazil. Thus, Lebanon, Ukraine, Russia, Kenya, Tunisia, Nigeria, and Indonesia were the most obvious outliers, with figures in those countries falling below 20 percent of their populations (Pouchster and Kent 2020).

In the so-called "Western" nations, however, increasing numbers of persons now not only "tolerate" LGBTQ behavior but even embrace it. In a surprising survey released in early 2022, a remarkable 7.1 percent of the United States population now self-identified as members of the LGBTQ+ community. According to Jeffrey Jones, reporting the results of a Gallup poll, "[t]he percentage of U.S. adults who self-identify as lesbian, gay, bisexual, transgender or something other than heterosexual has increased to a new high of 7.1 percent, which is double the percentage from 2012, when Gallup first measured it." While 86.3 percent identified as straight or heterosexual, an intriguing 6.6 percent did not even offer an opinion. "The results," according to Jones, were "based on aggregated 2021 data, encompassing interviews with more than 12,000 U.S. adults." But the detailed results of the poll, broken down by different age groups, were even more surprising. Thus, Jones reported that the

> increase in LGBT identification in recent years largely reflects the higher prevalence of such identities among the youngest U.S. adults compared with the older generations they are replacing in the U.S. adult population.
>
> Roughly 21 percent of Generation Z Americans who have reached adulthood—those born between 1997 and 2003—identify as LGBT. That is nearly double the proportion of millennials who do so, while the gap widens even further when compared with older generations.

Only 0.8 percent of people born before 1946 self-identified as LGBTQ. For "baby boomers" (those born between 1946 and 1964), the percentage was 2.6 percent; for members of "Generation X" (people born between 1965 and 1980), the percentage was 4.2; for "Millennials" (people born between 1981 and 1996) the percentage was 10.5 percent; and for "Generation Z" (those born between 1997 and 2003), the percentage was 20.8 percent. Not only is this last figure intriguing, but so is the steady increase in such identification since the end of the Second World War.

Especially interesting is Gallup's further finding that

> [m]ore than half of LGBT Americans, 57%, indicate they are bisexual. That percentage translates to 4.0% of all U.S. adults. Meanwhile, 21% of LGBT Americans say they are gay, 14% lesbian, 10% transgender and 4% something else. Each of these accounts for less than 2% of U.S. adults.
>
> (Jones)

The large percentage of self-identified bisexuals would not surprise anyone familiar with life in ancient Greece and Rome, nor would it surprise many readers of the present book, in which bisexuality has played such a large part in the literature described, even if most academic studies have focused mostly on "gay" or "lesbian" identities. Many of the authors and characters discussed in this book engaged in behavior, or expressed feelings, that could more properly be called "bisexual" rather than either simply "gay" or simply "lesbian." For decades, gays and lesbians often considered bisexuals cowards who were simply unwilling to admit, or come to terms with, their "real" identities as either gays or lesbians. The 2022 Gallup figures, however, suggest—along with much of the evidence assembled in the present book—that bisexuality is today (and perhaps was also in the past) much more common than many people have cared to consider or admit. The bisexual feelings and behavior suggested by the Gallup findings, and also suggested by much of the evidence presented in this book, imply that human sexual behavior, at least in some societies, is far more fluid than has commonly been assumed. Bisexuality can be seen as amounting to a rejection of rigid "binaries" in which people identify as either homosexual *or* heterosexual. Again, the ancient Greeks and Romans would not have been surprised by such a rejection.

In a further fascinating breakdown of the Gallup findings, Jones reports that

> Bisexual is the most common LGBT status among Gen Z, millennials, and Gen X, while older Americans are about as likely to say they are gay or lesbian as to say they are bisexual.
>
> Overall, 15% of Gen Z adults say they are bisexual, as do 6% of millennials and slightly less than 2% of Gen X. Women (6.0%) are much more likely than men (2.0%) to say they are bisexual. [In the general population], [m]en are more likely to identify as gay (2.5%) than as bisexual, while women are much more likely to identify as bisexual than as lesbian (1.9%).

Particularly noteworthy in Gallup's findings is the following statistic: 2.1 percent of people who belong to "Generation Z" identify as "transgender," while only 2.0 percent of them identify as lesbians.

As the evidence surveyed in the present book has suggested, very little has so far been written by or about literary authors and characters who might be called transgender or transsexual. This fact will almost surely begin to change as increasing numbers of literary authors identify as "trans" and/or as they write about "trans" characters or situations. Indeed, it seems possible that interest in gay or lesbian authors, characters, and identities may diminish as more and more persons identify as bisexual. A book such as this, written twenty or forty years from now, will almost surely allot much more discussion to bisexuality than the present one does, if only because the proportion of LGBTQ persons who identify as "bi"—either as authors or as characters—seems likely to continue to grow. It is, in fact, entirely possible to imagine that the letters in the standard acronym may need to be rearranged as "BGTLQ" to better reflect the proportion of persons in the community who identify with distinct groups within it.

As Jones notes in his closing comments,

> The proportion of U.S. adults who consider themselves to be lesbian, gay, bisexual or transgender has grown at a faster pace over the past year than in prior years. This is occurring as more of Gen Z is reaching adulthood. These young adults are coming of age, including coming to terms with their sexuality or gender identity, at a time when Americans increasingly accept gays, lesbians and transgender people, and LGBT individuals enjoy increasing legal protection against discrimination.
>
> Given the large disparities in LGBT identification between younger and older generations of Americans, the proportion of all Americans who identify as LGBT can be expected to grow in the future as younger generations will constitute a larger share of the total U.S. adult population. With one in 10 millennials and one in five Gen Z members identifying as LGBT, the proportion of LGBT Americans should exceed 10% in the near future.

If literary trends follow demographic developments, as they often seem to do, the nature of "Western" literature seems definitely likely to change in the next few decades, and the same may be true of "LGBTQIA+" literature itself.

Bibliography

Ackerman, Susan. *When Heroes Love: The Ambiguity of Eros in the Stories of Gilgamesh and David*. New York: Columbia University Press, 2005.

Adams, Stephen. *The Homosexual as Hero in Contemporary Fiction*. Lanham, MD: Rowman and Littlefield, 1980.

Aldrich, Robert, and Garry Wotherspoon, editors. *Who's Who in Contemporary Gay and Lesbian History: From World War II to the Present Day*. New York: Routledge, 2001.

Aldrich, Robert, and Garry Wotherspoon, editors. *Who's Who in Gay and Lesbian History from Antiquity to World War II*. 2nd edition. New York: Routledge, 2002.

Anders, John P. *Willa Cather's Sexual Aesthetics and the Male Homosexual Literary Tradition*. Lincoln: University of Nebraska Press, 1999.

Andreadis, Harriette. *Sappho in Early Modern England: Female Same-Sex Literary Erotics, 1550–1714*. Chicago: University of Chicago Press, 2001.

Austen, Roger. *Playing the Game: The Homosexual Novel in America*. Indianapolis, IN: Bobbs-Merrill, 1977.

Becker, Amy B. "Examining 25 Years of Public Opinion Data on Gay Rights and Marriage." *OUP Blog*, Oct. 5, 2014, https://blog.oup.com/2014/10/examining-25-years-public-opinion-data-gay-rights-marriage/.

Bergman, David. *Gaiety Transfigured: Gay Self-representation in American Literature*. Madison: University of Wisconsin Press, 1991.

Bloom, Harold, editor. *Lesbian and Bisexual Fiction Writers*. Philadelphia: Chelsea House, 1997.

Bly, Mary. *Queer Virgins and Virgin Queans on the Early Modern Stage*. New York: Oxford University Press, 2000.

Boswell, John. *Christianity, Social Tolerance, and Homosexuality: Gay People in Western Europe from the Beginning of the Christian Era to the Fourteenth Century*. Chicago: University of Chicago Press, 1981.

Boswell, John. *Same-Sex Unions in Premodern Europe*. New York: Villiard Books, 1994.

Bram, Christopher. *Eminent Outlaws: The Gay Writers Who Changed America*. New York: Twelve, 2012.

Bray, Alan. *Homosexuality in Renaissance England*. London: Gay Men's Press, 1982.

Bredbeck, Gregory W. *Sodomy and Interpretation: Marlowe to Milton*. Ithaca: Cornell University Press, 1991.

Bristow, Joseph, editor. *Sexual Sameness: Textual Differences in Lesbian and Gay Writing*. New York: Routledge, 1992.

Bristow, Joseph. *Effeminate England: Homoerotic Writing after 1885.* New York: Columbia University Press, 1995.

Bullough, Vern L. "Attitudes toward Deviant Sex in Ancient Mesopotamia." *The Journal of Sex Research*, vol. 7, no. 3 (Aug. 1971), pp. 184–203.

Burger, Glenn. *Chaucer's Queer Nation.* Minneapolis: University of Minnesota Press, 2003.

Canning, Richard, editor. *50 Gay and Lesbian Books Everybody Must Read.* New York: Alyson Books, 2009.

Cantarella, Eva. *Bisexuality in the Ancient World.* New Haven: Yale University Press, 1992.

Carbado, Devon, et al., editors. *Black Like Us: A Century of Lesbian, Gay and Bisexual African American Fiction.* San Francisco: Cleis Press, 2002.

Castle, Terry. *The Apparitional Lesbian: Female Homosexuality and Modern Culture.* New York: Columbia University Press, 1993.

Castle, Terry. *The Literature of Lesbianism: A Historical Anthology from Ariosto to Stonewall.* New York: Columbia University press, 2003.

Charles, Casey. "Heroes as Lovers: Erotic Attraction between Men in Sidney's 'New Arcadia.'" *Criticism*, vol. 34, no. 4 (Fall, 1992), pp. 467–96.

Clarke, W. M. "Achilles and Patroclus in Love." *Hermes*, vol. 106 (1978), pp. 381–96.

Clum, John M. *Acting Gay: Male Homosexuality in Modern Drama.* New York: Columbia University Press, 1992.

Conner, Randolph P., et al. *Encyclopaedia of Queer Myth, Symbol, and Spirit.* London: Cassell, 1997.

Cook, Matt. *London and the Culture of Homosexuality.* New York: Cambridge University Press, 2003.

Cornelius, Michael. *Edward II and a Literature of Same-Sex Love: The Gay King in Fiction, 1590–1640.* Lanham: Lexington Books, 2016.

Craft, Christopher. *Another Kind of Love: Male Homosexual Desire in English Discourse, 1850–1920.* Berkeley: University of California Press, 1994.

Crawford, Julie. "Sidney's Sapphics and the Role of Interpretive Communities." *ELH*, vol. 69, no. 4 (Winter, 2002), pp. 979–1007.

Crompton, Louis. *Byron and Greek love: Homophobia in 19th-century England.* Berkeley: University of California Press, 1985.

Crompton, Louis. *Homosexuality and Civilization.* Cambridge, MA: Harvard University Press, 2003.

Davidson, James N. *The Greeks and Greek Love: A Radical Reappraisal of Homosexuality in Ancient Greece.* London: Weidenfeld and Nicolson, 2007.

De Jongh, Nicholas. *Not in Front of the Audience: The Making of Gay Theatre.* New York: Routledge, 1991.

DeKoven, Marianne. *A Different Language: Gertrude Stein's Experimental Writing.* Madison: University of Wisconsin Press, 1983.

Dellamora, Richard. *Masculine Desire: The Sexual Politics of Victorian Aestheticism.* Chapel Hill: University of North Carolina Press, 1990.

Dellamora, Richard. *Apocalyptic Overtures: Sexual Politics and the Sense of an Ending.* New Brunswick, NJ: Rutgers University Press, 1994.

Dellamora, Richard. *Friendship's Bonds: Democracy and the Novel in Victorian England.* Philadelphia: University of Pennsylvania Press, 2004.

DiGangi, Mario. *The Homoerotics of Early Modern Drama.* New York: Cambridge University Press, 1997.

Dollimore, Jonathan. *Sexual Dissidence: Augustine to Wilde, Freud to Foucault.* New York: Oxford University Press, 1991.

Donoghue, Emma. Passions between Women: British Lesbian Culture, 1668–1801. London: Scarlet Press, 1993.

Donoghue, Emma. *Inseparable: Desire between Women in Literature.* New York: Alfred A. Knopf, 2010.

Dover, K. J. *Greek Homosexuality.* London: Duckworth, 1978.

Dowling, Linda. *Hellenism and Homosexuality in Victorian Oxford.* Ithaca: Cornell University Press, 1994.

Downing, Christine. *Myths and Mysteries of Same-Sex Love.* New York: Continuum, 1989.

Drake, Robert. *The Gay Canon: Great Books Every Gay Man Should Read.* New York: Anchor Books, 1998.

DuBois, Paige. *Sappho Is Burning.* Chicago: University of Chicago Press, 1995.

Dynes, Wayne, editor. *The Encyclopedia of Homosexuality.* New York: Garland Press, 1990.

Dynes, Wayne R., and Stephen Donaldson, editors. *Homosexuality in the Ancient World.* London: Routledge, 1992.

Efrati, Carol. *The Road of Danger, Guilt, and Shame: The Lonely Way of A.E. Housman.* Madison, MJ: Fairleigh Dickinson University Press, 2002.

Faderman, Lillian. *Surpassing the Love of Men: Romantic Friendship and Love between Women from the Renaissance to the Present.* New York: Morrow, 1981.

Faderman, Lillian. *Chloe Plus Olivia: An Anthology of Lesbian Literature from the Seventeenth Century to the Present.* New York: Viking, 1994.

Fincher, Max. *Queering Gothic in the Romantic Age: The Penetrating Eye.* New York: Palgrave Macmillan, 2007.

Fone, Byrne. *Homophobia: A History.* New York: Metropolitan Books, 2000.

Fone, Byrne R. S. *A Road to Stonewall: Male Homosexuality and Homophobia in English and American Literature, 1750–1969.* New York: Twayne, 1995.

Fone, Byrne R. S., editor. *The Columbia Anthology of Gay Literature: Readings from Western Antiquity to the Present Day.* New York: Columbia University Press, 1998.

Foster, Jeannette H. *Sex-Variant Women in Literature: A Historical and Quantitative Survey.* New York: Vantage Press, 1956.

Frantzen, Allen J. *Before the Closet: Same-Sex Love from Beowulf to Angels in America.* Chicago: University of Chicago Press, 1998.

Frontain, Raymond-Jean, editor. *Reclaiming the Sacred: The Bible in Gay and Lesbian Culture.* 2nd edition. New York: Harrington Park Press, 2003.

Garber, Marjorie B. *Vested Interests: Cross-Dressing and Cultural Anxiety*. New York: Routledge, 1992.

Garber, Marjorie. *Vice Versa: Bisexuality and the Eroticism of Everyday Life*. New York: Simon & Schuster, 1995.

Goldberg, Jonathan. *Sodometries: Renaissance Texts, Modern Sexualities*. Stanford, CA: Stanford University Press, 1992.

Goldberg, Jonathan, editor. *Queering the Renaissance*. Durham, NC: Duke University Press, 1994.

Goldberg, Jonathan. *Desiring Women Writing: English Renaissance Examples*. Stanford, CA: Stanford University Press, 1997.

Goodich, Michael. *The Unmentionable Vice: Homosexuality in the Later Medieval Period*. Santa Barbara, CA: ABC-Clio, 1979.

Green, Ellen, editor. *Re-Reading Sappho: Reception and Transmisson*. Berkeley: University of Chicago Press, 1996a.

Greene, Ellen, editor. *Reading Sappho: Contemporary Approaches*. Berkeley: University of California Press, 1996b.

Griffin, Gabriele. *Heavenly Love?: Lesbian Images in Twentieth-Century Women's Writing*. New York: St. Martin's Press, 1993.

Guy-Bray, Stephen. *Homoerotic Space: The Poetics of Loss in Renaissance Literature*. Toronto: University of Toronto Press, 2002.

Guy-Bray, Stephen. "'Unknowne mate': Sidney, Motion, and Sexuality." *Sidney Journal*, vol. 26 (2008), pp. 35–56.

Haggerty, George, editor. *Gay Histories and Cultures: An Encyclopedia*. New York: Garland, 2000.

Halperin, David M. *One Hundred Years of Homosexuality, and Other Essays on Greek Love*. New York: Routledge, 1990.

Halpern, Richard. *Shakespeare's Perfume: Sodomy and Sublimity in the Sonnets, Wilde, Freud, and Lacan*. Philadelphia: University of Pennsylvania Press, 2002.

Hammond, Paul. *Love between Men in English Literature*. New York: St. Martin's Press, 1996.

Hammond, Paul. *Figuring Sex between Men from Shakespeare to Rochester*. New York: Oxford University Press, 2002.

Heacock, Anthony. "Wrongly Framed? The 'David and Jonathan Narrative' and the Writing of Biblical Homosexuality [sic]." *Bible and Critical Theory*, vol. 3, no. 2 (2007), pp. 22.1–22.14.

Held, George F. "Parallels between *The Gilgamesh Epic* and Plato's Symposium." *Journal of Near Eastern Studies*, vol. 42, no. 2 (Apr. 1983), pp. 133–41.

Herzog, Katie. "Where Have All the Lesbians Gone?" *Andrewsullivansubstack.com*, Nov. 27, 2020, https://andrewsullivan.substack.com/p/where-have-all-the-lesbians-gone-0a7?utm_source=url.

Hine, Daryl. *Puerilities: Erotic Epigrams of the Greek Anthology*. Princeton, NJ: Princeton University Press, 2001.

Hogan, Steve, and Lee Hudson. *Completely Queer: The Gay and Lesbian Encyclopedia.* New York: Henry Holt, 1998.

"Homosexuality." British Social Attitudes. bsa.natcen.ac.uk, [1998], https://www.bsa.natcen.ac.uk/latest-report/british-social-attitudes-30/personal-relationships/homosexuality.aspx.

Hoogland, Renée C. *Lesbian Configurations.* New York: Columbia University Press, 1997.

Hubbard, Thomas K. *Homosexuality in Greece and Rome: A Sourcebook of Basic Documents.* Berkeley, CA: University of California Press, 2003.

Hubbard, Thomas K. *A Companion to Greek and Roman Sexualities.* Oxford, UK: Wiley-Blackwell, 2014.

Jones, Jeffrey M. "LGBT Identification in U.S. Ticks Up to 7.1%." *Gallup.com*, Feb. 17, 2022, https://news.gallup.com/poll/389792/lgbt-identification-ticks-up.aspx.

Kaplan, Morris B. *Sodom on the Thames: Sex, Love, and Scandal in Wilde Times.* Ithaca: Cornell University Press, 2005.

Keiser, Elizabeth B. *Courtly Desire and Medieval Homophobia: The Legitimation of Sexual Pleasure in* Cleanness *and Its Contexts.* New Haven, CT: Yale University Press, 1997.

Kellogg, Stuart, editor. *Essays on Gay Literature.* New York: Harrington Park Press, 1985.

Kent, Kathryn R. *Making Girls into Women: American Women's Writing and the Rise of Lesbian Identity.* Durham, NC: Duke University Press, 2003.

Klawitter, George, editor. *The Complete Poems of Richard Barnfield.* Selinsgrove, PA: Susquehanna University Press, 1990.

Klawitter, George. *Andrew Marvell, Sexual Orientation, and Seventeenth-Century Poetry.* Madison, NJ: Fairleigh Dickinson University Press, 2017.

Klawitter, George, and Kenneth Borris, editors. *The Affectionate Shepherd: Celebrating Richard Barnfield.* Selinsgrove, PA: Susquehanna University Press, 2001.

Klein, Fred. *The Bisexual Option.* 1979. New York: Haworth Press, 1993.

Kopelson, Kevin. *Love's Litany: The Writing of Modern Homoerotics.* Stanford, CA: Stanford University Press, 1994.

Larson, Jennifer. *Greek and Roman Sexualities: A Sourcebook.* London: Bloomsbury, 2012.

Levin, Richard A. "What? How? Female-Female Desire in Sidney's 'New Arcadia.'" *Criticism*, vol. 39, no. 4 (Fall, 1997), pp. 463–79.

Lilly, Mark. *Gay Men's Literature in the Twentieth Century.* Basingstoke: Macmillan, 1993.

Lochrie, Karma. "Configurations of Gender and Sexuality in Medieval Europe." *The Cambridge History of Gay and Lesbian Literature*, edited Mikko Tuhkanen, et al. Cambridge: Cambridge University Press, 2014, pp. 89–106.

Malinowski, Sharon, editor. *Gay and Lesbian Literature.* Detroit: St. James Press, 1994.

Martin, Robert K. *The Homosexual Tradition in American Poetry.* Austin: University of Texas Press, 1979.

McCallum, E. L., and Mikko Tuhkanen, editors. *The Cambridge History of Gay and Lesbian Literature*. Cambridge: Cambridge University Press, 2014.

McFarlane, Cameron. *The Sodomite in Fiction and Satire, 1660–1750*. New York: Columbia University Press, 1997.

Meyers, Jeffrey. *Homosexuality and Literature, 1890–1930*. London: Athlone Press, 1977.

Miller, Carl. *Stages of Desire: Gay Theatre's Hidden History*. New York: Cassell, 1996.

Miller, Neil. *Out of the Past: Gay and Lesbian History from 1869 to the Present*. New York: Alyson Books, 1995.

Moore, Lisa. *Dangerous Intimacies: Toward a Sapphic History of the British Novel*. Durham, NC: Duke University Press, 1997.

Murphy, Timothy F., editor. *A Reader's Guide to Lesbian and Gay Studies*. Chicago: Fitzroy Dearborn, 2000.

Nelson, Emmanuel S. *Contemporary Gay American Novelists: A Bio-Bibliographical Critical Sourcebook*. Westport, CT: Greenwood Press, 1993a.

Nelson, Emmanuel S. *Critical Essays: Gay and Lesbian Writers of Color*. New York: Haworth Press, 1993b.

Nelson, Emmanuel S., editor. *Contemporary Gay American Poets and Playwrights*. Westport, CT: Greenwood Press, 2003.

Nelson, Emmanuel S., editor. *Encyclopedia of Contemporary LGBTQ Literature of the United States*. Santa Barbara, CA: Greenwood Press, 2009.

Nissinen, Martti. *Homoeroticism in the Biblical World: A Historical Perspective*. Translated by Kirsti Stjerna. Minneapolis: Fortress Press, 1998.

Nissinen, Marti. "Are There Homosexuals in Mesopotamian Literature?" *History Journal of the American Oriental Society*, vol. 130, no. 1 (January–March 2010), pp. 73–7.

Norton, Rictor. *The Homosexual Literary Tradition: An Interpretation*. New York: Revisionist Press, 1974.

Orgel, Stephen. *Impersonations: The Performance of Gender in Shakespeare's England*. New York: Cambridge University Press, 1996.

Palmer, Paulina. *Contemporary Lesbian Writing: Dreams, Desire, Difference*. Philadelphia: Open University Press, 1993.

Pendergast, Tom, and Sara Pendergast, editor. *Gay and Lesbian Literature*, vol. 2. Detroit: St. James Press, 1998.

Pequigney, Joseph. *Such Is My Love: A Study of Shakespeare's Sonnets*. Chicago: University of Chicago Press, 1985.

Percy, William A. *Pederasty and Pedagogy in Archaic Greece*. Urbana: University of Illinois Press, 1996.

Poushter, Jacob, and Nicholas Kent. "The Global Divide on Homosexuality Persists." Pew Research Center, 25 June 2020, https://www.pewresearch.org/global/2020/06/25/global-divide-on-homosexuality-persists/.

Rambuss, Richard. *Closet Devotions*. Durham, NC: Duke University Press, 1998.

Reisman, Rosemary Canfield, editor. *Greek Poetry*. Ipswich, MA: Salem Press, 2012.

Richlin, Amy. *The Garden of Priapus: Sexuality and Aggression in Roman Humor*. New York: Oxford University Press, 1992.

Robinson, David M. *Closeted Writing and Lesbian and Gay Literature*. Burlington, VT: Ashgate, 2006.

Rohy, Valerie. *Impossible Women: Lesbian Figures and American Literature*. Ithaca, NY: Cornell University Press, 2000.

Rule, Jane. *Lesbian Images*. Garden City, NY: Doubleday, 1975.

Saad, Lydia. "U.S. Acceptance of Gay/Lesbian Relations Is the New Normal." *Gallup.com*, May 14, 2012, https://news.gallup.com/poll/154634/acceptance-gay-lesbian-relations-new-normal.aspx.

Sarotte, Georges Michel. *Like a Brother, Like a Lover: Male Homosexuality in the American Novel and Theater from Herman Melville to James Baldwin*. Translated by Richard Miller. Garden City, NY: Anchor Press/Doubleday, 1978.

Schulman, Sarah. *Stagestruck: Theater, AIDS, and the Marketing of Gay America*. Durham: Duke University Press, 1998.

Schwarz, A. B. Christa. *Gay Voices of the Harlem Renaissance*. Bloomington: Indiana University Press, 2003.

Sedgwick, Eve Kosofsky. *Between Men: English Literature and Male Homosocial Desire*. New York: Columbia University Press, 1985.

Sergent, Bernard. *Homosexuality in Greek Myth*. Translated by Arthur Goldhammer, pref. Georges Dumezil. Boston: Beacon Press, 1986.

Showalter, Elaine. *Sexual Anarchy: Gender and Culture at the Fin de Siècle*. London: Virago, 1992.

Sinfield, Alan. *Cultural Politics—Queer Reading*. Philadelphia: University of Pennsylvania Press, 1994.

Sinfield, Alan. *Gay and after*. London: Serpent's Tail, 1998.

Sinfield, Alan. *Out on Stage: Lesbian and Gay Theatre in the Twentieth Century*. New Haven: Yale University Press, 1999.

Smith, Bruce R. *Homosexual Desire in Shakespeare's England: A Cultural Poetics*. Chicago: University of Chicago Press, 1991.

Snyder, Jane. *Lesbian Desire in the Lyrics of Sappho*. New York: Columbia University Press, 1997.

Stewart, Alan. *Close Readers: Humanism and Sodomy in Early Modern England*. Princeton, NJ: Princeton University Press, 1997.

Summers, Claude J. *Gay Fictions: Wilde to Stonewall: Studies in a Male Homosexual Literary Tradition*. New York: Continuum, 1990.

Summers, Claude J., editor. *Homosexuality in Renaissance and Enlightenment England: Literary Representations in Historical Context*. New York: Haworth Press, 1992.

Summers, Claude J., editor. *The Gay and Lesbian Literary Heritage: A Reader's Companion to the Writers and Their Works, from Antiquity to the Present*. New York: Routledge, 2002.

Surber, Nida. *The Fierce Parade: Chaucer and the Encryption of Homosexuality in The Canterbury Tales*. Genève: Slatkine, 2010.
Tigay, Jeffrey. *The Evolution of the Gilgamesh Epic*. Wauconda, IL: Bolchazy-Carducci, 1982.
Tóibín, Colm. *Love in a Dark Time: Gay Lives from Wilde to Almodóvar*. London: Picador, 2002.
Traub, Valerie. "Recent Studies in Homoeroticism." *English Literary Renaissance*, vol. 30, no. 2 (2000), pp. 284–329.
van Leer, David. *The Queening of America: Gay Culture in Straight Society*. New York: Routledge, 1995.
Wahl, Elizabeth Susan. *Invisible Relations: Representations of Female Intimacy in the Age of Enlightenment*. Stanford, CA: Stanford University Press, 1999.
Walen, Denise A. *Constructions of Female Homoeroticism in Early Modern Drama*. New York: Palgrave Macmillan, 2005.
Wilhelm, James J., editor. *Gay and Lesbian Poetry: An Anthology from Sappho to Michelangelo*. New York: Routledge, 1995.
Williams, Craig A. *Roman Homosexuality: Ideologies of Masculinity in Classical Antiquity*. Oxford: Oxford University Press, 1999.
Woodhouse, Reed. *Unlimited Embrace: A Canon of Gay Fiction, 1945–1995*. Amherst: University of Massachusetts Press, 1998.
Woods, Gregory. *Articulate Flesh: Male Homo-eroticism and Modern Poetry*. New Haven: Yale University Press, 1987.
Woods, Gregory. *A History of Gay Literature: The Male Tradition*. New Haven: Yale University Press, 1998.
Zimmerman, Bonnie. *The Safe Sea of Women: Lesbian Fiction, 1969–1989*. Boston, MA: Beacon Press, 1990.
Zimmerman, Bonnie, editor. *Lesbian Histories and Cultures: An Encyclopedia*. New York: Garland, 2000.

Index

Achilles 7, 9–10, 17, 21
Aeschylus 17
aesthetes 101
AIDS 108, 198–9, 202
Alan of Lille 31
Albee, Edward 195–97
Alcaeus 10
Alcman 10
Alcuin 27
Alfred of Rievaulx 29
Amazons 23, 37
ambivalence 56, 61, 94, 102–3, 110, 117, 130, 140, 143–4, 148, 151, 166, 171, 178, 183
Anacreon 15
anal sex 15, 194
androgyny 29, 37, 46, 48, 64, 79, 80, 82, 90, 94, 137
Anzaldua. Gloria 204
Archilochus 10
Aristophanes 17
asexuality 3
Ashbery, John 192, 194
Athenaeus 25
Auden, W. H. 114, 164–5

Baldwin, James 157, 173, 178–85, 201
Barnes, Djuna 145–7
Barnfield, Richard 51, 55, 57–60
Baudri of Bourgeil 28
Beckford, William 71–2, 76
Behn, Aphra 63–4
Bentham, Jeremy 72
Beowulf 28
Bernard of Cluny 29–30
Bietris de Romans 31
bisexuality 1–3, 11, 15, 17, 20–4, 32–3, 44, 48–9, 63–7, 75–6, 83, 88–90, 96, 104, 122–3, 131, 140, 142–5, 147, 149, 153, 158, 162, 163, 164, 166, 177–8, 180–4, 187, 190–1

Bishop, Elizabeth 166–7
Blake, Williams 194
Boccaccio, Giovanni 33
Boswell, John 27
Bowen, Elizabeth 151–2
Bowles, Jane Auer 177
Byron, George Gordon, Lord 72, 75–8, 104

Callimachus 18
camp 23, 105, 116, 132, 159, 170, 175–7, 181, 188–90, 192, 194, 196
Capote, Truman 169, 185–8, 191, 192
Carpenter, Edward 83, 84, 92, 99–100, 127, 128, 130, 132, 142, 157
Cather, Willa 117–21
Catullus 20, 22
Cavafy, Constantine 111–15, 126, 129
celibacy 23, 60
Chaucer, Geoffrey 33
Cleaver, Eldridge 180–1
Cleland, John 67–9
Crane, Hart 152–4
cross-dressing 38, 45, 51–3, 75–6, 90. *See* transvestites
Cullen, Countee 157–8, 159

dandies 70, 85, 101
Dante Aligheri 32, 78
David [his only name] 29
David and Jonathan 7–8, 10
Debate Between Ganymede and Hebe 31
Debate Between Ganymede and Helen 30
Dickinson, Emily 87–9
Don Leon 75, 77
Don Leon, Author of 77–8
Donne, John 13, 55–7, 62
drag 196
Duffy, Maureen 201
Duncan, Robert 197

effeminacy 17, 20, 22, 23, 24, 33, 38, 40, 41, 60, 68, 69, 70, 71, 72, 73, 80, 85, 92, 93, 95, 101, 105, 108, 119, 129, 130, 139, 145, 156, 157, 162, 177, 182, 183, 186, 187, 189, 190, 191
Eliot, T. S. 113
Enkidu 8
Euripides 17

feminism 62, 133, 135, 138, 144, 147, 149, 163, 167, 185, 188, 198–202
Forster, E. M. 100, 105, 113, 126–32, 135, 140, 141, 142, 177
Foucault, Michel 92
Frank, Waldo 145
Freud, Sigmund 43, 80, 143, 173–4

Ganymede 17, 29–31, 38, 40, 47, 57–8, 60
Genet, Jean 193, 203
Gide, Andre 103, 181
Ginsberg, Alan 192–4
Godfrey of Winchester 28
Gosse, Edmund 94
Gottschalk [his only name] 27
Gray, Thomas 69
Greek Anthology, The 16–19
Gunn, Thom 197–9
Gurney, Ivor 84

H. D. [Hilda Doolittle] 142–4
Hall, Radcliffe 127, 132–7, 146, 150
Harlem Renaissance 158
hermaphroditism 63–4, 90
Hildebut of Lavardin 29
homosociality 8–9, 27–8, 45, 49, 79, 82, 126
Hopkins, Gerald Manley 83, 84, 98–9
Horace 21, 45
Housman, A. E. 109–11, 120
Hrabanus Maurus 27
Hughes, Langston 155–7, 158, 159

Ibycus 16
incest 73, 90, 95, 143
Inge, William 196
intersexuality 3
Isherwood, Christopher 159–62, 188

James, Henry 87, 94–7, 117, 146, 185
Jewett, Sarah Orne 100

Jonathan and David 7–8, 10
Juvenal 24–5

Kureishi, Hanif 205
Kushner, Tony 205–6

Lawrence, D. H. 84, 122, 128, 139–42
Leavitt, David 161–6
Lewis, Matthew ("Monk"), 72–3
Locke, Alain 157
Lorde, Audre 201–2
Lowell, Amy 122

Mansfield, Katherine 144–5
Marbod of Rennes 28–9
Marlowe, Christopher 37–42, 59
Martial 23–4, 56
Marvell, Andrew 60
masochism 73, 90, 101, 137, 139, 167, 171, 175, 193, 197
masturbation 60, 70, 72, 81, 86, 98–9, 105, 140
Maugham, W. Somerset 123
McKay, Claude 145, 159
Meleager 18
Melville, Herman 80–2, 206
Michael Field [pseudonym for two women writing together] 97–8
Millay, Edna St. Vincent 149
misogyny 13, 24, 31, 38, 43, 49, 60, 92, 103, 105, 110, 130, 133, 188, 196–7

Notker Balbulus 27
Nugent, Bruce 158, 159

O Admirabile Veneris Idolum 27
O'Hara, Frank 192
oral sex 5, 15, 20, 24, 56, 98, 161, 164
Ovid 22–3, 56–7
Owen, Wilfrid 150

passivity, sexual 7, 8, 15, 17, 19, 37, 80, 92, 95, 198
Pater, Walter 90–1, 104, 120
pathics 20
Patroclus 7, 9–10, 17, 21
penetration, sexual 15, 19, 20, 24, 50, 62, 64, 67, 69, 70, 81, 139, 140
Peter Abelard 29
Petronius Arbiter 23

Philips, Katherine 61–3
Philostratus 25
Pindar 16–17
Plato 12, 43, 52, 61–2, 79, 80, 91–3, 101, 127–8, 131, 142, 152–3, 165, 190
Plautus 20
pornography 19, 57–8, 62, 67–8, 90, 97, 109
prostitution 17, 19, 24–5, 68, 102, 106, 112
Proust, Marcel 115–17

queer 90
queers, queerness 1–7, 33, 40, 48–9, 60, 62, 70–3, 77, 81, 85, 90, 97, 117, 123, 141, 143, 155, 169, 174, 177, 192, 194

race 82, 158, 178–9, 184, 201–2
racism 82, 158, 181, 201–2
Renault, Mary 162–4, 174, 176, 179, 180, 188–92
Rich, Adrienne 199–201
Robinson, Edwin Arlington 145
Rossetti, Christina 89

Sackville-West, Vita 137, 147–9
sadism 80, 90, 93, 101, 139, 175
sadomasochism 197
Sappho 11–14, 20, 55–7, 90
Sarton, May 152
Serlo of Wilton 30
Shakespeare 4, 36, 42–53, 59, 102
Sidney, Sir Philip 36–7
slaves, slavery 15, 17, 19, 20, 21, 22, 23, 24, 25, 70, 85
Smollett, Tobias 70–1
sodomy 28–33, 38–42, 45–50, 56, 58, 60, 64–71, 79, 93, 106, 141, 175
Solon 10
Sophocles 17
Spender, Stephen 166

Spenser, Edmund 35–6, 59
Statius 25
Stein, Gertrude 123–6, 137, 147
Story of Amis and Amile 33
Story of Lancelot and Galehaut 32–3
Straton of Sardis 18–19
Swinburne, Algernon 83, 89
Symonds, J. A. 83, 84, 91–4, 96–7, 99, 129

Teleny 108
Tennyson, Alfred, Lord 78–80
Theocritus 18, 21
Theognis 15–16
Thurman, Wallace 158
Tibullus 21–2
transsexuality 22, 189–91
transvestites 2–3, 9, 17, 24, 37–8, 48, 50, 56, 72, 94, 167. *See also* cross-dressing
Two Lesbian Love Letters 30

Vidal, Gore 163, 174, 176, 179, 180, 188–92, 203
Virgil 20–1, 57, 75–6, 86

Walafrid Strabo 27
Waldo [his only name] 27
Walker, Alice 204–5
Walpole, Horace 69–70
Walter of Châtillion 30
Warner, Sylvia Townsend 150–1
White, Edmund 202–4
Whitman, Walt 82–7, 88, 92–4, 99, 100, 109, 141, 152, 153, 155, 162, 193–4
Wilde, Oscar 4–5, 88, 91, 96, 101, 109, 120, 123, 129, 132, 135, 152
Williams, Tennessee 94, 167–76, 191, 196
Wilmot, John, Earl of Rochester 64–5
Wilson, Angus 176–7
Woolf, Virginia 123, 126, 136–9, 149

www.ingramcontent.com/pod-product-compliance
Lightning Source LLC
Chambersburg PA
CBHW052108300426
44116CB00010B/1581